Praise for
Into the Fullness of
A Spiritual Autobiography

"Join Dov Elbaum, one of Israel's most creative thinkers, on a year-long spiritual journey, whose itinerary follows the map of the ten *sefirot*, the aspects of God's personality. Reading along, you'll soon find yourself on your own voyage of discovery."

—**Daniel C. Matt**, author, *God and the Big Bang: Discovering Harmony Between Science and Spirituality*, *Zohar: Annotated and Explained* and the multi-volume annotated translation *The Zohar: Pritzker Edition*

"[A] wise intertwining of personal journey and Jewish direction, textual richness and struggle to glean ancient meaning and finally, fear with faith.... A deep read!"

—**Rabbi B. Elka Abrahamson**, president, The Wexner Foundation

"Masterful ... reflects the quiet truth, 'The hardest journey is the journey inward.' In chronicling his [journey of] taking Jewish tradition seriously while not literally, [Elbaum] charts a path for us all."

—**Edwin Goldberg, DHL**, Israel and Ida G. Bettan Professor Emeritus of Midrash and Homiletics, HUC-JIR; author, *Saying No and Letting Go: Jewish Wisdom on Making Room for What Matters Most*

"In the best of Jewish interpretive tradition ... illuminates not only the depth of the author's inner life, but the wealth and complexity of Jewish religious experience through the generations."

—**Moshe Halbertal**, Gruss Professor of Law, NYU School of Law, professor of Jewish thought and philosophy, Hebrew University; fellow, Shalom Hartman Institute

"[From] one of the great Jewish visionaries of our time, [a] stunning and unique ... Kabbalistic map for all of our inner journeys."

—**Yossi Klein Halevi**, senior fellow, Shalom Hartman Institute; author, *At the Entrance to the Garden of Eden: A Jew's Search for God with Christians and Muslims in the Holy Land*

"A wild spiritual ride! ... Through Elbaum's magic touch the Torah once again sings."

—**Rabbi Bradley Shavit Artson, DHL**, dean, the Ziegler School of Rabbinic Studies, American Jewish University; author, *Passing Life's Tests: Spiritual Reflections on the Trial of Abraham, the Binding of Isaac* and *God of Becoming and Relationship: The Dynamic Nature of Process Theology*

"With rare sincerity, from within his own sufferings and revelations woven into carefully selected ancient texts, Elbaum peels away worn-out expressions and summons us to dare to enter into the mist of the Sacred, to follow our ancestors into the Void in the quest for God, for faith, for life."

—**Rabbi Tamar Elad-Appelbaum**, vice president, Masorti Rabbinical Assembly

"Magnificent and challenging.... A book of depth, offering no pat answers to deep religious questions. In the honest struggle that emerges, Elbaum demonstrates his deep learning and gentle soul.... For those who care about the deepest theological issues ... an important guide and fellow traveler."

—**Rabbi Elie Kaunfer**, executive director, Mechon Hadar; author, *Empowered Judaism: What Independent Minyanim Can Teach Us about Building Vibrant Jewish Communities*

"Renders accessible engimatic Kabbalistic ideas, turning them into windows into the human soul. An intellectually rewarding and emotionally satisfying work."

—**Micha Goodman**, director, Ein Prat Academy for Leadership; author, *Secrets of the Guide to the Perplexed*

"On the journey of faith, the true seeker must have the courage to stand in a place of uncertainty and ask difficult questions. [Elbaum] explores the landscape of faith, subjecting his experience to a comprehensive and profound analysis that is informed by meticulous scholarship and the determination to know God and live in the light of that mystery. This book is the inspiration for each of us to take that awesome journey."

—**Rabbi Shefa Gold**, author, *The Magic of Hebrew Chant: Healing the Spirit, Transforming the Mind, Deepening Love*

"A powerful, erudite meditation on faith, doubt, the nature of God. Dov Elbaum's ability to harness traditional Jewish scholarship while making himself wholly vulnerable in his spiritual quest is both illuminating and deeply compelling."

—**Rabbi Danya Ruttenberg**, author, *Surprised by God: How I Learned to Stop Worrying and Love Religion*; editor, *The Passionate Torah: Sex and Judaism*.

"Elbaum, a relentless God-wrestler, shares his high and low states while teaching applied Kabbalah and the flow of the Jewish year. Will stimulate you ... to look deeply into your inner life."

—**Rabbi Zalman Schachter-Shalomi**, author, *Davening: A Guide to Meaningful Jewish Prayer* and *Jewish with Feeling: A Guide to Meaningful Jewish Practice*

"Biography–as–theology is a powerful way to explore the inner spiritual struggles in which all of us engage, and Dov Elbaum's memoir is among the best of these. His insights into faith and his wrestling with God, religion and the meaning of life will resonate with anyone seeking a deeper walk with truth."

—**Rabbi Rami Shapiro**, author, *Amazing Chesed: Living a Grace-Filled Judaism*

"Leads us on a powerful journey out of the void to ... the mysteries of faith and hope.... Articulates a deeply meaningful system of belief for the modern thinker struggling with the challenges of our tradition."

—**Naamah Kelman-Ezrachi**, dean, HUC-JIR's Jerusalem School

"Brilliant, courageous and innovative.... Serves as a modern continuation of the literary and scholarly work of Martin Buber [and] follows in the footsteps of Abraham Joshua Heschel's work.... Makes present and internalizes the ancient Kabbalistic perceptions in his personal life [and] creates a renewed understanding—both personal and spiritual—of a Jewish tradition that today non-Jews and non-Israelis worldwide are also fascinated by."

—**Moshe Idel**, Max Cooper Professor of Jewish Thought,
Hebrew University, Jerusalem

Into the Fullness of the Void

A Spiritual Autobiography

DOV ELBAUM

Translated by Azzan Yadin

For People of All Faiths, All Backgrounds
JEWISH LIGHTS Publishing
Woodstock, Vermont

Into the Fullness of the Void: A Spiritual Autobiography

2013 Quality Paperback Edition, First Printing
© 2013 by Dov Elbaum

All rights reserved. No part of this book may be reproduced or reprinted in any form or by any means, electronic or mechanical, including photocopying, recording, or by any information storage and retrieval system, without permission in writing from the publisher.

For information regarding permission to reprint material from this book, please write or fax your request to Jewish Lights Publishing, Permissions Department, at the address / fax number listed below, or e-mail your request to permissions@ jewishlights.com.

Originally published in Hebrew in 2007 by Am Oved, Tel Aviv.

Library of Congress Cataloging-in-Publication Data
Elbaum, Dov, 1970-
 [Masa' be-halal ha-panui. English]
 Into the fullness of the void : a spiritual autobiography / Dov Elbaum.
    pages cm
 Includes bibliographical references.
 ISBN 978-1-58023-715-4 (alk. paper)
 1. Elbaum, Dov, 1970- 2. Authors, Israeli—Biography. 3. Orthodox Judaism—Relations—Nontraditional Jews. 4. Jews—Israel—Identity. 5. Secularism—Israel. 6. Faith (Judaism) I. Title.
 PJ5055.2.L356Z4613 2013
 892.4'36—dc23

                          2013018858

10 9 8 7 6 5 4 3 2 1

Manufactured in the United States of America
Cover Design: Heather Pelham
Interior Design: Kelley Barton
Cover Art: ©iStockphoto.com/konradlew

For People of All Faiths, All Backgrounds
Jewish Lights Publishing
A Division of LongHill Partners, Inc.
Sunset Farm Offices, Route 4, P.O. Box 237
Woodstock, VT 05091
Tel: (802) 457-4000 Fax: (802) 457-4004
www.jewishlights.com

Contents

chapter one

Keter
Invisible Beginnings

1

It was the eve of Yom Kippur. At the synagogue with my five-year-old daughter, both of us dressed in white, I was given the honor of opening and closing the Torah ark for one of the Yom Kippur prayers. I went up and tried to open the velvet curtain covering the ark, but it remained stuck in its runner, refusing to budge. The cantor stood behind me, clearing his throat and waiting impatiently for the Torah scrolls inside to be revealed so that he could chant, "Who shall ascend the hill of the Lord? And who shall stand in His holy place? Those who have clean hands and pure hearts, who do not lift up their souls to what is false, and do not swear deceitfully" (Psalm 24:3–4). But the curtain did not move. Embarrassed, I could sense the other congregants' thoughts: "Just another one of those guys that only come to synagogue on the eve of Yom Kippur. He receives honors he doesn't deserve, while we make the effort and come here each and every day."

Finally back in my seat, I struggled to regain my composure. I could not stop replaying the mistake of a synagogue novice who attends once a year and does not even know how to open the curtain of the ark. After all, only a short time earlier, along with the rest of the congregation, I had recited *Kol Nidrei*, the "absolution of vows"

1

liturgy that opens the Yom Kippur services, and my heart was filled with the hope that I was on the threshold of a truly new year, a year of revelation and change. I had stood and recited intently, "*Kol nidrei* ... All vows and oaths we take, all promises and obligations ... we hereby publicly retract ... and hereby declare our intention to be absolved of them." I wanted desperately to shake loose from of the detritus of the previous year and the old fears, anxieties, and preoccupations. But here I was, unable even to open the Torah ark. I could not ascend the hill of the Lord.

There had been times when I did not fast, desecrating the most sacred Jewish holiday. But for years now I have been fasting and praying, studying traditional Jewish sources, writing and teaching about these sources, meditating on their minute details, even down to the letters of the texts. I am not religiously observant, but I venerate the Hebrew Bible and honor and revere Jewish intellectual history, and I try to live according to Jewish and ethical ideals.

On our way home after the service, my daughter and I walked in the middle of the street, reveling in that particular freedom of Yom Kippur, when the streets are free of motor vehicles. I released her hand from my grip so that she could run among the hundreds of young bike riders who enjoyed a world without motorized threats. Their cries of joy did not disrupt the great calm that had descended. My thoughts turned to a practical question of *halakhah*, Jewish religious law. For almost a year I have been taking medicine every night to ease severe facial pains. Doctors have told me that they do not know either the cause of the condition or when the pain will go away. The prescribed medication only slightly dulls the torment. I looked at my watch, knowing that if I did not take the medication in the next hour, my left cheek and jaw would begin to burn. I wondered how I was to take it without water and then recalled the halakhic rulings governing fasts, which I had learned some time ago: a small mouthful of water, less than the amount referred to as *melo logmav*, "a full mouthful," is not considered a drink, and its consumption does not constitute breaking the fast. I was surprised to find myself again considering halakhic minutiae that had long ago lost significance for me.

Later that evening, I learned that the daughter of one of my best friends had been hit by a car and gravely injured. Her father is the only friend I have kept from my days in the ultra-Orthodox community. He was home at the time of the accident and heard the sound of the car as it struck his child. He then heard the shouts of the passersby, and then he heard his family name. He rushed outside and, seeing his daughter lying unconscious, asked the gathered crowd to recite the verse "O God, please heal her"—Moses's prayer for his sister, Miriam. The girl's little brother, who had seen the accident, was sent to school to recite psalms with his classmates for the recovery of his sister. The doctors cannot estimate her chances for survival or her future condition should she live.

The next afternoon, as the sun descended toward the horizon, I wrapped myself in the prayer shawl that my father gave me on my wedding night, stood in the corner of my bedroom, and began to recite the concluding prayer of the Yom Kippur liturgy. "Open the gate for us though it is the time of the closing of the gate, for the sun hangs low," I prayed weeping, trying to say the words with fervor; but my heart was elsewhere. I remembered other days of atonement and other atonements, other prayers of forgiveness and other moments of forgiveness. The time had come for me to confront my faith. Who is the God I believe in? What is my relationship with Him? Where will my faith lead me? Again and again I asked myself: Am I able to look at these questions directly and still pray on Yom Kippur?

I decide to devote the new Jewish year to a journey in which I will use classical Jewish sources to explore my identity and my faith. No need to trek to distant, snow-covered peaks carrying a heavy pack, no need for an extended absence from my home, my wife, and my daughters. Everything I need is at hand: library, intellect, memory. Where then is the starting point?

Delving deep into my childhood, I struggle to retrieve the early experience of faith. A series of images: On a late afternoon, a five-year-old boy leaves his house and disappears for hours. He walks away from his neighborhood and reaches a riverbed, into which the waste of Jerusalem flows, frothy and acidic. He climbs to the top of a hill overlooking the city's northern edge, a hill that would eventually be covered with tall buildings and ringed by highways. The boy lies down and watches in wonder as the pine and cypress trees sway in prayer in the wind.

Perhaps this is the starting point I have sought, perhaps the first moment of amazement, of spiritual elevation. I do not recall my gaze rising to the heavens as if fulfilling the prophetic injunction to "lift up your eyes on high and see: Who created these?" (Isaiah 40:26). But I do remember the respite from the hustle and bustle of the small apartment in which my parents raised their nine children, the relief from the shouts and the tensions, from the secular-religious rupture within Israeli society that found such clear and tangible expression in my neighborhood.

Is this all I can retrieve? Having devoted most of my adult life to the study of faith, prayer, and the relationship between God and man, I would have expected to have at least one solid childhood memory involving some experience of the sublime, at least one uplifting moment of wonder that impacted my life. But I am unable to uncover from my early childhood even a trace of such an experience. I could, of course, invent one, as many writers and philosophers perhaps have done. I could insert into my childhood an image of a boy gazing to the heavens, the sun or the moon and stars washing over him, swallowing him up, touching him. Another possibility: a boy straining to raise himself up above the windowsill in his parents' home, lifting his eyes on high to see a tattered cloud shifting shape in the wind, slowly taking on the form of an elderly father, his beard white as snow.

The Talmudic sages, followed by Maimonides and others, have instilled in us a collective memory of Abraham, "the father of the believers."[1] Already as a child of three, recounted Maimonides, Abraham "began to wander in his thought,"[2] asking himself who created the sun and the moon and the stars, until, by the power of deductive reasoning, he concluded that a single God had created all these.

But my childhood offers not a single memory of some experience of faith. Instead, my entire childhood was a package of fear, loss, pain, cruelty, weariness, and helplessness—which seemed related not to God but to my family and circumstances.

In the drawer of the desk in my study I find a photograph; the rounded script of one of my older sisters provides the date. It is a close-up portrait of a seven-year-old boy, a colorful yarmulke resting on his reddish hair, his somber face tilted diagonally toward the horizon, gazing off like Abraham lifting his eyes on high. I staged the photo—the pose, the camera's distance, the proper borders for my image. Only my collar and my face looking out into the distance should be visible, I told my sister. Even then I was aware of the vacuum of my faith and sought to fill it with constructed images.

I do not think that I believed in God back then or thought that the commandments I studied and observed really had anything to do with Him. Even when I transgressed some religious commandment, there was neither guilt nor fear of God. My only real concern was that my parents and teachers would find out.

Perhaps it was God's will that faith remained hidden from me as a child, lest I cling to it now only out of habit rather than embarking on a long and tortuous journey at the end of which I may find a conscious, adult faith.

This is not my first foray into the terrain of faith. Religious faith never served as a refuge for me, only a fragile way station teetering on the brink. Questions of faith have plagued me for years. As long as I interpreted the concept of faith in its broadly accepted sense, I could not reach even a provisional conclusion that accurately reflected my emotional and ethical sensibilities. I read tirelessly about religious belief. I prayed, and I retreated into solitude, but I never experienced true faith. But now I feel that I am ready to undertake this journey with a determination that was lacking in my earlier campaigns.

I ponder my mother's faith. Born into a venerable Jerusalem family, she grew up in the hermetically sealed world of early-twentieth-
century pre-State Jerusalem. She was like a butterfly in its protective
cocoon; the world of her childhood had not yet been breached by the
forces of enlightenment and secularization sweeping the West, so it
maintained a certain wholeness or integrity. Throughout her life,
my mother's faith in God was always clear and self-evident, like the
white rice she used to cook us. No contemplation required: simply
pour, sift, transfer into an oiled pot, cover with water, lightly salt,
turn on the flame, and wait as the rice absorbs the water.

Her parents never taught her the meaning of faith or how she
ought to think about God. The only theological topics she would
discuss, though she found them boring, were old age and death,
occasionally wondering aloud: What is the nature of life after death?
What happens in paradise? She wanted to know if she would meet
her family and her righteous forebears there. What happened to her
mother, who died young? And, most importantly, what awaits her in
the final, heavenly judgment?

My father, by contrast, emerged from the ruins of Jewish life in
Eastern Europe. Born in a small Polish town in the interwar period,
he was exposed from a young age to Jewish secularism and enlightenment, to the full spectrum of Jewish Socialist and Communist factions,
and to the secular Zionist ideologies that circulated through his town.
While still a young boy, his family managed to flee to Palestine, just
before the gates of Poland slammed shut. While he had seen different
ways of life and thought, my father ultimately chose the Jerusalem
Breslov Hasidim. His faith included sadness and muted joy, prayer
and quiet religious fervor, and messianic hope. The return of the
Jews to their ancestral homeland was proof that God had returned to
history. But this faith was eroded by the hardships of his life. He was
never able to declare his faith publicly, confidently, without hesitation or qualification. His faith in God was marred by memories of
the terrible poverty that he suffered as a child and that instilled in
him a devotion to money and steady employment. My father would
pay lip service to the Jewish God who bestows livelihood from the

heavens—"O fear the Lord, you His holy ones, for those who fear Him have no want" (Psalm 34:10)—but God was an integral part of my father's thought and life. He was always anxious about livelihood and, through force of habit, continued to be troubled even when there was nothing really to worry about. To him, money and the very term *parnasah* (livelihood) were guarantors of a secure life. He never could grasp why I gave up an assured livelihood for a murky dream.

I was born into a shattered and fragmented world. This was the 1970s in a new Jerusalem neighborhood, populated mostly by newly secular North African Jews. Most people struggled to eke out a living and could not meaningfully engage the new truths set forth by Israel's founding fathers in all their European secularist glory. The families in our apartment building were forever apologizing for maintaining some of their traditions ("It's just out of respect for Mom and Dad"), but in their hearts they admired my family's religious devotion.

The chasm between Israel's secular and religious populations was plainly evident in our neighborhood, which was built after the Six-Day War and bordered an older, more established, religious neighborhood. It was if an invisible barrier separated the two. Few of the residents of the religious neighborhood entered the secular neighborhood to shop, and vice versa. While secretly yearning to join the game, the religious kids watched and shouted insults as the secular kids played soccer. Though I lived in the secular area, I was also part of the religious community. I shopped there, and I knew all its residents.

I never understood why my secular neighbors could drive to the beach on the Sabbath, while I, a fellow Jew, lived such a different life; for me, even tearing toilet paper in the bathroom was prohibited on the Sabbath. The other kids in the neighborhood thought of Orthodoxy almost as a separate race, while I saw it as a way of life they had miraculously managed to avoid by declaring their secularism and thus unburdening themselves of the yoke of religious observance. When he caught me in a lie, one of my secular friends said, "You're Orthodox, for you it's really forbidden." My secular friends reacted vigorously to an infraction in a neighborhood soccer game but blithely dismissed their own religious transgressions. For them, Orthodox Judaism was less a set of rules than a kind of genetic mutation.

As a child without personal freedom or choice about my way of life, I seethed with a sense of deep injustice. My frustrations began to be reflected in my behavior, as I started to reject the moral and social boundaries I had been raised to respect. I beat up my friends, I stole and cheated, and I lied to my parents, to my teachers, and to everyone else around me. I was always a good student, but my teachers complained that my wild misconduct was corrupting my classmates. Finally, my parents decide to send me to a yeshiva at the other end of Jerusalem a year earlier than normal in our circles.

I was twelve and a half when I arrived at the yeshiva. My first year was a jumble: living with dozens of young men, three roommates, intensive study from the break of dawn until late in the night, constantly closed off in one place—with only a few hours at home on Fridays. The yeshiva was permeated with an atmosphere of fierce competitiveness. And there were the usual travails of adolescence, including the awakening to sexuality, masturbation, and the ensuing guilt. But by my second year, I had adjusted to the fullness of the yeshiva's religious life.

On one of the nights of Elul, the last month of the Jewish year, a time when the yeshiva was suffused with the spirit of the imminent High Holy Days, I was sitting on the back bench of the empty *beit midrash* (study hall), staring at a volume of Maimonides's masterful *Code of Jewish Law* (*Mishneh Torah*). With a pang of jealousy, I wondered if I would ever be as great a Torah scholar as he. Maimonides, after all, had written a commentary on the Mishnah when he was thirteen! My thirteenth birthday had come and gone, and I felt that I still knew nothing. The sins and desires of my body and mind were keeping me from reaching my goal: to become the Maimonides of my generation. Rosh Hashanah was upon us, and I was about to stand in judgment before God. I needed to make haste and move forward quickly on the path toward *scientia Dei*, knowledge of God, which, according to Maimonides, is the obligation of every man who does not want to be counted among the commoners.

Years later I learned that Maimonides had only begun to write his commentary when he was twenty-three and completed it when he was thirty, but I resolved that second year in yeshiva to radically alter my way of life. I wrote about some of the intense experiences of that time in my first book, *Zeman Elul* ("Elul Term").[3] I decided that many of my transgressions were the result of the time I was wasting on empty chatter with friends, so I took a vow of silence for the entire month of Elul and the period of the High Holy Days that followed. I limited my speech to discussion of the Talmud. I followed the yeshiva's curriculum meticulously, even adding independent study in the late-night hours.

As my silence continued, prayer was less and less a mechanical ritual divorced from my thoughts and feelings. I began to articulate every word in the prayer book with great intention, *kavannah*, trying to grasp the deepest meaning of every word and trying to relate to the praises and petitions that flowed from it. This kind of prayer takes a lot of time. Not wanting to draw attention to my long and agonized prayers, I would sneak out of the communal services held in the main sanctuary of the yeshiva and head off to the empty classrooms for solitude. Each prayer intensified my awareness of God's power and glory and my absolute dependence on God's will for the atonement of my sins and transgressions (which had taken on monstrous proportions in my frightened conscience). I prayed through tears and sobs, swaying wildly, embracing the pain in my soul and the sharp regret for the life I had lived thus far.

Though my prayers often began in pain and fear, often love and thanksgiving began to wash over me, filling me with a sense of inner purity and atonement. The alienation of so much of my childhood gave way to a daily sense of intimacy with God. For the first time in my life, I felt protected. I was guided by a loving, affirming, and forgiving power that still allowed me my freedom of choice.

Late at night, sometimes after midnight, I would sneak into the library—the "book treasury," as it was called—of the nearby adult yeshiva, where I worked to acquire a deeper belief in God. I tried to read *The Book of Principles* by Rabbi Yosef Albo—whose last name, I noted, was very similar to mine—as well as Rabbi Saadia Gaon's *Book of Opinions and Beliefs*, Maimonides's *Guide for the Perplexed*, and Rabbi Yehudah Halevi's *Kuzari*, a *vade mecum* in today's religious curriculum. At first, I was fascinated by the logical arguments in these tractates—so similar to my yeshiva's rational approach to Talmud study. But as I read on, I began to realize how foreign their philosophical definitions of faith were to my own very intimate relationship with God, who had become for me a personal guide, loving and beloved, a living presence during my hours of devotional prayer.

I stopped studying the great Jewish philosophers of the Middle Ages—Maimonides, Rabbi Yehudah Halevi, Rabbi Hesdai Crescas, Rabbi Solomon ibn Gabirol, and Gersonides, among others. Instead, I devoted myself to exploring my personal feelings for and faith in God. I felt a God who is both father and king, a supreme power hovering attentively over me, hearing my prayers and answering them. God became a partner to my loneliness, which was intensifying as my silences grew longer and deeper. I felt that my friendship with God was contingent upon my meticulous observance of the Jewish commandments, His unmediated and unequivocal instructions to anyone seeking His presence.

I spent the next several years studying at the yeshiva, experiencing peaks and valleys, sins and attempts at atonement, as well as continual struggles with my maturing body and increasingly powerful sexual urges, which I tried to overcome through regular Monday and Thursday fasts. My fear of God did not center on the punishment I would receive if I transgressed His Torah so much as the fear of losing His protection in this world.

Over the years, the terms of God's patronage became increasingly tangled, as they grew both more complicated and demanding every day. I wrapped myself in more and more vows, prohibitions, and requirements not required by Jewish law. I renounced pleasure, leisure, all levity and playfulness, and I suppressed any impulse toward free and unbridled joy. I could not even share with friends and teachers my feelings of religious elevation, knowing they would consider it peculiar, an abnormality to be dealt with, nipped in the bud. But the more I denied myself all that this world has to offer, the more my curiosity and desire grew. The sweet internal freedom I felt in moments of religious elevation only whetted my sense of being trapped within my world. The various formulations of faith I encountered in the yeshiva could not compare with my vivid religious experiences. A yawning chasm opened between my knowledge and learning on the one hand and my sense of self on the other. The walls were closing in, day by day, until I had no oxygen, until I had no choice but to try to break free.

At seventeen I resolved to leave the yeshiva. Again, it was the month of Elul, a period of intense repentance and supplication. I packed my belongings in a suitcase and waited until my friends were in the classroom, then snuck out to the bus station and boarded a bus to my parents' house.

I will never forgive myself for my cruelty toward my mother when I told her I had decided to change course and no longer be observant. I woke her from her afternoon nap and recited the phrase I had rehearsed en route from the yeshiva. Her eyes were cloaked in sadness, the sadness of many generations, of hope suddenly extinguished. A profoundly Jewish sadness that can only be expressed through an uttered sigh—a *krechtz*—that is itself burdened with a long history.

A few weeks later, on Yom Kippur, I fled the synagogue and returned to my parents' empty house. As if possessed, I wolfed down food, breaking the Yom Kippur fast.

I never shared with my parents the real factors that led to this radical change in my way of life; it was easier to declare that I no longer believed in God or the Torah. Foolishly, I thought it would be easier for them to understand a clear and unambiguous argument than the true but recondite motivations, many of which were not clear to me at the time. Shocked, my parents enlisted the help of the greatest rabbis in the ultra-Orthodox world. A renowned secular actor, who had made his own turn to Orthodoxy a public spectacle, warned me of all manners of infernal punishment. Hunched over his prayer lectern, drawing upon all his thespian skills, he growled at me through the dark room. The spiritual overseer of my former yeshiva believed he could give me large sums of money that would allow me to carouse until I had sated my carnal desires, after which I would return to the fold. Prominent rabbis tried to provide me with proof positive that God exists and that both the Torah and the Rabbinic oral tradition are God's truth. In the course of our conversations, these great rabbis rolled out the full range of arguments put forth by the medieval Jewish philosophers. I again immersed myself in the works of Maimonides, Rabbi Saadia Gaon, and Rabbi Yehudah Halevi, hoping to formulate a proper response to these rabbis. I was able, I felt, to rebut the rabbis' claims or, at the very least, to reach a compromise position: though it might not be possible to prove the existence of God, it is also impossible to prove the opposite. Finally, after endless conversations with rabbis, my parents despaired. My father excommunicated me with his silence.

In the years that followed, I was busy learning the codes and language of my new, secular world. I was no longer occupied with matters of faith and God. My mind revised its memories until I was convinced that I had abandoned the world of my youth as a result of disbelief in God or in the divinity of the Torah. This, in any case, is what I told myself and my new friends.

It was self-deception. I may not have been sure that the Torah is divine, but I never stopped believing that God exists.

It was the loneliest time of my life, and today I think of it as the most difficult time in my life. It had been a few short months since I left the Orthodox world of my family and what had been my community. My parents and siblings were completely estranged from me; they communicated only their anger and their rejection. In one of the more difficult confrontations, my older brother—overcome by emotion and, perhaps, his great love for me—declared that he would rather I die in a car crash than commit spiritual suicide. I did not respond to these harsh words and have long since forgiven him. In my loneliness, I would leave my parents' house every evening and wander the empty streets of our neighborhood until the wee hours of the night, all the while contemplating my future, the possibilities that lay before me in this new world, dreaming of becoming an author, lurching from a sense of grandeur and manifest destiny to feelings of inadequacy and dejection.

One Friday night in the windswept Jerusalem winter, I marched along the main thoroughfare toward Mount Scopus. My gaze wandered to a large, lit window in one of the apartments to my left. Through the open shutters I could see a family, seated together in the living room, watching a weekly variety show. I drew as near to the window as possible, hoping to watch with them. I surveyed the family: parents, perhaps forty years old, a teenage girl, and a young man with kind eyes. Then I saw that the young man was sitting in a wheelchair, his twisted hands resting on his stomach. I quickly retreated from the window but remained on the sidewalk, staring through the open window under the cover of darkness. In that moment, I would have traded places with the young man, despite his terrible disability. I was jealous of him, surrounded as he was by what appeared to be his warm and loving family.

My walking routes always had the same starting point: the prestigious cemetery of the Sanhedria neighborhood, located at one of the busiest intersections in northern Jerusalem, not far from my parents' home. A large inscription was emblazoned over the cemetery entrance: "The Destination of All Living Things." From there I passed to the edge of Ammunition Hill, a former Jordanian army stronghold that now commemorates the courage of the Israeli paratroopers who conquered East Jerusalem during the Six-Day War. Sometimes, if the night was not too dark, I mustered up the courage to enter the site, wandering through Jordanian trenches, now a memorial to the bloody battle that took place there. I thought of the brave paratrooper who said after the battle that all he wanted was to get home in one piece. Then I jumped over the ditches and dugouts until I returned to the main road.

A few hundred yards later, my route ended at a large intersection, dwarfed by a huge, two-story statue made of giant metal plates that form odd geometric shapes suspended in midair, taunting gravity. There I would sit, gathering strength for the walk back.

The Jewish artist, Alexander Lieberman, named that statue "Faith."

So I would begin my walk at the cemetery and reach Faith.

—

2

The first stage of my journey I will call *Keter*—"crown"—the highest of the kabbalistic *sefirot*. The *sefirot* (*sefirah* in the singular) are the ten spiritual steps, or potencies, through which God created and continues to create the world. In Kabbalah, God is revealed by means of these ten manifestations of His essence, ten distinct glimmerings of the creative power within Him. The *sefirot* are the harmonic rhythm of the divine life-process and of His ever-renewing act of creation. Each is defined by unique powers and characteristics, and only when they are properly aligned and properly united is our worldly reality in a state of abundant blessedness and beneficence.

At the highest, most hidden end of this structure is *Keter*, the divine essence that lies closest to God's infinite being; at the lowest, most revealed end is *Malkhut*—"kingdom"—a *sefirah* that manifests itself in our material existence and governs mundane reality.

I do not know if there truly are ten *sefirot* floating out there, and in any case they would be divine and so by definition beyond the grasp of human minds. But I accept the Hasidic interpretation that the *sefirot* exist in my body and soul, and it is in this sense that I want to engage them.

Each *sefirah* embodies a different narrative. The derivation of the word *sefirah* is a matter of controversy among Kabbalah scholars.[4]

For me, the *sefirot* are first and foremost *sipurim*, stories both about God and the various meanings we find in the concept "God" and about us as creatures made in the image of God.

Over the centuries, kabbalists have characterized *Keter* as representing the primordial stirrings of God's will within the divine Infinite, the initial awakening of a desire to be, to become manifest. For me, *Keter* represents a very human experience—the inchoate impetus toward motion, toward change. *Keter* has no discernible "content," no desire for anything already known; it is rather the yearning for all possible content. That is why kabbalists often speak of it as *ayin*, nothingness, an intermediate state between an absolute, undifferentiated unity that defies definition and the first spark of distinguishable existence.

Keter is the starting point of the cosmic creation process. Because it has no distinct content or self-awareness, *Keter* can be described as an absolute openness toward the transition from potentiality to actuality. The ten *sefirot* are commonly represented in the form of a human body. Kabbalists describe *Keter* as "the supernal crown," God's diadem. It rests on and is bound to God's head but is not the head itself. The base of *Keter* reaches down into the world of creation, where the divine Infinite undertakes a preliminary crystallization that precedes the creation of material reality, while its upper spires point up toward the Void Space of the radical unity of *Ein Sof*, the Infinite that admits no division and is still innocent of even the most primal stirrings of will and self-consciousness.

It all begins there, they say: God's creation of the world and man's creation of himself. In most kabbalistic traditions, God's starting point is as the *Ein Sof*, infinity, that is, the totality of God's forces. These infinite forces are actually a single force, without limits or borders, unfettered by time, space, or want. This force defies predication and description, since any possible attribute originates in our thoughts and language, which by their nature are limited.

The divine Infinite is "one," for infinite power is not divisible into distinct elements or essences. Maimonides was responding to this infiniteness when he developed his doctrine of negative attributes, according to which God can only be defined negatively: God is *not* human, God is *not* bound by space and time, and so forth. According to Maimonides, we cannot make any positive assertion—God is *this* or *that*—since such a statement places boundaries on God's infinite power.

But if God's power is infinite and encompasses space and time, how is the material world possible? The question perturbed sixteenth-century kabbalists. Only two answers appear viable: either God is not infinite, or reality does not truly exist and we and the world we inhabit are an illusion, a dream.

Kabbalists tried for centuries to resolve this enigma using the doctrine of *tzimtzum*, "contraction," whose earliest and arguably most poetic formulation is found in a manuscript by Nahmanides, a great thirteenth-century scholar and key figure in early Spanish Kabbalah who composed commentaries to the Bible and the Talmud. He writes:

> How did He form and create His world? As when a man draws in a breath, contracting himself, so that a small space can contain a great deal. In this manner God contracted His light in the span of His hand and the world remained in darkness. Within that darkness he hewed rocks and carved boulders, in order to produce from them the paths of Mystical Wisdom.[5]

Nahmanides suggests that in order for creation to take place, God first had to leave the place of creation. Prior to the creation of the world, God departed from a particular space, thereby emptying it, that is, freeing it up for the cosmos He was about to create. The infinite God forced Himself to converge within a set space and so allow the formation of a space external to Him, that is, not permeated by Him. Only within this God-vacated space could physical creation take place, a region Nahmanides characterizes as "darkness," since it is devoid of divine presence.

Comprehensive and detailed discussions of God's contraction emerged from sixteenth-century Safed, especially in the writings of

Moshe Cordovero and in the teachings that Rabbi Isaac Luria passed down to his circle of disciples, chief among whom was Rabbi Hayyim Vital. In the eighteen months prior to his death at the age of thirty-eight, Luria expounded to his disciples a rich and penetrating analysis of God's contraction. In the Lurianic tradition, this is described as the creation of the Void Space.

After God contracts, opening within Himself a bubble known as Void Space, He pours His creative potencies into this space, and these eventually take the form of the ten *sefirot*. The potencies in question are highly concentrated and constrained in comparison with God's infinite essence, and after a long transformative process, they initiate the creation process, beginning with the divine "nothingness," that is, infinite being, and working down to the physical world.

Gershom Scholem, the greatest Kabbalah scholar of the last generation, characterized the doctrine of contraction as the most significant intellectual revolution effected by the Kabbalah. The doctrine of contraction posits that there is no existence, no aspect of reality that is not somehow confined and demarcated. No power can manifest itself that does not carry within it its own finitude.

Just as we cannot perceive sound waves whose frequency is too high for our ears, our inability to perceive God empirically does not signify God's absence, but merely that our grasp of reality is limited. Our universe is governed by limits and borders and finitude, and this is, alas, all that we can know. We cannot experience the infinite aspect of God prior to its contraction and delimitation.

The concept of contraction applies not only to empirical reality. There is a gap between the abstract and its practical realization. The journey the abstract must make before it becomes an actuality is not merely a matter of its maturing in one's thoughts; even this maturation means taking leave of some of the elements originally present in the idea. It is a process of shedding layers of possibility, of continuous self-delimitation to a reality that is governed by borders and limits.

We also experience contraction in the way our feelings and perceptions find expression in language. In our dreams, the laws of space and time are not binding, and events need not occur in chronological sequence. But to describe a dream means using spatial-temporal language that is limiting and cannot duly convey the experience. In other words, in order to "translate" the dream from my internal experience to an external communicable reality, we must pay the price of contraction, a payment we make every time we express our thoughts in language; every sentence, every word—contraction. But without contraction there is no creativity. The world of thought is rich and colorful, but exteriorizing our thoughts means channeling and constricting them.

Let us return to God's contraction: when the infinite power named God or *Ein Sof* decided to create the material world, it had to shed an infinite number of infinite possibilities, manifesting as a concrete reality with boundaries and limitations. This is the kabbalistic interpretation of the Genesis creation narrative, where the world comes into being through divine speech, that is, the world is articulated, as opposed to the abstract and diffuse divine thought that can never exteriorize itself as a created reality.

When I first studied the kabbalistic doctrine of contraction, I wondered: If God is infinite, why was He compelled to contract and create the physical world in the first place? What is the telos of creation, of the many disappointments described in the Bible, of the world's suffering and pain? I am, of course, not the first to raise these questions. But I have always found the kabbalists' standard response wanting—namely, God wished to realize His giving powers, to manifest His goodness and His mercy, and so had to create a reality distinct from His infinite essence upon which to lavish His beneficence and grace. The kabbalists have said, "There is no king without a nation." For God to manifest His kingship, He must have—that is, create—mankind, over whom to reign. This answer used to seem to me to be almost crass and insulting: was the creation of the cosmos really nothing more than a way to satisfy God's hunger for power?

Today I understand the daring of the idea that despite His infinite power, God cannot fully realize Himself without someone to govern.

God creates subjects for Himself in order to more fully become God. God without creation is God without self-consciousness.

Just as there is no life that is not bounded by death, just as the infant will not grasp that he is an independent being without separating from his mother, so too there is no reality without contraction. The infinite, radically one God lacks awareness of Himself as extant. It is only through the external agency of the radically other—the finite, limited, created reality—that God can fully manifest His being. In creating the world, God also created Himself.

The creation of the heavens and the earth, and the creation of man above all, are not free acts of divine beneficence. If God does not create, He does not exist. In *Sefer Yetzirah* ("The Book of Creation"), the earliest kabbalistic work and the foundation for generations of future kabbalists, a similar idea appears. God made "nonexistence into existence,"[6] that is, created existence and in so doing forged His own existence.

Another conclusion: God's essence and the essence of the created world are profoundly interconnected and reflected one within the other. At the moment of creation, God relinquished His infinite freedom. His relationship with mankind—the only creature with an awareness of God—is a matter of mutual self-interest.

The path from no self-consciousness to self-determination is long and fraught with suffering. Someone who possesses awesome powers can create something small and circumscribed and clearly delineated with relative ease. But in fact this task is no less difficult than that facing a powerless person who must perform a task far beyond his ability. The effort is the same, but the direction reversed. Both are compelled to change in a way that goes against their nature: the powerful and talented person to focus his abilities in order to accomplish something comparatively paltry; the weak and untalented person to acquire new knowledge and develop new tools to accomplish something previously beyond his abilities. No wonder, then, that Luria's disciples describe God's transformation from the Infinite, in all its splendid isolation, to the Creator of a finite and delimited world as a series of struggles and crises.

I have compassion for this infinite God who must undergo such a radical contraction. I have compassion for Him and for us—all mankind, indeed all living things, for our pains and our contractions, those forced upon us in the past, and those that await us in the future. We are forever faced with choices, every decision precluding so many other possibilities.

When I was a child, my parents made most of the decisions for me—first and foremost the decision to be my parents. They chose the physical landscape in which I would grow up, the kindergarten and religious elementary school I would attend, and they often chose not to choose. They did not choose to be involved with my friends; they did not choose to nurture my talents in extracurricular activities; they did not choose to better instruct me how to find a path to another person's heart; they did not choose to teach me how to express my feelings. All this used to anger me, but today I am merely saddened by the choices they made and those they did not make. Both constricted my physical, psychological, and intellectual space. Now that I am a father myself, I cannot blame them. Am I doing any better? Though my skills are more developed than my parents', all the same I find myself constricting my daughters' space, intentionally or otherwise.

My life fans out in a sequence of contractions. How best to set limits for my daughters? How do I instill in them respect for human beings? Should I scold? And how, if necessary, do I punish? In what school should I enroll them, and in what extracurricular activities? Myriad choices, some marginal, others central, all of which determine the direction of their lives. Other questions I must address: Which talents should be nurtured, and how best to identify latent talents? When is what I see in them true talent, when a product of my wishful thinking? Should I prevent them from spending time with children I think are a bad influence? Should I let them be exposed to negative experiences to strengthen them for life's adversities? With every choice, we abandon other paths that may be no worse than the path taken. All these possibilities—some of which I am conscious of, others not—are sacrificed upon the altar of the one choice I myself made.

At some point, we have to decide on a path lest we lose ourselves in the labyrinths of our lives. We must choose a profession, a source of livelihood, and perhaps confront a more decisive choice—do we raise a family, and if so, with whom?

And what of the heart, which yearns to experience the thrill of love, to be set aflutter, to meet new souls and thus renew our own. Every choice of a partner means relinquishing other potential partners. Even now, in writing these words, I am rejecting other phrases and formulations, for the inherently finite medium of language will never fully express my thoughts and feelings.

Though muted by the irenic Genesis creation narrative, God expressed the words "Let there be light!" in a terrible cry that reverberated through the cosmos. That is why, projecting my own trifling sufferings onto the Creator, I am filled with pain and compassion every time I think of the divine contraction. I make no apologies for this analogy, which follows a long and distinguished Jewish tradition.

The appeal of Hasidic thought lies in the ability of its masters, from its eighteenth-century founder, the Baal Shem Tov, down through his great disciples, to reformulate the conceptual vocabulary of Kabbalah in psychological terms. The teachings and homilies of the Hasidic masters infuse the most basic kabbalistic symbols—the structure and interrelations of the *sefirot*—into the recesses of the human psyche. These symbols, originally developed as a way of offering a more concrete vocabulary with which to explain how divine power created the world, are in Hasidic thinking transposed into a psychological key, and so have bearing on all the debates and deliberations that make up the fullness of human life. Each of us is constituted by the same basic forces, by the same *sefirot*, so that when a person descends into the depths of his own soul, he traverses all these realms. Eastern European Hasidism transforms Kabbalah into a unique tool for psychological insight and self-reflection.[7]

The beauty of the Hasidic approach is that it not only provides a set of symbols and tools for understanding the human soul, but it also enriches the image of God at the same time. The kabbalists and

Hasidic masters repeatedly refer to Job 19:26, "from my flesh I shall see God." Introspection provides a pathway to understanding the processes within the divine universe. Man is a miniature world in all senses of the word,[8] and since man was created in the image of God, he is also a microcosm of the divine.

God's birth pangs did not end with the decision to create the world. God suffered a series of horrific failures in the creation process itself. In kabbalistic terms, these failures are referred to as "the breaking of the vessels." The Zohar—the foundational text of mystical Judaism—and Luria and his disciples describe a series of massive cosmic-mythological events in which God, through His divine potencies, created worlds that were immediately annihilated. God did not destroy these worlds because He was dissatisfied with them; rather they collapsed into themselves and shattered. This cycle continued until God could repair the broken vessels and use them to create the reality we know today, though this world too hangs by a thread, sustained only by a series of very complex checks and balances.

The Lurianic doctrine of "the breaking of the vessels" can be traced back to a midrashic motif from the Talmudic period that underwent considerable elaboration. According to the original midrash, "the Holy One blessed be He would repeatedly create worlds and destroy them, until He created ours."[9] In the opening of the famous *Idra Rabba* ("the Great Assembly") section of the Zohar, Rabbi Shimon bar Yohai and his disciples midrashically link this tradition to an apparently unrelated verse: "These are the kings who reigned in the land of Edom, before any king reigned over the Israelites" (Genesis 36:31). What follows is a curious genealogical list of kings that seems to have little or nothing to do with the rest of the Genesis narrative.

According to the Zohar, embedded in these verses is the great narrative account of "the breaking of the vessels." On this reading, the phrase "before any king reigned over the Israelites" refers to the cosmic destruction of the previous worlds, while each named king refers to one such world. The Zohar's unique interpretive approach does not identify the plain meaning of the biblical text; the plain sense is only an external garment covering the arcane processes occurring within the unknowable Godhead, or *Keter*. The Zohar further decodes the kings of Edom passage by marking "Edom" as representing the unstable state that resulted from the breaking of the vessels. The dead kings are the vessels that burst under the pressure exerted by "Edom," the quality of "redness" that generally symbolizes the power emanating from the *sefirah Gevurah*. In the Zohar's terminology, the restraining potency of *Gevurah* can become destructive if it is unbalanced.

What is the meaning of the litany of kings? What was the purpose of the "broken vessels"? Here too we can approach the question mechanistically—and this is indeed the most common view—and recognize that the vessels were a necessary element in the creation process, boundaries containing the contracting infinity of God's creative power. These boundaries (i.e., vessels) channeled and contained the divine energy as it burst into space, allowing for the creation of an enduring reality within it. But since God was not yet accustomed to setting boundaries, the vessels were too rigid and did not allow for any development or growth, or perhaps God erred and channeled too much power into the vessels, causing them to break—like a fine glass cup that shatters when boiling water is poured into it.

I try to understand the notion of the "breaking of the vessels" through the filter of my own experience. Why can't I decipher the period leading up to the break with the Orthodox world of my family? I often feel lumps of emotion and thoughts related to that period inside, but I cannot contain them. They are still too raw, so they elude me. I lack the tools to fully grasp and actualize them. I need the proper implements. Indeed, I cannot even give these inchoate memories a proper name; I do not yet have the tools to grasp them, to break down their complexity. Yet I remain aware of their presence, lurking beneath the surface.

There are, however, experiences whose negative impact is so great that they break us, so that we lose the ability to employ these tools. Sometimes a person feels such powerful feelings of love that when he experiences its sudden and unexpected loss, he has great difficulty loving again—the vessels containing his love have shattered. Negative experiences are etched in the soul, traumatic scars in our very being.

This view is strikingly similar to Lurianic Kabbalah's description of creation's transformation from the *nihil* to the reality we inhabit. There are divine forces in our world, but without the requisite vessels they can be neither contained nor even perceived. In this sense, the advancement of human knowledge over the centuries can be seen as an effort to formulate new definitions, new taxonomies, "vessels" to contain the divine forces.

As odd as it may sound, Lurianic Kabbalah asserts that forging the vessels is the easy part. Far more difficult is the mending of the shattered vessels, whose fragments are scattered throughout all of reality—physical, psychological, and spiritual. Man must set out in search of God's broken vessels, collecting the life force—"sparks"—stored within them, then try to repair them. This is the process of *tikkun*, repair or emendation, which, according to Lurianic Kabbalah, is incumbent upon each of us.

But shattered vessels have become negative, even evil forces. Anything that is evil or negative or difficult or sick is a shard of these broken vessels. Absent the mitigating influence of positive and creative forces, the vessels became destructive. All the harsh borders within the world and within ourselves—death and disease, wounds of the flesh and the soul and the memories of both—all the destructive forces of denial and chaos that work to keep us from fully realizing our abilities and our desire to grow and to live a meaningful and creative life—all these originate in the broken vessels. When I meet a negative person, I should recognize that this behavior has its roots in the broken vessels within him, that is, in difficult experiences that leave him in dark shadows not lit by some positive force. In kabbalistic terminology, these are called "harsh judgments," forces of negation that have not been mitigated by the positive and creative forces of *Hesed* (mercy or compassion). Not everyone can repair the broken vessels scattered around their daily life, but we are nonetheless expected to repair and reconstitute the shards in our bodies and our souls over the course of our lives. The redemption of the world and of human society—the Hasidic ideal of *tikkun olam*—will come about only when every individual has personally undertaken a *tikkun atzmi*, the repair of the self.

⁓

Every fiber of knowledge buried within me is crying out, telling me that the nervous pains that began last year are rooted in the shattered worlds within me, in the shards that I cannot yet redeem from the smoldering rubble. My doctors may laugh at me, and I cannot yet identify the broken world in question, but I have no doubt this is so.

Generations of Kabbalah sages charge me with a difficult, two-fold task. First, I must repair my own shattered vessels, mending past events whose overwhelming force prevented me from experiencing them at the time. Second, I must increase the capacity of my internal reservoirs so as to better receive and contain a new reality. A gradual increase in the volume of my vessels will allow me a wider range for understanding new concepts and experiences.

I do not know how to go about repairing myself, and as my frustration grows, a troubling question occurs to me: why doesn't God repair the broken vessels Himself? Why must we, such terribly limited mortals, be burdened with the task of confronting the terrible consequences of the rupture within the divine? Why must we live in a flawed and tattered reality suffused with suffering and evil?

This is a bold question for religious believers, and the kabbalists do not explicitly engage or even acknowledge it. But when I try to cut through the jumble of obscure, torturous formulations of kabbalistic thought, I find the following answer: God does not repair the broken vessels that are in our world because He is incapable of doing so. This task is beyond His power as Creator. God cannot do this work for me, and less can He do it without me.

When God introduced His powers into the universe in order to create a defined world, He was forced to find a very fine balance between His infinite unity, transcending division and contraction, and the need to create a reality subject to borders—borders that define His own being; in other words, a balance between the unfettered overflow of divine light that bursts into the space of creation, and the vessels—the borders and definitions—that bestow on the light a this-worldly reality. This balance—which allows God's powers, infinite in their process, to exist as an undifferentiated "one," even while being manifested in the world—is couched in terms of male and female imagery of flowing and reception. When the male and female were separated, the (female) vessels were shattered and scattered about, severed from the overflow of light they were intended to contain. As a result, our world became *olam ha-perud*, "the world of separation," sundered from the infinite divine power.

God cannot repair the "world of separation" alone, since His unity is infinite and absolute and so cannot participate in the divisions required to enter into the depths of this world. God could only enter the world of separation by severing an aspect of Himself from Himself, and God, it seems, does not do so.

The collection of the sparks and the mending of the vessels remain, then, almost exclusively human enterprises, undertaken as we strive to repair our world and our selves. The esoteric or mystical significance of "repairing the broken vessels" is that we must rebuild God. As long as the world of separation endures, a world sealed off from God's reach and influence, God is not whole.

This is how the many kabbalists (following the Talmudic sages on this point) interpret the eschatological passage in Zechariah 14:9: "And the Lord will become king over all the earth; on that day, the Lord will be one and His name one."[10] In our unredeemed reality, God is not one, not whole. Elements of the divinity are shattered and dormant, and it is our goal as human beings to rehabilitate and reconstitute them. God needs a dynamic dialogue with humanity that alone will help heal the wounds and fractures that are at once His and ours.

Up come feelings of rebellion and refusal. God's desire to live forced Him to undergo contraction—and now we are expected to harvest the bitter fruit of His failure? Is this the reason Judaism considers suicide the most grave transgression of all—as though a man who chose to end his own life were saying, "I do not wish to be a partner in the project of divine *tikkun*"? But can we be expected to commit to a partnership in a project in which we have no say and that ultimately stems from God's own selfish needs? The question remains even if God's actions are motivated by a desire to benefit His creatures, though this impulse seems paradoxical in light of what we know of human life and human history.

I submit that all the kabbalistic discussions of the shattering of the vessels, and of feeling compassion for God as He contracts, are attempts to blur the painful truth: there can be no justification for why so many people experience so much suffering.

3

We are in the middle of Sukkot, the Festival of Booths. On the eve of the holiday I visit my close friend and his wife, who have not budged from their daughter's bedside in the pediatric ICU. The doctors have given up hope of the girl ever awakening from her coma. Her pupils are dilated and the intracranial pressure is potentially lethal. One of the best neurosurgeons in Israel has strongly recommended opening the girl's skull to release the pressure on her brain, but my friend will not sign the consent form. The doctors are upset with him for further jeopardizing his daughter's life. His father has demanded that he relent, but my friend is adamant.

Is this faith or madness?

I return home from the hospital, and just before the beginning of the holiday I take my daughter to the ultra-Orthodox city market in Bnei Berak, where we can purchase the four species that are part of the holiday ritual. For a trifle in these final hours, we buy a palm frond (*lulav*), a citron (*etrog*), three myrtles (*hadas*), and two wilted willows (*aravah*) that were about to be thrown out. The holiday of Sukkot is about both stability and impermanence, between the palm frond that can last for many years and the willows that wither within days. But halakhic technology has solved even the wilting willows: the vendors offer vacuum-sealed packages of the Four Species—a package of Void Space, for only in the void can time stand still. On our way home, my daughter inhales the scent of her golden citron. The Zohar describes Sukkot as the holiday of faith.[11] It is the holiday in which, like the Israelites following God through the desert, one departs his home to take refuge in faith, seeking shelter under the wings of the *Shekhinah*, the aspect of God immanent in our world. I see my father's sukkah in my mind's eye—old planks and boards cobbled together. My father taught me to strike a hammer on the head of the nail—the proper grip at the end of the handle, the importance of the first blow landing with a full and accurate swing of the arm. He was always so proud of the sturdy sukkah he built, boasting that it could stand firm for all eternity.

An eternal sukkah, eternal faith ... I laugh bitterly.

Longing to escape the confusion that has gripped me the past few days, I decide to take my family to the Negev, the desert region in southern Israel, where we will spend the holiday Shabbat. The forecast is for cold and clear weather. I want to stare at the ripples of otherworldly sunsets, listen to the night silence, encounter the merciful and compassionate God once again in the harmonious, glittering light of countless stars and the cold mountain wind blowing over me, soothing my fears.

I did not foresee that after the Negev sunset, with night falling quickly, I would see nothing but evil. I met an evil, fire-breathing God; a God of plotting and provocation.

But I *was* prepared, I thought to myself later. I *was* familiar with the theological systems that portray the world's creator and ruler as cruel and fickle, almost like a moody teenage boy. This Gnostic view was widespread in the Mediterranean during the first centuries CE—the belief in a good god who is not involved with the material world, and an evil demiurge who governs our world. With no small amount of condescension, I viewed these theologies as primitive, bizarre heretical cults, precursors of medieval Christianity.

But in the desert twilight that Sabbath eve during the Festival of Faith, I saw only evil. My core sense of myself and of the world collapsed then and there.

I am so naive, I said to myself. Inveterate optimist that I am, whenever I think of God, I never consider that He might, in fact, be evil. But now a God has been revealed to me who has not yet decided who and what He wants to be, a God who discovered the evil within Him and, enraged by it, continually lashes out at us. I saw a God laughing maliciously, an evil wizard who enjoys watching us suffer. A God who relishes watching us surrendering ourselves naively to His impetuous folly. And after all that, He wants us to bow and worship.

On a visit to the hospital two days earlier, I felt helpless in the face of the pain of my friend and his wife as they stood vigil for their unconscious daughter, her head shaved, surrounded by machines. My friend, whose life is governed by the norms of the ultra-Orthodox world, spoke with me about the medical reports. But his wife remained crouched in the corner of the intensive care unit, reciting psalms. When his wife saw we were engaged in a prolonged conversation, she began loudly berating her husband for wasting time on idle chatter instead of praying for his daughter's life.

The deep darkness of the Negev night brought another of the piercing, stress-induced headaches that have wracked me since early childhood. And now it came with a facial nerve pain that struck me like a hammer on an anvil. I saw that God was enjoying Himself— my pain a source of divine amusement. How foolish I am, I thought, a naive man seeking to anchor his sense of self in an ideal of harmony and progress, and even writing in this vein to encourage others to see the world in this light. *Just another person trying to mask the true nature of God with a blanket of lies*, I taunt myself in my pain.

A terrible wound opens in my soul, compounding my intensifying physical pain. The twinkling of the stars only focuses my mind on the pain flashing through my upper jaw and temple.

After the pain subsides a bit, I can think more clearly. How right they were, the worshippers who peer at us from across the generations, seekers of God who tried to appease and propitiate, offering Him blood sacrifices, flattering Him with incense and myrrh morning and night, singing hymns of praise and glory. What caused intelligent people to try to appease God with sacrifices—what has God to do with sacrifices? Well, they did it because they knew the truth. God is not a merciful father, but a vulgar king who thirsts for blood and suffering. Even when the believers praised Him, they did not tell the truth. We were all led astray by their effusive words of praise, but the laudatory hymns actually expressed a hidden hope that God would be swayed by these prayers and reform His ways. They must have thought: *If we call Him compassionate and merciful, a king who loves justice and righteousness, perhaps He will forget for a moment that He is "a God who rages every day"* (Psalm 7:12) *and not rain blows upon us daily.*

My entire life has been a mistake! Even when I distanced myself from the commandments of my ancestral religion, it never occurred to me that God is evil! My pains swell up again; I am lost and know not where to turn. There is no consolation, I know that now. If this be God, there is no escape, nowhere to run. My loneliness grows. Not only have I lost the last vestiges of faith in a heavenly father, I have discovered that He is and has always been violent and abusive.

After that Sabbath experience in the Negev, when I encountered a zealously vengeful God, I returned home terribly depressed. I told my wife I was disappointed with the accommodations, that there had been too much noise, and so forth. I could not tell her the truth, that the last traces of my faith in life had been shattered and that I had become spiritually and emotionally unmoored. I feared she would mock me. It frightened me to think that perhaps all of us feel something like this but suppress it in our daily lives lest we plunge into the darkest pits of despair.

"Well, of course," some will ask, "haven't you heard the question 'Where was God during the Holocaust?'" Yes, I have heard it; I have heard it countless times. But I never listened. At almost every one of my lectures over the past few years, some elderly man stands up and throws down the same gauntlet: "Where was God during the Holocaust?" and I, foolishly, respond with the same vague and noncommittal answer: "I don't know where God was during the Holocaust, just as I don't know where God was yesterday, when a car ran over a four-year-old child," suggesting there is no real difference between evil on a historical scale and the more circumscribed daily evils. I then add, "True, there is evil in God; evil is part of creation." But it never occurred to me that there is only evil, nothing but evil, with no good to balance it. Evil rules, the evil God rules. There is no consolation.

4

My journey has stopped dead in its tracks. Over the past three weeks I have been unable to write. I spend most of my time reading the works of Kabbalah scholars, wondering where I went wrong, what is the core misunderstanding that has so broken my spirit. But the reading only confirms and fans my fears. Once again I take up *The Doctrine of Evil and the Husks* (Kelippot) *in Lurianic Kabbalah*,[12] a thin volume published years ago by the Kabbalah scholar Isaiah Tishby. I had read it once as an undergrad, but as usual I let my optimism sweep me along, without asking myself what the text is truly trying to say. I had found in the kabbalistic corpus only what I was looking for, quickly passing to the consoling doctrines of Hasidism.

Isaac Luria had several disciples, each of whom understood the doctrine of divine contraction differently. Most familiar, perhaps, is the version promulgated by Hayyim Vital, whose widely disseminated writings constitute the core of what is today considered Lurianic Kabbalah. But there were other disciples who heard Luria's teachings and transmitted very different traditions that for generations were purposely obscured by Vital's followers. One of these disciples was Joseph ibn Tabul, who wrote a scandalous essay in Luria's name, "*Derush Heftzi Bah*," an essay Isaiah Tishby considered the deepest and most authentic expression of Lurianic Kabbalah.

According to Ibn Tabul, Luria holds that creation occurred as a result of God's desire to cleanse Himself of tiny particles of evil that were intermingled in His infinite self. So He concentrated all these particles in a single space within Him and proceeded to abandon it. God's contraction, in other words, involved the concentration and the cathartic evacuation of the evil within Him. Our world, our entire reality, comes out of that concentrated space and is suffused with the detritus of evil. The infinite God cannot stand even trace elements of evil, but we receive intense doses that fill our finite lives, blanketing and permeating our earthly existence.

We are the trashcan for God's evil.

Ibn Tabul's kabbalistic formulation is no less bleak:

> That force [of evil] was admixed throughout God's being ... and when the desire presented itself to emanate the world, he gathered together all the roots of harsh judgment embedded within him ... and mercy departed from the location of those roots. By way of analogy, a speck of dust within the ocean does not make the waters murky, and cannot be detected, and it is only when the water is drained that the dust that was mixed in it is revealed. So too here ... all the power of harsh judgment was gathered in a single place, so [it] grows denser, and as a result the light of the Infinite One, may He be blessed, departs.[13]

To be sure, this is only a partial description, and all the great kabbalists, including Ibn Tabul, agree that this is only the first step—the primordial origin of a reality into which God will eventually introduce His powers of beneficence. But if reality is rooted in evil and God's primary desire is to cleanse Himself, to rid himself of the evil within Him, what can we possibly hope for from such a reality? Why must we be the victims of this divine ablution?

⌐

chapter two

Hokhmah
The Abyss from Which None Ever Returns

In times of trouble, I always find my way back to Rabbi Nahman of Bre-
slov. Even as a child, when my father gave me "Rabbi Nahman's
Stories" in the Yiddish original, I was drawn to this enigmatic figure.
The stories—the lost princess, the wondrous beggars, the giant eagles
who gather in a tall tower and compete about who possesses the most
ancient memory—filled the storerooms of my imagination, even
though at the time I did not understand their significance.

My parents' shelves were always littered with material about
Rabbi Nahman's life and teachings: a collection of his sayings, the
epistles of his disciples, even secret travel instructions to his grave in
Uman, Ukraine, which in my youth was under Soviet sovereignty
and so closed to Israelis. The booklets described how to obtain a visa
to the Soviet Union, how to bribe border guards, how to find the
house of the old widow in whose yard Rabbi Nahman is buried—
even the widow's irritation when the prayers of the Hasidim disturb
her rest. But the effort will be rewarded, the booklets promised:
before he died, Rabbi Nahman promised to watch over anyone who
makes a pilgrimage to his grave and recites ten psalms and, should
it come to that, seize the pilgrim by the hair and drag him up out of
the pits of hell.

When the Soviet regime collapsed and the gates of its former territories burst open, I too made a pilgrimage to Rabbi Nahman's grave. I had no high hopes for the promises Rabbi Nahman made— my trip was for journalistic and anthropological reasons, to observe the mass prayer of Rabbi Nahman's followers on Rosh Hashanah. I watched in wonder as an otherwise marginal Ukrainian town was transformed for a few glorious days into a bustling Hasidic city.

I do not expect Rabbi Nahman to save me now. But I do know that if there was a Hasidic master capable of experiencing true suffering and using it as a spiritual and intellectual stepping-stone, it was Rabbi Nahman. When, as a child, I prayed with my father in the great yeshiva of the Breslov Hasidim in the Me'ah She'arim neighborhood in Jerusalem, there was a huge sign: *"Gevald, zey zach nisht meyo'esh"*—"*Gevald*, do not despair, there is no despair whatsoever in the world." At the time I did not understand what despair Rabbi Nahman was referring to or why the synagogue officials saw fit to hang this great banner in the sanctuary. I was particularly interested in Rabbi Nahman's chair, displayed in the synagogue in a glass case. I scrutinized it, tracing the floral engravings in the brown wood. Today I know much more, having read a great deal about Rabbi Nahman's physical and emotional *via dolorosa*—his grave illness, the death of his children, and his ongoing determination to remain in a state of joy even in the face of awful circumstances.

But I am not speaking of joy right now. I am headed toward Rabbi Nahman precisely because he is one of the few figures in Jewish history who dared to ask the kinds of questions that so trouble me and to subject them to such a comprehensive and profound analysis. Jewish history knows many deep thinkers who have produced complex halakhic innovations or sublime philosophical systems. But Rabbi Nahman moves beyond the cold abstractions of theological and philosophical discourse. His literary and intellectual production—doctrines, homilies, stories—is always rooted in his personal life and set unembellished before the reader.

Rabbi Nahman's discussion of the Lurianic doctrine of contraction is found in *Likkute Moharan*, a homiletic elaboration of Exodus

10:1: "Then the Lord said to Moses, 'Go to Pharaoh; for I have hardened his heart and the heart of his officials, in order that I may show these signs of Mine among them.'" Kabbalistic interpretations generally understand this as a veiled meditation on the meaning of evil in its various manifestations.[1] Rabbi Nahman, typically, begins the homily expressing a widely accepted sentiment: "God created the world out of His compassion. For He wanted to reveal His compassion, and if creation had not taken place, to whom would He have shown His compassion?"[2] This is a common kabbalistic notion, though coming from the mouth of Rabbi Nahman, it sounds almost satiric.

> He therefore created the entire creation, from the inception of the divine emanation (*Atzilut*) all the way down to the center point[3] of the corporeal world [that is, from the primordial stirrings of the contraction process to the depth of corporeality], in order to display His compassion. Yet when God wanted to create the world, there was no place in which to create it, since there was nothing but *Ein Sof* (the Infinite). He therefore contracted the light to the sides and through this contraction the Void Space was made. Then, within this Void Space, all days and measures[4] came into existence—this being the creation of the world. The Void Space was necessary for the creation of the world, since without the Void Space there would have been no place in which to create the world.[5]

Rabbi Nahman's description so far is familiar to me from Lurianic Kabbalah, with the exception of the neologism "Void Space" as a term for the Lurianic space from which the Infinite removes itself prior to creating reality within it. But here Rabbi Nahman changes course, tacking in a new and daring direction:

> But full comprehension of the contraction that produced the Void Space will only be possible in the future, since it requires that we apply to it two contradictory attributes: being and nothingness. The Void Space is the result of the contraction; that God, so to speak, withdrew His divinity from that place. Thus

there is, so to speak, no divinity there, so it is not at all possible
to comprehend the concept of the Void Space until future days.[6]

If I understand him correctly, Rabbi Nahman is saying that our intellect cannot grasp the meaning of this Void Space until the Messiah
comes and resolves all Torah enigmas. Apparently, the question is:
can there even be divine presence in our world? After all, the creation
of the world was inaugurated by God's contraction—that is, God's
departure from the world. And yet, there must be some immanent
presence of God, since all living beings draw on God's vitality.

This is precisely the difficulty that Luria's doctrine set out to
resolve. God channeled His infinite powers, setting limits and borders
for them, and they find expression in the ten *sefirot* that ultimately
bring about the creation of the world. On this reading, then, God has
an unquestionable presence in creation, albeit circumscribed within
the Void Space, the area devoid of the infinite power that constituted
God's essence prior to the contraction. What, then, is Rabbi Nahman
asking, and why is his question so difficult that it can be answered only
in the messianic age?

To Rabbi Nahman, this question seems to be the greatest challenge to religious faith. All the other challenges to the Jewish belief
system can be answered, he says, for example: If God knows the
future, can there be free will? What about the description of God's
character in human terms, so evident in just about every chapter of
the Bible? Or the fact that even Maimonides was not able to prove
that the world is not eternal but rather created? According to Rabbi
Nahman, all these challenges can be resolved eventually: "For he will
be able to find God in that place, provided he seeks and searches for
Him there.... For there exists [in these lesser difficulties] divine vitality, that is, the intellect and letters[7] that fell into that place."[8]

His own question, in contrast, comes from the "Void Space,"
which, according to his own definition, cannot contain answers, since
it transcends the intellect:

For the questions that arise from this heresy stem from the
Void Space in which, so to speak, there is no divinity. There

is therefore absolutely no way that one can find an answer for these questions that come from there, from the aspect of the Void Space, i.e., no way to find God there. For if God were found there as well, it then would not be vacated and it would consist of nothing but the Infinite. And from this heresy Scripture says, "none ever return [*yashuvun*]" (Proverbs 2:19). For there is absolutely no repentance [*teshuvah*] for this heresy since it stems from the Void Space, from which, so to speak, He contracted His divinity. But through faith, the Jewish people cross[9] all wisdoms and even this heresy that stems from the Void Space, for they believe in God without philosophical inquiry and intellection, through perfect faith alone.[10]

I ask myself if I have fallen into that very abyss from which, according to Rabbi Nahman, "none ever return." Is he referring to the cruel God who, once encountered, can no longer be thought of as a merciful and compassionate father? Is the heresy of the "Void Space" the existential loneliness to which simple faith is the only possible response?

A number of important Breslov scholars have concluded that Rabbi Nahman was referring to God's absence from the world[11]— that the only way to explain the presence of evil in the world is to declare that God is not present in it. Better to suppose that the father has traveled to a distant land than to admit that he is present but brimming with violent malice.

But I cannot despair of Him yet, and I reflect on the following passage:

> For God "fills all the worlds and encircles all the worlds."[12] Thus we find that He is, so to speak, within all the worlds and around all the worlds. Yet there has to be a gap, so to speak, between the filling and the encircling, otherwise it is all one and the same.... Thus the Void Space surrounds the entire world, and God, who encircles all the worlds, encircles the Void Space as well. Thus one may state that "He fills all the worlds"—i.e., the entire creation that was created within the Void Space, and also that "He encircles all the worlds"—i.e., He encircles the

Void Space. In between, the Void Space acts as a gap, since God, so to speak, contracted His divinity from there.[13]

Rabbi Nahman no longer echoes the Lurianic doctrine of contraction, which he had earlier described as God's departure from the circular space, but rather addresses the next stage, in which God introduces the essences of the ten *sefirot* into the Void Space. Rabbi Nahman's description of this space is unique. The Void Space is like a ring of emptiness that continues to surround the material world after it was created.[14] The empty ring is the excess Void Space left over after creation, a gap, so to speak, between the filling and the encircling. Otherwise it is all one and the same. The gap in question is not a difference so much as a breach or lacuna. Without such a gap between God's infinite essence and the created world, the material world would be lost, absorbed into the Infinite.

God is infinite, says Rabbi Nahman, but the infinite God contains finite, demarcated aspects actualized in the created world. Between these different aspects—the infiniteness and finitude of the divine—is the Void Space.

What is this gap, this ring of emptiness? How does it contain "being" and "nothingness" simultaneously? The ring serves as an insulating layer, the point of no contact, as it were, between God's infinity and the emerging reality of creation. This insulation is not wholly devoid of both divinity and creation. It is not a cosmic vacuum, but neither does it contain the fully infinite aspect of God or created reality as grasped through our conceptual apparatus and then formulated in language. It is, rather, an intermediary state, simultaneously "being" and "nothingness."

This liminal area is characterized by an absence of created reality, even in its most subtle manifestation, as the contraction of the Infinite into the spatial and temporal categories that give rise to the familiar space and time is still waiting to happen. In this sense, the intermediary state does not even entail "contraction" of letters or language, since these are the primordial elements of human thought and such a contraction constitutes a phase of creation. This is why Rabbi Nahman asserts that there can be no speech in the Void Space:

For these perplexities and questions [raised] by the heresy that stems from the Void Space are the aspect of silence, since there is above them no intellect[15] or letters to answer them, as explained above.... Speech is the demarcation of all things. God circumscribed His wisdom in the letters, such that certain letters demarcate one thing, while other letters demarcate something else. But in the Void Space—which surrounds all the worlds and which is, so to speak, vacated of everything, as explained above—there is no speech at all, and not even intellect without letters. Thus the perplexities that stem from there are in the aspect of silence. This is analogous to what we find regarding Moses: When he inquired about the death of Rabbi Akiva, "Such is Torah and such is its reward?" God answered him: "Be silent, thus it arose in my thought." That is, you must be silent and not ask for an answer and solution for this question, since "thus it arose in thought," and thought is more elevated than speech. Therefore you must keep silent regarding this question, because it is in the aspect of "arose in thought," indicating there is no speech that can answer it.[16] The same holds true of the questions and perplexities that stem from the Void Space, where there is no speech or intellect, as explained above, and they are thus in the aspect of silence— there one must simply believe and keep silent.[17]

This passage, which reveals the source of Rabbi Nahman's theological perplexity, deals with the difference between God's thought prior to its contraction and individuation and the conceptual nature of human thought and intellect. Since the traditional kabbalistic view states that the world was created through speech, it follows that speech is located beneath the lower limit of the vacuum ring, that is, beneath the Void Space that divides infinity from the created world. It is in principle impossible for human thought to transcend created reality. Human thought is ineluctably discursive—it is grounded in language and in the concepts of space and time, which are God's creative speech.

The question then arises: what *does* exist within divine thought? On the one hand, the first three *sefirot* are devoid of the unfettered infinity of divine potencies, since their infinite presence would negate the finitude of creation. On the other hand, they are devoid of creation qua intellect and language.

These baffling recesses engender many other theological perplexities that Rabbi Nahman does not mention, perhaps because they would only worsen his already poor standing in the Hasidic world of his day. For instance, how can God's providence reach into the created world? How does the fact that the world lies on the other side of a God-less vacuum affect our understanding of the pain we suffer in this world? These issues, says Rabbi Nahman, lie beyond the reach of the human intellect: "one must simply believe and keep silent."

I consider my own theological questions to be of the sort Rabbi Nahman characterized as originating from the Void Space, in which case he offers me a stern warning: anyone who raises such heretical questions has no recourse but to set them aside or suppress them in the depths of his mind. But I have traveled too far in my life, in my Jewish faith, to have someone tell me to refrain from asking. Can Rabbi Nahman provide nothing more than a stock response on the need to embrace a simple faith? Where are all the "divine and human secrets" that no less a sage than S. Y. Agnon promises Rabbi Nahman's readers?[18]

Rabbi Nahman alternated between assured self-confidence and abject worthlessness, joy and sorrow, uplifting optimism and crushing pessimism. Other Jewish thinkers have experienced similar oscillations, but none has been as expressive and as open as Rabbi Nahman. His truth burns more brightly than that of any other Jewish thinker, its brilliance undimmed by two centuries. I will never forget the Hasids' prayers in the great Breslov synagogue in Jerusalem. I am forever grateful to my father for making what was for him a long trip with me every year during the High Holy Days to that synagogue, which was located in a distant Jerusalem neighborhood. Even as a child I could sense the truth suffusing that synagogue. The Breslov synagogue did not have a mellifluous cantor, but rather a prayer leader, a prominent Hasid who led the congregation in prayer with an imploring, rent voice. My uncle (Rabbi Yaakov Meir Schechter, prominent in the Breslov community) recited psalms before blowing the shofar on Rosh Hashanah. I owe my most cherished moments in the prayers I experienced later in my youth to Rabbi Nahman.

All of the sources Rabbi Nahman cites reinforce the notion that some questions have to stay questions, because they stem from the Void Space. One of these sources is a famous Talmudic midrash that deals with the meaning of human suffering as the Babylonian Talmud defines it in *Berachot* 7a—"the wicked man prospers; the righteous man suffers."

In this Talmudic legend (Babylonian Talmud, *Menahot* 29b), Moses ascends to heaven to receive the Torah and there finds God adorning the letters of the Torah with crowns, that is, graphic flourishes. Moses asks God why he is delaying for these trivial flourishes, and God answers that they will serve as the basis for legal rulings by the future sage Rabbi Akiva. Moses's curiosity is piqued, and he wants to learn more about this Rabbi Akiva for whom God so labors and asks to see him. God transports Moses into the future, directly into Rabbi Akiva's *beit midrash*, where Moses sits humbly in the last (and least prestigious) row and is unable to follow the discussion. Moses grows weary and is troubled that Rabbi Akiva is expounding the Torah in a way that he cannot grasp. He is reassured only when he hears that Rabbi Akiva's teachings are based on his, Moses's, own words. Moses goes back in time and asks God, "If Rabbi Akiva is so great that even I cannot follow his teachings, why does God not give the Torah through him?" God replies, "Be silent, thus it arose in My thought." Moses then asks to see the rewards bestowed on this wondrous man, and he again travels to the future where he witnesses the Romans raking Rabbi Akiva's flesh and hanging it on meat hooks. Moses hurries back to the past and asks God if this is the reward due a great Torah scholar. Again God replies, "Be silent, thus it arose in My thought."

Rabbi Nahman does not understand God's repeated silencing of Moses as rebukes but rather as God informing Moses that this is not a place of speech but of silence. The answer to these questions originates in the Void Space, where God's thought cannot be expressed discursively. In other words, God cannot provide an answer through the medium of human speech, suited for the human intellect.

But even as Rabbi Nahman is telling me that I should not dwell on unanswerable questions, advocating, like my mother, a simple Jewish faith, he has provided me with a hint as to the meaning of the silence of the Void Space. Two hints, in fact: first, that there exists a "place" within the ten *sefirot* that is the source of unanswerable questions; and second, that this place is called *mahshavah*, "thought."

There is a rich online database of kabbalistic and Hasidic texts. The word "thought" appears often, but then I find a few citations that link the Void Space, the source of unanswerable questions, to God's thought, which is identified in kabbalistic sources with the two *sefirot*—*Hokhmah* and *Binah*—through which God reveals Himself as creator and that appear immediately after the hidden *sefirah Keter*.

Hokhmah, the most subtle and most primordial point of all existence, emanates from *Keter*. Everything that was and is and will be, all the souls and all the times, are contained within this compressed primeval point in the form of pure thought, a point that is unthinkably small and large at the same time. *Hokhmah* is like a geometric point that occupies no physical space—unlike the infinite lines that can be drawn from it. The transition from *Keter* to *Hokhmah*, the first step in the cosmic emanation process, is a transition from "nothingness" to "being," from absolute potentiality to primordial actuality, albeit an actuality that is entirely abstract, lacking even the most preliminary definition.

Hokhmah represents the elemental Torah, the divine intellect, the Torah that precedes the existence of words and letters. The kabbalists anchor this view in their interpretation of Job 28:12: "From where [*me'ayin*] shall wisdom [*hokhmah*] be found, and where is the place of understanding [*binah*]?" This verse is usually read as a question regarding the provenance of wisdom (i.e., from God). But the Hebrew word *ayin*, which in this verse means "where," can also mean "nothingness" and can thus refer to the *sefirah Keter*. On this reading, the verse is not a question ("from where?") but a statement: wisdom, that is, the *sefirah* Wisdom (*Hokhmah*) emerges from *ayin*, from *Keter*. All that is and all that may yet be, all the unfathomable multifaceted variety of reality, is contained in the primordial point known as *Hokhmah*.

Perhaps this is why the kabbalists see creation and revelation as parallel processes, why reality and language emerge conjoined from God's veiled and impenetrable wisdom. As the first point of reality, *Hokhmah* is designated by the Hebrew letter *yod*, the smallest in the Hebrew alphabet, a tiny mark from which the other letters will later emerge. The entire Torah—the biblical text itself as well as all the interpretations and midrashim generated by the desire to understand it, indeed all of human wisdom—is contained in this little *yod*. It is also the first letter of YHWH, the Tetragrammaton, or four-letter name of God.

Hokhmah carries with it its counterpart, *Binah*, which emanates from it. These two *sefirot* can be grasped as distinct aspects of mind: *Hokhmah* is the initial spark, the creative insight, which is generally visual; *Binah* is reflective thought that absorbs and processes. *Hokhmah* is likened to a point of light in a hall of mirrors, its image endlessly reflected.

Hokhmah and *Binah* are symbiotically linked, and neither can be grasped independently of the other. The kabbalists refer to them as "two companions that never part." *Hokhmah* is so ethereal, its essence so elusive, that it can only be grasped as it is reflected in *Binah*, while *Binah*—the mirrored hall—would remain shrouded in darkness without the light of *Hokhmah*. This is why the kabbalists refer to these *sefirot* as the primordial couple, *Abba* and *Ema*, father and mother, a duality that reflects the opposition between the male and female aspects of the divine and the human. In other words, the "point" and the "hall" are the elemental manifestations of the masculine and the feminine, both profoundly altered and most fully realized when in a state of union. *Hokhmah*, the point, is also associated metaphorically, even poetically, with overflowing light and water, images by which the Jewish mystics seek to explore the most abstract levels of consciousness. No less common are descriptions of sexual union, with the emanating light of *Hokhmah* understood as the *sefirah*'s ejaculate—*Hokhmah* full to the point of bursting with the potential energy of all that is and all that will be. This abundance fills *Binah*'s womb, creating a more reflective and individuated intellect, which in turn gives birth to all the remaining *sefirot*, that is, the seven lower *sefirot*. These seven "foundation" *sefirot*, which are the foundation for the limited reality to which we have access, are *Hesed*, *Gevurah*, *Tiferet*, *Netzah*, *Hod*, *Yesod*, and *Malkhut*.

Kabbalah texts generally devote a more comprehensive and richer discussion to *Binah* than to any other *sefirah* (except for *Malkhut*, who is represented as *Binah*'s twin sister). *Binah* is the highest of the *sefirot* that can be grasped by the human mind. It is within *Binah* that the first contraction occurs that draws the divine toward the principles that govern human thought; it is within her that the concepts of time and space begin to crystallize. As a result, it is only at the bottom of *Binah*, at the point where it comes in contact with the seven lower *sefirot*, that we find the divergence into different forces such as compassion (*Hesed*) and harsh judgment (*Gevurah*).

Binah is also the most important point of transition between the human and the divine, the narrow rope bridge that the Jewish mystics must traverse first on their way to revelation and that then leads them back to the terra firma of this world. Those who venture out into the Void Space to be reenergized by a vitality that has not yet undergone contraction are in so doing returning to *Binah*. It is *Binah* that they leave behind when setting out to interpret this newfound vitality and to forge the tools needed to realize it within the most constricted reality of all—our life here on earth. *Binah* is the supernal, overflowing mother, who gathers those who yearn for ever-renewing life into her being, and in her they gestate and are ultimately born, writhing in agony and shouting in a raw, embryonic language.

Rabbi Moshe Cordovero, a great kabbalist who was a contemporary of Isaac Luria, said that one cannot speak of *Hokhmah* and *Binah* at all.[19] Cordovero taught:

Speech is prohibited in *Binah*. But one can meditate on *Binah*, for it is called *Mi*, "who,"[20] a question that has no answer. But in *Hokhmah* even contemplation and questioning are futile, since we are unable to grasp its attributes. Thus Moses was told: "Be silent, thus it arose in My thought."[21]

The pair *Hokhmah* and *Binah*—the former transcending language and even thought, the latter that cannot be spoken of but can be contemplated—are discussed at great length in *Gates of Light* by Rabbi Joseph Gikatilla, an important thirteenth-century kabbalist:

Now listen closely and hear what can be heard in this matter: every occurrence of the phrase "thus it arose in thought" is in fact the statement "be silent," for you will find the gates locked regarding this matter, since it is locked and sealed in the highest chamber that no creature can enter, namely the chamber of profound thought that is referred to as endless desire,[22] so "check your mouth from speaking." And thus it is written with regard to Rabbi Akiva, when he was seen by Moses our Master, peace be upon him, who saw that they were combing his flesh and said, "Such is Torah and such is its reward?" and He replied, "Be silent, thus it arose in My thought." That is to say, Your question is not in a place in which you can grasp anything, so simply be silent. Why? Because thus it arose in thought. For it is located in a place to which you cannot ascend, nor can it descend from its place and set out toward you ... and now we have provided you with a great rule concerning any occurrence of the phrase "thus it arose in thought," for these are obscure matters and no creature can contemplate them, since there is absolutely no contemplation in thought. And since there is no path of entry into it, and it has no end or limit, how then can a finite being grasp an infinite matter? And it is about such matters that Scripture states, "Your thoughts are very deep" (Psalm 92:5). And the question of "the wicked man prospers; the righteous man suffers" is also related to this matter.[23]

From this passage we learn that Rabbi Nahman's Void Space is not located in the terrestrial realm, the world you and I inhabit, but rather in the most rarified realms of the *sefirot* whose existence predates the separation of speech and thought. *Hokhmah* and *Binah* form that insulating "ring" that is free of the Infinite, since the first emanation of divine power into the Void Space has already occurred. But they are also free of the created world familiar to us, which begins with divine speech that first stirs and begins to unfold within *Binah*.

The kabbalists caution against trying to discuss or even contemplate the content of these *sefirot*, since they contain unanswerable questions. Rabbi Nahman warns that this is an "abyss from which none ever return." Only Moses, he writes, could contemplate the nature of the Void Space, and even he could not express these thoughts in language; he had to be silent. But silence in the realm of the *sefirot* that correspond to highest Thought is not the silence of the absolute *nihil*. It is, rather, a knowing silence, which recognizes that this realm affords no space for human thought and speech:

> One can ascend to the World of Thought, and this is called elevating all the worlds, for thought is very exalted. Anyone who wants to enter the World of Thought must remain silent. Even if he speaks proper words at that moment, Thought escapes him. This is because Thought is so exalted that even proper speech diminishes it. This is the aspect of "Be silent, thus it arose in My thought"—one must be silent to ascend to thought....[24]

So says Rabbi Nahman.

But even as a child I asked questions rooted in the Void Space. On the way home from my religious studies, I would play the "omniscience game" with God. If God knows all my future actions, I thought to myself, clearly He knows which way home I will choose. So I would reach the starting point of my regular route, only to turn around and choose another. But when I reached that path, I thought to myself that God no doubt knew I would choose this route, so I immediately returned to the first path. And so I would continue to struggle—with myself or with my God—until evening fell and I despaired of it all. But in truth there was no danger in this game; more like a waste of time. So I decided that if I cannot grasp the true essence of the Void Space through my intellect, I would try to do so through my body.

When we experience pain, the muscles in the hurt region contract. This is an autonomic response; the blood vessels around an open wound constrict to reduce the blood flow. Paradoxically, muscle contractions have the opposite effect on internal pains, trapping them in the body and ultimately prolonging them. The contraction does not allow the wounded area to receive nourishment and thus heal.

Perhaps this is how one feels upon finding onself in the metaphysical space of evil: pain followed by an instinctive contraction that traps the pain inside. This cramping of the soul not only results in pain and suffering to those around us, but the increasingly violent constrictions causes the evil that suffuses us to become more acute.

———

Hokhmah—the primal source of all the worlds that will grow increasingly constricted as divine emanation proceeds—contains evil to the same extent that it contains good; the two coexist, without border or distinction. This is the space that has not yet undergone contraction, where everything is still in a state of potential, without definition or demarcation, encompassed by the primordial point in a state of primordial chaos. After all, "good" and "evil" are words that we assign different types of drives or entities, but none of these yet exist within *Hokhmah* in the same way we encounter them on earth. Within *Hokhmah* there is no distinction between good and evil, time and space; nothing within it can be expressed in speech. Only in *Binah* do we find the first stirrings of linguistic individuation.

In this sense, says Rabbi Nahman, silence is the only appropriate response for anyone located in *Hokhmah*. Perhaps this type of silence is like experiencing pain without contracting our muscles, that is, without attempting to shield ourselves from it by contracting it into human language and thought. If I do not attempt to protect myself from pain and reduce it by means of words and thoughts, I will be able to transform it from good to evil or, in this particular case, from evil to good. Perhaps, in other words, the desired transformation can be effected within a realm of pure experience that transcends speech. When, on the other hand, I try to enunciate the experience of pain in discursive thought and writing, I find myself at the bottom limit of *Binah*, where the contraction process begins. Here, at the pulse that marks the initial moment of contraction, evil crystallizes into evil, and good crystallizes into good. Within my life, the two are distinct realities; no longer interchangeable, the one cannot be transformed into the other.

Rabbi Nahman's silence, like God's rebuke of Moses who inquires after the fate of Rabbi Akiva, is apparently not passive acquiescence to an insuperable reality. To the contrary, only silence is transformative. Remain silent so that you can remain within *Hokhmah* long enough to convert evil into good.

This is not some vacuous magic trick. Many people who have tried to deal with intense pain over an extended period of time understand the significance of such silence, as it is the basic condition for transforming the pain in a profound and meaningful way. That is why a person who is located in the *Binah* within his soul may ask questions, but answers are precluded. For speech too quickly transforms potential experience into actual, at which point experience is again plunged into the depths of constriction and definition that exclude the possibility of deep transformation. One must wait patiently during the entire gestation period in the womb of *Binah*, the great mother, until the resulting being, having completed the natural process of growth and ripening, is discharged from the Void Space.

The secret of silence in the Void Space is "will without effort," that is, intentionally entering the Void Space without attempting to overcome the pain. One must experience the pain without giving in to the instinctive tendency to tense up and contract, which in this case means resorting to speech and so failing to inhabit a space of silence.

Rabbi Nahman knew well the agony of the Void Space and the pain of its silence. He suffered greatly in his short life: the torment of tuberculosis that ended his life at thirty-eight; the misery of his children's death; the sorrow and frustration of being misunderstood. Rabbi Nahman also had struggles of faith and was torn between rationality and mysticism, between the old world and the new. Here is Rabbi Nahman's own description:

> Man is a microcosm that contains the entire cosmos.... And so it can happen that a person who sits alone in the forest may become insane. This is because he is alone and all the nations are contained within him, and they are at war with one another, so that every time he must change to suit the aspect of a different nation, all according to the fortunes of the different nations, all of which are contained within him alone. As a result he can go completely insane due to the constant turbulence of ideas within him, because of the warring nations contained within him alone.[25]

But silence, as well as the internal dialogue, is part of a transformative process:

> Know too that controversy is the aspect of creation ... for if all Torah scholars were one, there would be no place for the world's creation. However, as a result of their controversies and their distinction from one another, with each withdrawing to a different side, the aspect of the Void Space is produced between them. This is the aspect of the contraction of the light to the sides, within which the world is created by means of the spoken word.[26]

Rabbi Nahman reassures those who easily despair and suggests ways out of the darkness. The analogy between the Void Space and controversies between sages implies that the divine process of contraction and creation is reproduced by the sages, who fall silent when points of disagreement emerge. By being silent in a space of controversy, the sages create a Void Space and dwell within it, which eventually makes possible the birth of a new type of human speech, analogous to the creation of the world through God's divine speech: "For whatever each one of them says is only for the sake of creating the world, which they bring about within the Void Space between them. For Torah scholars create everything through their words."[27]

The speech of the sages after the silent suspension of debate is a further iteration of God's founding act of creation within the Void Space. God's speech insulates the divine Infinite from the Void Space in which were created the *sefirot* beneath *Binah*, while the sages' conversation reconstructs this space when their disputes have ended and a place exists for a new, creative speech: "For the scholars' interpretations and discussions are not adduced for the sake of biblical interpretation as such, but rather for the resulting actions,[28] namely that they will form and create the world."[29]

Rabbi Nahman valued conversation and dialogue. But authentic or "new" speech must be preceded by silence that ensures that no evil is born from the Void Space. The silence is a vital component in the incubation process, the time of gestation in *Binah*'s "womb." True speech, speech that will convert evil into good, can properly emerge from *Binah* and proceed to the seven lower *sefirot* of action only when its birth is preceded by silence.

The Void Space contains both being and nothingness, both good and evil, as of yet indistinguishable. But we must not be intimidated, we must not flee the silence or decamp from this space. The controversies and disputations of sages do indeed cause a Void Space to open between them, but by nonetheless dwelling in this space I help this new, ripe speech emerge (which, in turn, mitigates my fear of residing in the Void Space). A new reality materializes as the Void Space, known as the world of thought—which up to now was devoid of all language and speech—is gradually suffused with linguistic creativity eventually referred to as "action." The new speech, then, begins to press on the empty gap, closing it and, as it were, clearing it away so as to make room for creation.

We are not dealing with the silence of the "ineffable" so often addressed in classical Jewish mysticism and in the works of the great rationalist philosopher Maimonides, who endorsed a God so abstract that predication that takes God as grammatical subject is tantamount to idolatry.[30] Rather, this silence aims to carve out a space for my earliest and most elusive memories of physical and spiritual birth, to recover the most obscure site of being and nothingness from which my body and my consciousness emerged. This silence is not an end unto itself, but rather paves the way for an attempt at slowly and ever so gently giving birth to these memories so that—aided by my discursive self-consciousness—it emerges, infant-like, into the world of action. The process cannot be rushed, lest the memory be stillborn.

According to Rabbi Nahman, we must undertake our own *tikkun* at the very heart of the problem, at the initial spark of divine speech from which the world was created, by "conquering" region after region within the world of thought ("the aspect of *Hokhmah*"), that is, the Void Space. This allows us to transform our inner Void Space into a creative force in our soul. This can be achieved only by utilizing the new language that emerges from the Void Space. In so doing, we can mend our own soul.

Rather than invoke a simple faith innocent of doubts and unanswerable questions, Rabbi Nahman emphasizes that the most meaningful faith, "the supreme faith," is located precisely within the Void Space:

> For in the future days, when "[God] will change the speech of the people to a pure speech, that they may all call on the name of the Lord" (Zephaniah 3:9), and they will all believe in Him, then the verse "come gaze from the peak of Amana" (Song of Songs 4:8) will be fulfilled. Specifically "from the peak of Amana," i.e., the aspect of the aforementioned faith (*emunah*) which is the peak of all faiths."[31]

The heart of faith is located at the highest reaches of the Divinity, in the silence of the Void Space, "for *Ein Sof* (the Infinite) is God Himself, and His wisdom is altogether incomprehensible. In that place there is only the aspect of faith."[32] At the lower end, in *Binah*, lies the egress of God the creator's primordial speech. In between faith and speech is the Void Space.

The language that emerges out of the Void Space, Rabbi Nahman unequivocally states, *is* silent faith.

But what is this silent faith? What faith is possible for me, now that I have been exposed to the terrible paradoxes of the Void Space from which none return? How can I believe in a place where the human intellect is already so thoroughly determined? Perhaps I can keep silent, but can I believe in a place that contains an indiscriminate mix of being and nothingness? Is the highest faith indeed located in a place that contains no rational and discursive thought? And if so, have I returned once again to the simple faith of my mother?

chapter three

Binah
The Sound of a Serpent
Shedding Its Skin

1

I try to practice silence to the extent my daily life allows. Sukkot has passed; my daughters are back in kindergarten. Rabbi Nahman of Breslov did not survive Sukkot. He died on the third day of the festival, his eyes fixed on the ceiling of his rented home in the Ukrainian city of Uman. His lungs ravaged by tuberculosis, he died in a fit of violent coughs, far from his family and his home. Moments before his death, he instructed his disciples to burn his unpublished manuscripts and managed a brief complaint: "I have no one to consult."[1]

My present silence is not the silence of my youth. Then I took a vow of silence, but my thoughts raced endlessly. Now, for the first time, I am trying to maintain myself patiently in a state of not understanding. All my old habits cry out in protest. The Jewish culture in which I am steeped focuses on words—divine revelation manifested through language, study, and prayer that find expression in the written and spoken word. In such a world, a person's achievements are measured by his capacity for discursive thought, and these paradigms are embedded in my consciousness. I acquired my most basic analytic and conceptual tools in the Orthodox educational system of my childhood. I learned to study on my own, to honor the views of my predecessors. I developed confidence in my ability to decipher any text, even if it required great effort and perseverance, and to recognize that there is nothing so complex that it cannot ultimately be overcome. I am proud to be part of this tradition.

However, the yeshiva curriculum is based on the principle that there are no contradictions in the Torah, no conflicts or dissonance among different biblical sources. We were quoted ad nauseam the famous Rabbinic gloss of Deuteronomy: "'This is not a trifling matter for you' (Deuteronomy 32:47)—Rabbi Mana said, 'This is not a trifling matter for you,' that is, if it is trifling it is only so for you. Why? Because you do not labor in Torah."[2] In other words, if and when I come across a textual difficulty, or if the Torah appears illogical or contradictory, I am to blame, not Scripture. My task is to redouble my efforts to understand the harmony between the different sources. I was conditioned that even if there are contradictory statements, there is a third verse that mediates between them, and in this mediation lies the truth. Any sustained period of reconciliation with non-understanding, any respite from one's efforts to overcome this state, was viewed as a mark of laziness and a fundamental betrayal of reason—almost the greatest sin we can commit against ourselves. The only sin greater was "taking a break," going out to have a good time. Even today I find myself fearing such free time. The yeshiva phrase is *bitul torah*—that is, time not spent in study is "the nullification of Torah."

Now I must confront a profound silence bereft of mediating positions—only radical, intractable contradictions. I will not understand the circle in which being and nothingness dance so long as I strive to reconcile them. I must be able to not understand, to remain in a place of insistent silence: silence of speech and silence of thought, in the calm expectation of the dawning of something else, the precise shape of which is as of yet unfamiliar to me.

To cease speaking, and writing, and thinking ... to merely be silent and feel! How does one feel without words? Through the body, perhaps? I have no idea how to do this. My culture is verbal through and through; all my skills are tied to words, to language. I cannot calm my consciousness for even a moment. My thoughts collide, pursue me, chase the sleep from my eyes. The God within me murmurs and roars restlessly. One moment He gazes upon me with a glowing face; in the next his countenance bespeaks evil and malevolence.

I try to pay close attention to the silence of the body, but I have a hard time deciphering its language. I cannot link the words referring to my body and my body itself. Twice a week I find out how far I still am from understanding its silence. My yoga teacher explains how and where to move my knees, but the words, recalcitrant, refuse to penetrate my consciousness. Were my yoga teacher trying to communicate a complicated philosophical doctrine I probably would have understood her immediately. But "the right knee moves to the left" I find incomprehensible, and I am reduced to rolling about awkwardly, imitating the movement of the other students.

⟋⟍

A strange dream haunts my restless sleep the past few nights: I am standing in a wide valley beneath the great Himalayas. Above me towers a huge mountain, its snow-capped peak penetrating the clouds. A wide stone stairway winds up from the bottom of the valley for the benefit of the many travelers who want to reach the summit, but I am unable to pass through the stone gates leading to these steps. Guards are stationed on either side, inspecting all who wish to enter. When they examine my bags, they find in my backpack a large metal sword in a leather sheath. I turn away, trying to hide the sword under the bushes along the path. Then I wake up.

After several days of silence, while poring over Himalaya guidebooks in search of a mountain similar to the one in my dream and toying with the idea of actually setting out in search of one, I understand that I must rid myself of the swords I have carried with me thus far, which have protected me over the course of my life.

My search for faith has always been conducted by means of arguments and counterarguments, definitions and analysis. But perhaps I need to search in a different way altogether. To leave my sword by the side of the road and replace it with other instruments that will help guide me to faith.

My silence is no longer a conscious choice. It forces itself upon me, and I am powerless to resist. I am eager to continue reading and writing, but my hands refuse to translate my wishes into thoughts and my thoughts into words.

I want my body to be silent as well, to stop burdening it with all the painkillers I keep taking. When my prescription runs out, I seize on the opportunity and do not refill it. I want to feel the pain that is in this place of silence so I can, perhaps, reinterpret it.

After two days without medication, I experience a tremendous sense of liberation. Even when the pain awakens me at night, I try to put into practice what I have been taught, drawing full breaths into it, examining it as if an outside observer, trying to grasp its nature. But I am not attending so much to the discomfort from my facial nerves as to the muted currents of pain flowing though my entire body, and especially through my arms. A dull, low-level ache pulses through my bloodstream, as though carried by the red blood cells themselves. In the split second suspended between inhaling and exhaling, I hear the pain's continuous whisper, like God seeking out Adam in the garden: *Ayeka*—"Where are you?"

I am supine in bed, startled and suddenly concerned by this hidden pain that had thus far escaped my notice. Can it be that I never felt it until now? Is this why I cannot fall asleep without intentionally stretching one of my limbs—a hand or a foot—into an uncomfortable position? Perhaps I have been trying to channel the pain into one of my limbs, concentrating it in one clearly delineated location, allowing the rest of my body to sleep.

What is the root cause of this pain? Where does it come from?

The frenzy of thoughts gradually abates, giving way to steadier images and memories. One of them appears over and over: a long metal ruler striking my fingertips, which are curled up like a pinecone. I remember immediately. The ruler belongs to my elementary school teacher. I am nine or ten years old, and my teacher is hitting me. Corporal punishment was common in the ultra-Orthodox school system in those days, but Mr. Podolsky's cruelty was exceptional. My glare exposed his weaknesses, his stunted being—both physical and spiritual. He wanted to break me, to hear me cry out in pain, at least once. So he beat me with his ruler, but I never cried out. I waited for him to lose hope, to call me "elephant skin" and send me back to my seat. I employed my old trick—dissociating myself from my fingernails and from the awful pain. The ruler never did "straighten me out." Instead, I donned the thick skin of an elephant, and even today I can defeat my daughters in tickle fights. I can numb my sensory nerves in an instant; I could have had a brilliant career as a faqir.

Is this, then, the root cause? The ruler blows that my body absorbed without protest, so many years ago?

Another day passes, and again I try to fall asleep, but my right ear begins to twitch. Blood flows into my earlobes ... and a still earlier corporal memory begins to bubble up to the surface, though still opaque and indistinct. No. The root cause was not ruler blows or the cries of joy from my fellow classmates, who wondered who would emerge victorious from this horrible contest. It began with the humiliating slaps I suffered at an earlier age, six or seven, administered by teachers who did not yet dare to terrorize us with the ruler. The memory of these slaps sends boiling blood rushing to my ears even to this day.

My right ear confirms the discovery. The twitching stops.

A stifled cry rises in my chest. My fists clench in rage, sadness, bewilderment that such cruelty could be acceptable. The pain in my hand shifts direction, now moving up, toward my chest, enters the chambers of my heart, and begins to squeeze, pressing and constricting, pressing and constricting. Something is pinching me, slapping me, gripping my arms and hitting my hands against one another, hitting me with a wooden and then a metal ruler. Is it the pain itself? Or perhaps the pleasure I saw in my teacher's eyes at the spectacle of this cruel humiliation? No, I say to myself, don't return to the clear feelings of humiliation that were undoubtedly branded into my consciousness. Don't neglect the pain of the body. Yes. The body. The skin. The nerve endings, beaten, incited, scorched.

I am crying again, shouting at the heavens the pains of a little boy who refused to shed a tear. I am in the eye of a storm of interlaced pains that I cannot untie—how awesome to set out this way on a journey of faith.

2

Perhaps the object of faith is not the person or thing in which we believe, whether the belief in question is the result of rational understanding or of vivid emotional experiences. Perhaps faith begins precisely where trust is wounded. Perhaps my faith is nothing more than the designation of a particular state, a place in my psyche or consciousness. Perhaps it is the emotional space that spurns unambiguous definitions, a state in which I can encounter God simultaneously as a merciful, compassionate father and as a cruel, capricious king.

Perhaps faith does elude definition, but not because it transcends words and feelings, as many mystics claim. Perhaps my faith is a stormy state within, a place of permanent turbulence where different winds constantly batter each other—a site of constant motion, constant change, without words or direction. An internal space that is, paradoxically, "empty" and "void" precisely because it is so full of contradictory emotions and dreams, of yearnings and painful memories, that cannot be contained in waking consciousness.

Perhaps true faith is anchored in a sense of uncertainty, a place that contains all the bits of information that make up my world— knowledge of God and His denial, my willingness to bear the yoke of the kingdom of heaven and to reject it, love and hate, fear and anxiety alongside security and inner peace—in a frenzied state of perpetual motion, seething and frothing, interconnected and interpenetrated, their radical fullness overflowing the others' borders, until there emerges a whirlpool of new being, of overwhelming insight, of unfamiliar feeling. Authentic creation.

Rabbi Nahman of Breslov's hints lead me on a journey, searching for this strange faith about which I cannot speak but can only experience within the Void Space. I begin to search for descriptions of faith as an unstable state, as a stormy space with collapsing borders. I return to the books and find, to my amazement, a characterization of faith I had never encountered:

> Rabbi Shimon said, "When the Holy One blessed be He created the world, He engraved engravings of the mystery of faith ... engraving both above and below, all are part of a single mystery. ... Seven palaces above, and they are the mystery of supernal faith, and seven palaces below, as above. All are part of the supernal mystery."[3]

This is just one of many similar verses in the Zohar, the first attempt I know of at a novel interpretation of faith, one that may shed new light on my earlier struggles. The seven sanctuaries of the Zohar may refer to the dynamic between the different *sefirot* that make up the Godhead. Whatever their precise nature, the critical issue for us is that we are no longer dealing with an understanding of faith in the standard lexicographical sense of belief in a particular doctrine. What we have here is a *credo* in the etymological sense, an "I believe," situated within the landscape of faith that is "world," and "place," and "space," a faith that encompasses processes that elude pat definition or fixed description. We are not dealing with physical space, of course, but with an intellectual and emotional place called faith, a place that finds expression even in physical pain and distress. According to the Zohar, faith is not a matter of upholding particular religious laws or accepting certain precepts, but of remaining steadfast in this place, being willing to dwell in it, with all of the attendant anxieties. According to the Zohar, faith is the place where everything is created, so all creation is ultimately rooted in this faith. It is a creative faith—not a comforting faith that affords people the inner peace needed to remain fixed in the same place.

I sense the danger of dwelling in the "place" of this faith. I cannot know now how it will appear to me or the ultimate results of such a dwelling. After all, all of us have our individual sites of faith, our own anxieties and tempests. If I allow myself to remain in the place of faith for a long time, will I be able to continue living my life as I have up to this point? Will the truths that have anchored me thus far retain their validity? Will those who love me now continue to do so? Will I be able to maintain my standing in the eyes of those who surround me and (a more dangerous possibility) in my own eyes?

Suddenly I understand the simple faith Rabbi Nahman mentions in connection with dwelling in the Void Space. I must possess a particular kind of faith if I am to respond to faith and dwell in its space without fear. This is a space of many doubts; no exit is visible. "I believe," in this sense, means that I accept the storm that will rage within me. I agree to live in a chaotic space, without knowing when or how I will emerge from it. This agreement is itself faith.

I resume my visits to the hospital, standing by my friend's daughter as she lies in her bed. Was he occupying this place of faith when he saw his child on the hard sidewalk and began to pray while waiting for an ambulance to take her to the hospital? Is this the faith in question—when a man's world is uprooted in an instant, and he knows not where to turn for help? Or was his prayer little more than a reflex, the conditioned response of a person accustomed to supplication? But it is now, when his daughter's life hangs in the balance and every doctor issues a different recommendation, that he decides to overrule the strenuous objections of his wife and parents and reject all the doctors' suggestions, even though he can see nary a glimmer of hope. Is this the Void Space of faith?

Supreme faith may be a process of renewal, a shift from a "nothingness" overflowing with potential and possibility that as of yet contains no conscious distinctions. Or perhaps it is the ability to remain within the womb of the Void Space and to be reborn from within it. In the writings of one of the great early kabbalists, Rabbi Azriel of Gerona, it is a clear statement of this understanding of faith. He lived in thirteenth-century Spain, but the manuscripts were only discovered in the mid-twentieth century.

> One who produces being from nothingness is not lacking, for being is nothingness with regard to nothingness, and nothingness

is being with regard to being. As it is written, God "made non-existence into existence" (*Sefer Yetzirah*, 2.6), rather than "created *ex nihilo*." This teaches us that nothingness is being and being is nothingness. And nothingness is called *amen*, and the place where being begins to be present from nothingness is called *emunah* ("faith")…. And since the creator is a root that is identical for all, the way of faith and the way of heresy come into existence in the place where nothingness and being are bound together.[4]

This is a very difficult passage. According to Rabbi Azriel, "the place where being begins to be present from nothingness is called *emunah* ('faith')." He refers to nothingness as *amen*, which is the place in which nothingness and being are bound together. But passage, birth, and transformation occur in the tempestuous regions of my self, regions that as yet have no meaning, since I have not yet forged of them insights, not yet established what is good and what is bad—inchoate drives that I have not yet named. Rabbi Azriel of Gerona refers to this place as the "abyss." He does not conceive of the abyss as negative—a place of chaos—but as positive. It is the being that precedes difference and contraction; a light so bright that our eyes can only register it as darkness. In such a place there is no meaning to "faith" or "heresy" in the traditional sense—all things have equal weight there. Faith is the state of suspension between being and nothingness, and it is there that I begin to forge the definitions of my life.[5]

This space of faith within me is so full of possibilities that I have difficulty finding the right path—or perhaps I am so hollow there, so weak, that I fail to find even a single path. Either way, I now refer to it as the faith of the Void Space. To my understanding, this is the only path that Rabbi Nahman espouses for mending the broken vessels (the source of evil in this world, according to Lurianic Kabbalah), a mending not only of man but also of God, who broke right along with those primordial vessels. Most kabbalists tend to concentrate on the path toward building new vessels and the slow and gradual growth of man over the course of his journey toward religious and spiritual perfection. But Rabbi Nahman dares to enter into the obscure and terrifying region of the broken vessels, and then on to the Void Space of unanswerable questions.

Even if I do not freely choose to reside in the space of faith, this faith will break through to me somehow, even if only opaquely and imperceptibly. Isaac Luria claimed that this is the true meaning of dreams:

> This is the esoteric meaning of "they are new every morning; great is your faith" (Lamentations 3:23), for *malkhut* is called faith (*emunah*) and she grows greater every night on account of the lower souls that ascend nightly to be included in her and gestate within her for their renewal. And then, come morning, they depart from there renewed.[6]

Here Luria interprets the well-known verse from Lamentations, the Scroll of Destruction, focusing on the meaning of the phrase "great is your faith." The verse, whose grammatical subject is God, seems to suggest that God's own faith increases every morning. But what does "God's faith" mean? In what does God have faith? And why would it increase? Does faith have volume that it might increase? According to Luria, faith is a divine space identified with the *Malkhut*, the lowest of the *sefirot*, which represents the immanent aspect of the Divine within our world.[7]

How so? In his imagistic, allegorical language, Luria argues that when a person goes to sleep, the deepest component of his personality, his soul, departs for a place known as *emunah*; there it is impregnated and renewed, returning to the person in the morning, when he awakes. The verse "they are new every morning; great is your faith," then, communicates to us that the divine element in man, the soul, is renewed nightly by its ascent to the space of *emunah*, faith.

Souls are impregnated every night—entering as they do into the very depths of the expanding womb. For Luria, then, faith is like a great womb in which the process of gestation occurs. When a person's soul exists in a state of gestation, the person is in a place of faith. It follows that faith is not a type of knowledge—be it intellectual or emotional—nor even some unprovable feeling; it is a place, a fertilized womb. Luria's interpretation reminds me of a verse from Psalms: "to declare your steadfast love in the morning, and your faith by night" (Psalm 92:3)—the space of faith is nocturnal, it is a dream landscape without the delimitations and fixations of waking consciousness. Only thus can one enter the world of faith and have the most hidden aspect of one's self be worthy of gestation and rebirth.

Luria is speaking of something called the soul, the *neshamah*, but I can no longer accept as self-evident this common term, which has occupied my thoughts for many years (sadly, I still have no idea what it means). Is it an invisible essence that God places within us during our earthly sojourn, by virtue of which we become "God's image," but that departs our mortal coil to wander about at the moment of death? What good is an invisible essence to me? How can it help me renew myself?

So many Jewish texts deal with the soul that I have a hard time deciding where to begin. This much is clear: I must not consult the books that speak of some human element being punished in hell or rewarded in heaven or that speak of a divine element that suffers its descent into the debased and tainted human body. My own body rebels against these views, against the repeated attempts at separating my soul from my body. The ascetic traditions that have polluted Judaism no longer suit me; my pains offer daily evidence of the futility of trying to isolate one from the other. I must find another understanding of *neshamah*, soul, better suited to the person I am and to what I have learned of the Void Space.

The Zohar hints at another approach, pointing toward an understanding of the soul not as an essence or an entity that resides within me, but as a particular state of activity affecting me, like breath itself.

The Zohar describes Abraham as the first human being to have a *neshamah*, a soul.[8] I am stunned. Did his progenitors—say Noah or Terah—not have a soul? Doesn't every person have a soul? Apparently not. The soul needs to be forged, or more accurately, the soul is itself a kind of activity. Abraham, recounts the Zohar, merited a soul because he was "the first *ger*," the first stranger—a man who left his homeland and his family and his father's house in order to become a stranger. Abraham's departure from his familiar and secure place, his willingness to break with his known customs, with known patterns of thought, and to set out into the unknown—that itself is the soul. If I set off to be a stranger, I create a soul for myself. If I do not, I have no soul. Rabbi Nahman of Breslov offers a profound characterization of the soul as the active essence that "searches through" God's treasures. He even plays on the shared letters of two Hebrew words, suggesting the *hofshi*, "free," refers to a person who never ceases *lehapesh*, to search anew time and again.[9]

My entry into the Void Space is *neshamah*, soul. For according to my understanding, "soul" refers to the force that draws me into a state of foreignness or otherness, a willingness to break with the familiar and the comfortable within which I have lived up until now, driving me toward a state of searching and of freedom. My soul is not a substance of any sort; it is the space between exhaling the old and inhaling the new, the willingness to tear asunder the warm comforters with which I have wrapped myself. Perhaps there is a divine element to the activity I call "soul," for as surely as we search, God searches too. All the same, the soul is not an invisible spirit residing within me, unawares. It is visible and tempestuous and painful and pressing.

Some days I am in constant flux, shifting from souled to soulless, and back again. The place of the soul's activity cannot contain the "perfect faith" of Maimonides's principles of faith, which is, by definition, fixed and static. A faith based on knowledge cannot but be static and so, to my mind, is a form of idolatry. Whoever states his *credo*, his "I believe," as a matter of certainty, it is as though he says to me, "I reside in a fixed place that never experiences renewal." He does not reside in the place of faith.

I recall Rabbi Nahman's statement: "If I knew I was now standing at the same level as I was last year, I would want nothing to do with myself."[10]

This much I know: The memories and the pains emerging within me are merely the first steps in my journey. I have not yet reached the depth of the Void Space, but must do so to experience full and authentic renewal, to "start anew" as Rabbi Nahman says. Alas, all this is contrary to my most reflexive response to crisis situations, which is to latch on to the existing vessels—to the known and the familiar—with all my might. If I am to break this cycle, I must shed the familiar and the known, as they have become my own dead husk to me, bereft of divine spirit.

Kabbalists liken the entrance into the depths of the Void Space to entering into a state of gestation within *Hokhmah* and *Binah*—whether understood as part of the Godhead or as part of the soul. This is the point of passage from nothingness to being. Man divests himself of all garments, returning to his most primordial form of existence, absolute freedom—preceding all costumes and images. Ultimately, this is a journey back to our most primitive selves, to the kernel of our personality, the root of our soul still in its inchoate state, before negative events and circumstances have wounded and scarred us. The journey leads us back to the place of the infant, who is inside the darkness of the womb, small and weak and helpless. But the infant is able to receive sustenance through his mother's umbilical cord until he is ready to emerge into the world, armed with the new vitality and the new vessels that evolved during the gestation period. It is a process of repair for broken vessels, but it is more than that. It allows us to create new vessels that up until then existed only as abstract potentialities within us, heretofore unrealized.

I am deep enough into the Void Space to recognize that it is dark and empty. The various forces roiling me remain indeterminate and amorphous, and I find dwelling within the Void Space of faith more difficult by the day. I sense the forces growing wilder and more violent. I am lost to myself; nothing is clear, nothing is understandable. I am hurled into the divine nothingness that lies in the inner recesses of my soul, a nothingness without form or shape. My consciousness begins to call up memories, wounds really, unbearably harsh. Only my belief consoles me—the belief that I am in the Void Space of faith. In this state, Rabbi Nahman says, we re-create the divine act of creation.

I sink deeper and deeper into shapeless forces, denuded of all sense and meaning, so that I can cast them anew into the new vessels

I must forge while in the Void Space—replacements for my old, broken vessels.

3

In the faith of my dreams I see myself walking the street between the Sanhedria cemetery and the white statue called "Faith." I am headed for the secular school near my childhood neighborhood. Midway through the dream journey, with my book bag and notebooks in hand, I realize that I am thirty-five years old and have no business there. The agony of missed opportunity spreads through my body. There are places I will never be able to visit or to mend.

Another dream follows. I arrive at the yeshiva where I studied and walk into the main study hall. I take a prayer lectern and try to place it across from the Torah ark, but my fellow yeshiva students— along with other young men I don't recognize—gather around me, forcing their own prayer lecterns into my space, until finally they push me away.

I have no place. If I spend too much time in the Void Space, there is no one there to accept me. If God is, in the Rabbinic phrase, "the place of the world,"[11] what kind of space is available when God has lost His place?

I cannot count the number of times I asked myself why I left my childhood world. As I write this book, I have spent more years in the secular world than the ultra-Orthodox. Was the path I chose the right one? I am not suggesting that the halakhic world of Orthodox or ultra-Orthodox society is free of doubt. Every society experiences changes and crises that spur self-examination. But the gaps between these events vary from group to group and from individual to individual within these groups. The leeway available to a secular individual, who does not accept the authority of a particular halakhic or spiritual system, is markedly greater than the latitude allowed a religious person.

We are in the midst of the month of Heshvan, and this year, Heshvan is the cruelest month. I have no place. No place. I recently left my work as the moderator of a television show. I had enjoyed that work very much, and the position served as an existential anchor in many ways: a source of livelihood for my family that situated me in one of the key arenas of Israeli culture and provided me prestige and influence. But after five straight years, I began to experience unremitting dissatisfaction, as though I were walking in place, while suspended. Enough is enough, I said to myself. My soul is drowning in its own inertia. No development, no dynamism. More than anything, I felt that my television persona was slowly taking hold of my consciousness and that I would soon forgo my authentic self and the places I yearn to reach. So I concluded that chapter in my life, all the while wondering where it would lead me next. Though I considered the move quite carefully and was aware of its ramifications—the loss of income, prestige, and power—I could not foresee how strongly my fears and anxieties would gnaw at me.

Now, with my family's livelihood in doubt and my public stature and influence diminished, I no longer have a clear sense of my own talents or of my direction. I have entered the realm of faith that I have referred to again and again in these pages as a space of change and uncertainty, a space that allows for rebirth and renewal. Well, this is all well and good, but I am not sure I am strong enough to pay the price. Though I experienced other periods of extended uncertainty in my life, I remember them as times of suffering and regret brought on by some change in my life circumstances: separation from a lover, being forced from a job, my own errors and shaky self-confidence, and so on. The common denominator is a state of heightened sensitivity—strong emotions and acute pain.

What kind of faith can I experience in such a state of uncertainty? I cannot shout, since I am not sufficiently pained. I cannot even cry, since I do not feel anything. "To declare your steadfast love in the morning, and your faithfulness by night" says the psalmist in a verse whose second half has been interpreted and reinterpreted many times over as a reference to faith in times of suffering and loss. But what could have prepared me for faith in a place devoid of feelings and will and yearning?

The greatest agony contains more life than this small death. I recall the kabbalistic concept of *ibbur*, "gestation," encountered in our earlier discussion of the soul's nightly renewal. Each of the *sefirot*—each of the instruments God uses to govern the world—must periodically undergo a period of gestation in order to renew itself and properly serve as a conduit for the divine influence into this world. For me, however, gestation was a symbolic reference to an individual gathering himself into a protected space, in which to grow and develop—and finally emerge reborn.

The new winds blowing within lead me to a startling new esoteric interpretation of gestation: the fetus, floating in the darkness of its mother's womb, cannot see anything. He only hears muffled noises from without but cannot reach the outside world. The mother must first carry him to term. So he waits. He rolls around, moving his limbs, and everywhere encounters walls. He cannot stretch out, cannot expand. He yearns but knows not for what, for he has not yet released the cry of salvation that will burst forth from his chest when he emerges from his mother's body and looks at the blinding, injuring light of the world—only then will he shout and cry and suffer. Only then will he experience cold and feel the eternal yearning for his mother's warm touch, for her breasts streaming consolation into his body. And his consolation-bringing cries will reassure him when he thinks back to the dense opacity of his mother's womb. But a day will come, after many years of crying and shouting and suffering, when he will feel as though his skin is being peeled from his flesh, and he will yearn for the womb's darkness. For on that day he will realize that this darkness contains the promise of great renewal. And if he desires to truly live, to reach out his hand and touch the spring of renewal, to draw from it new and therefore unknown life overflowing with joy and sorrow, elation and suffering, love and loneliness—he must return to his mother's womb. He must again survive months of gestation, months of stifling want and suffocation in which his lungs cannot expand to shout in joy or scream in fear. He must return to that state—to a non-existent existence, to a non-existence that contains seeds of existence. Within that space, simultaneously full and void, the waters of the "supernal mother" will slowly stream into him, into the *Binah* within him, and he will not be aware that he has absorbed them until he emerges from the womb and a primordial scream bursts out of his parched throat.

Small wonder, I think to myself, that the Jewish sages of the Second Temple period established *sod ha-ibbur*—the intercalation or, more literally, "the gestation of the month"—as one of the most important and closely guarded esoteric doctrines. The issue is not limited to mathematical complexity—the calculation of the initial appearance of the moon each month and calibration of the lunar and solar calendars so that the holidays are celebrated at the appointed times—Rosh Hashanah in the fall, Passover in the spring. The esoteric doctrine of intercalation and the preference of the lunar over the solar calendar are deeply rooted in the nature of the moon. The moon, never illuminating on its own, always reflecting the light of the sun; forever in flux, sometimes a waning sliver, other times a waxing fullness; at times completely invisible, other times completely exposed; at times at the celestial apex, other times at its nadir; some months visible for much of the night, other months but briefly.

The lunar cycle symbolizes our need for the cyclical manifestation of God's light. We crave the sun's radiance, its benign light, its healing and vitalizing power. But when our lives wane, we identify with the moon, never constant, never secure in its own being—but whose ongoing permutations are the secret of her beauty. The secret of the gestation of the month is ultimately the secret of our own gestation.

The Zohar gives the following parable for the suffering of the individual who is "gestating" within the world of faith and in need of constant flux:

> Come see, there are three sounds that never disappear: the sound of an animal giving birth; the sound of a man's soul departing his body; and the sound of a serpent shedding its skin.[12]

There is no doubt that the author of the Zohar drew on the following Talmudic passage, but while the three examples in the Talmud—for example, the crowds in Rome—highlight the physical sound that people often ignore, the Zohar adapts the two examples of silent change and adds a third not found in the Talmud.

> Our sages of the Talmud have taught, there are three sounds that span the entire length of the universe. They are: the sound of the sun; the sound of the crowds in Rome; and the sound of the soul as it departs the body. There are others who add—birth, while others add—the first rain. The Rabbis prayed for the soul at the time that it departs the body, and annulled it [i.e., the noise].[13]

The late editorial changes evident in the Zohar suggest a focus on internal, psychological changes that occur entirely within the individual and contain a clear psychological element. Moreover, the Zohar attributes great importance to changes that occur in the course of life and thus adds the example of the serpent that sheds its skin.

The list in the Zohar is short but precise. First comes the greatest of all changes, a child's entrance into the world; the cry of the pregnant woman as she gives birth—the transition from nothingness to being. This is followed by the transition from being to nothingness—the moment of death. But in between these two singular events, we encounter myriad smaller changes as well. These are perhaps the most interesting transformations of all, as they are the only ones that come about as the result of free choice.

Between birth and death, man often finds himself like a snake that has shed its skin. Exposed and vulnerable, he waits for the completion of his transformation. These can be times of sorrow and pain and suffering.

A person headed toward such a state of gestation will encounter pain but also many dangers, and not everyone is suited for such struggle. A person might shed his skin, but the new skin might not grow for a very long time, leaving him exposed and vulnerable. A person who sheds all the definitions that constituted his most basic worldview may be sucked into a Void Space that will collapse his personality altogether. I would encourage people to remove their masks, to do away with the husks that envelop them. Yes, they are husks, but there is no doubt that their personality has partially merged with them, in part to protect itself. After all, they did not come into existence for no reason. But why would I ask anyone to remove their walls and defenses?

I think that the deepest, most hidden secret of faith within the Void Space is knowing that you have to leave it. The Void Space is an abyss into which one can fall and never emerge. Whoever forgets his place and settles in the Void Space risks remaining there too long and emerging only after suffering severe distress.

While in the Void Space, I must remind myself to enjoy it, to accept and appreciate it, not to view it as a deficiency but as an abundance. I must always remember that I experience it as a void *not* because it is, in fact, empty. I am not truly in a black hole devoid of thought and will, of desire and pleasure. On the contrary, the reason I experience the Void Space in these terms is that it is full, overflowing with infinite possibilities and potentialities—love and grace, wisdom and creation—but I do not yet possess the vessels to contain them, so they remain invisible to me. I must slowly and confidently acquire the ability to perceive these qualities, to store them within me, and to gradually reveal them.

When dwelling in the Void Space, I must not forget my goal or my capacity to leave this temporary state at the appropriate time. The Void Space is a great treasure trove. I forage within it and I forge it into my being, moving constantly toward a clearer understanding, a deeper insight, than anything I have known thus far. Precisely because it is so new, I need this gestation period within it. I need to crystallize the new cells constantly forming in me and to allow the old ones to shift to a new place within my body and my consciousness, knowing that the Void Space constitutes a new and ineluctably temporary state of consciousness. I must resist establishing this confusion as a permanent state. The Void Space is the space of faith. In order to depart reborn, I must have faith; I must know that it is a place of abundance even when it appears empty. I will emerge from the Void Space in a new state of consciousness, but I know that even that state is not permanent; when it becomes too rigid, I will have to shed my earlier creation, like the serpent shedding its skin time and again over the course of its life.

But how will I know when it is time for me to shed my skin again? The serpent sheds its skin when it blanches and loses its distinctive sheen and sparkles. I will do the same when my consciousness, my life, the path I've chosen, no longer shines, no longer sparkles in the sunlight, and is no longer a blessing to others.

Everything beneath my skin will soon be exposed for all to see. This may reveal causes for celebration or shameful stains—memories from difficult moments in my childhood or perhaps repressed memories of people I've hurt over the years. Still, I have no choice but to illuminate everything.

4

A final moment of hesitation before I dive into the depths of my Void Space.

If I immerse myself in it completely, if I believe strongly enough to be silent and wait patiently to be reborn, how will I know that my new self has reached a state of ripeness? Perhaps I will still be seeking refuge behind all manner of defenses. After all, the mind can produce endless self-deceptions to prevent us from seeing through it. How will I identify the moment of my rebirth? Will it occur when I am able to write a new book—another word trap? Or perhaps when my pains subside completely? I am not sure my faith is that strong.

Isaac Luria and his students were able to identify the "root" of the soul, that is, the path that must be taken to repair the "broken vessels" within them. Luria never employed this psychological approach, but the meaning is clear. Thus, for example, Luria told his disciple Hayyim Vital that his—Luria's—soul stems from the soul of Abel, while Vital's is rooted in the soul of Cain, his killer.[14] That may have been when Vital understood that the fault lines of his own life lay in his love-hate relationship with his master.

I asked great scholars, a number of them kabbalists, whether they can they identify the root of my soul. What is the precise point requiring repair, the point on which I must focus? The request makes some of them feel uncomfortable. But is this not a legitimate question? I want to know my destiny, the reason I was placed on this earth. Does my life possess unique meaning or not? I ask them to help me find the proper path: what unique goal do I have in the world, what mission will make me happy and complete?

I regret having posed the question. Can such a question really be answered? Even a man with great spiritual perspicuity cannot know the answer. Every soul has its unique root, every person his own Void Space. Our purpose is to return to our root, to the precise location where we first felt our soul begin to break into tiny fragments.

Often after I realize something on my own, I can then see it alluded to in my books. Rabbi Meir Nahum of Chernobyl, one of the greatest Hasidic thinkers, defined the root of the soul as the place of the vital sparks and the seeds that scattered when his soul ruptured:

> Each individual root of a soul contains many myriad sparks. And one must repair the root of his soul and elevate the sparks that belong to his root, and inasmuch as he purifies his *nefesh*, and performs his actions, even the most mundane, for the sake of heaven, thereby elevating the sparks trapped in the inanimate world. Later, when his soul evolves he attains the level of *ruach* and begins to elevate the sparks trapped in the vegetable world. And when he attains the level of *neshamah*, he elevates the sparks trapped in the animal world—and all this is accomplished through repentance.[15]

The root of my soul has no single location, for it is myriad fragments scattered in me and in my immediate surroundings. The people close to me, and even my possessions all reflect something about the sparks and fractures of my soul, all communicate to me silently: "their voice goes out through all the earth, and their words to the end of the world" (Psalm 19:5). How could I have thought that another person would be able to recognize this shattered, scattered vessel? Just as no two people possess the same spiritual workings, so there is no spiritual teacher—no matter how great—who can peer deeply enough to recognize the root of another's soul. Even God, it seems, cannot instruct a person as to the root of his soul.

If a person cannot strive toward the root of his soul, even God cannot help him; God Himself does not know it.

Distressed, I return to the wise Rabbi Nahum of Chernobyl, who claims that my soul will grow and ascend from one state to the next as I repair my broken vessels and elevate the sparks that belong to the root of my soul. What Rabbi Nahum did not say was how to find the starting point in the search for these sparks. If I want to identify sparks that have scattered in every direction, I will need some sort of instrument to identify them as stemming from the root of my soul. Each of us must find our own Archimedean point, our own anchor when journeying into our Void Space, into the faith that will lead us to change and renewal and to the creation of a new self.

Hasidic masters understood the search for the root of one's soul as an ongoing individual process, not a brief, clearly defined, goal-oriented journey. Still, I note that one of the starting points mentioned for those seeking the root of their soul is to follow in the footsteps of the great Jewish interpreters and midrashists—in other words, to discover the root of the soul by means of deep study of traditional Jewish literature, study that begins by finding what paths resonate most deeply on an emotional and experiential level and then setting out to provide a new interpretation of these classical Jewish texts.

In previous generations, the Jewish commandments could also function as clefts in the boulders that line the abyss. All the great Jewish mystics demanded that any person nearing the moment he sheds his skin and dives into the abyss not relinquish the footing of the commandments. This despite the fact that, followed to its ultimate depths, this path demands that we not latch on to the commandments, since they bind the individual to a fixed and familiar life framework. The mystics' insistence was not born of their piety or their concern for the commandments as such, but rather of their (justified) anxiety for the fate of a person diving into an unknown abyss having severed all bonds to the borders that might lead him back to his world, to his daily life.

This is probably the deep motivation for the generations-long kabbalistic tradition of limiting entry into the world of Jewish mysticism to men of a certain age, who are steeped in the Babylonian Talmud and the vast halakhic literature, and who meticulously observe the Jewish commandments. The people who established these rules knew that it was only at the age of thirty or forty, after marrying and fathering children, and acquiring deep and broad knowledge of the halakhic world, that a novice could be exposed to the mystical world and still remain rooted in terrestrial reality.

My own path toward spiritual and emotional renewal follows this classical curriculum of immersion in the classical Jewish corpus. True, for me this study does not entail commitment to the *mitzvot*, but the deepest foundations of my selfhood lie in this tradition, and, like so many others, I use it to my advantage. This much I know: over the course of this journey I must not cling to any of the foundations that have traditionally supported me. I must search for my own unique interpretation, which itself constitutes the renewed growth I desire.

This is how Rabbi Hayyim Vital records the teachings of his master, Isaac Luria:

> Know that the community of all souls number six hundred thousand, no more. And it is the Torah that is the root of the souls of the Jewish people, for they were hewn from it and rooted in it. Thus we find six hundred thousand interpretations to the Torah, all of which conform to the plain meaning of the biblical text (*peshat*); and another six hundred thousand interpretations explicate matters alluded to in the text (*remez*); another six hundred thousand are produced by midrashic methods (*derash*); and yet another six hundred thousand are esoteric in nature (*sod*). Thus we find that each of the six hundred thousand interpretations engenders a single Jewish soul. And in the messianic era, each and every Jew will attain knowledge of the Torah in accordance with the interpretation that suits the root of his soul, the interpretation by which he was himself created and formed, as I just mentioned. And people will learn all this in the world to come, after their death, and also at night, when a person sleeps and surrenders his soul, which then departs and ascends—if he is worthy and his soul ascends on high, there

he learns the interpretation in question, i.e., the one on which the root of his soul depends. All this is according to his deeds that day—whether they teach him a single verse or a single pericope, for at a given time a particular verse will illuminate his soul more brightly than on other days. But another night a different verse will illuminate his soul, according to his deeds that day, but all the verses are understood in accordance with the interpretation upon which the root of his soul depends, as I already mentioned. My master [Isaac Luria], may his memory be a blessing, would survey his disciples every night as we stood before him, and he would see what verse glows more strongly in each one's forehead, with regard to the glowing trace of his soul. And he would explicate some issues regarding that verse, in keeping with the interpretation that belongs to the disciple's soul, as I already mentioned. And before that disciple fell asleep, he would focus on the interpretation that he [Luria] had briefly set forward, and would recite the verse in his mouth, so that when, in sleep, he surrenders his soul and it ascends on high, they will impart upon it an additional teaching.[16]

Every person who approaches Torah study has a unique interpretation suited for that person. Each of us has our own interpretation of the Torah, and it is incumbent upon us to find that interpretation. When you interpret the biblical text, you are interpreting yourself, and until you do so, you will not accomplish your life's goal, you will not discover the root of your own soul—of your own paradise. Luria goes on: "Thus, at night, when the soul departs during sleep, there are those who merit ascent, and there they read the interpretation that grips their root." During the nocturnal passage to the place of faith, the soul resides in a timeless, spaceless reality—much like a dream. In other words, we have the ability to draw near to the root of our soul, to faith, when we are in the true abstract space and time of dreams, without borders or boundaries, in a state that precedes the contraction. In this passage, Luria interprets faith as an entry into a place that has no rules or regulations. Only then can we begin to search for the root of our soul. Arrival at the place of faith is not a goal unto itself, for there permanent residence in a state of chaos is ultimately meaningless. Rather, it initiates a process in which we shed our skin as we travel toward the root of our soul, from which something new emerges. Faith is the ability, the courage to reach this site of chaos that precedes the formation of the "vessels," and to do so in order to create new vessels or repair broken ones. Only in chaos can we establish a pathway to the supernal abyss that comprehends the root of the soul and there ascertain what we must repair.

The kabbalistic sources interpret the biblical jubilee year as part of this dynamic. According to the biblical injunction, every forty-nine years there is a jubilee year, at which time all debts are canceled and ownership claims are annulled, and the land must lay fallow. Rabbi Moshe Hayyim Luzzatto, one of the greatest kabbalists of the seventeenth century, interprets the jubilee commandment as a symbolic reference to the search for the root of the soul. The purpose of our existence, says Luzzatto, is not only to discover and then develop the root of our soul. Sometimes it is necessary to go "beyond the root" in order to effect additional *tikkunim* (repairs). Luzzatto interprets the biblical injunction to return land to its original owners: "And you shall hallow the fiftieth year and you shall proclaim liberty throughout the land to all its inhabitants. It shall be a jubilee for you: you shall return, every one of you, to your estate and every one of you to your family" (Leviticus 25:10). In his interpretation, this verse refers symbolically to the root of the soul:

> Each and every soul has its own root, and though sometimes it is necessary to step beyond the root in order to bring about the necessary *tikkunim*, ultimately the soul returns to its root. This is the emendation that occurs in the jubilee year, "you shall return"—the esoteric meaning of which is that the souls return to their roots. That is why it was a sabbatical year, since the righteous experience true return to their roots as repose.[17]

Perhaps I need to stop trying to uncover my root and focus on other *tikkunim* I need to perform—some old, some new. Perhaps these emendations will lead me back to my estate, to the root of my soul.

Perhaps discovering the root of my soul is merely the reward hidden behind various *tikkunim*, even if at the time they do not appear to be hewn from any root materials.

———

I am returning to my estate. No, not to the promised, consoling estate that houses the root of my soul, but rather to a familiar state of study—to the sources, which will lead me to the *tikkunim* I must perform.

Many *tikkunim* await me on my journey, yet I find I cannot stay on the path. There are still plenty of anchors that keep me locked in place. I am responsible for my family. I cannot allow myself to set off on the journeys of Rabbi Moshe Luzzatto and Rabbi Nahman of Breslov—lives of wandering, self-imposed exile for the sake of a particular teacher or doctrine, often over the course of years, without concern for their homes and wives, for their parents and children. They traveled freely and they endured suffering and tribulations. As for me, I have lost myself in my search for a mere two days, yet I feel guilty for not having spent enough time with my family. Even if I try to block out the guilt, deep in my heart I know that I cannot accept the path they chose—to neglect their family for the sake of a journey.

———

chapter four

Hesed
The Fiery Sword of Abraham

1

I hope there is a middle path that will allow me to journey into the Void Space and find the root of my soul without shattering the souls of those who are dear to me. I am now trying to find an answer to this question from the greatest biblical traveler of all, Abraham, the father of the believers, the subject of the biblical injunction "Go forth!" (Genesis 12:1).

Even as a child I felt a special kinship with Abraham; in my imagination, I maintained a constant, secret dialogue with him. There was a small park by my parents' house, Sanhedria Park, where a number of graves from the Second Temple period were excavated and attributed to members of the Sanhedrin, the Second Temple Jewish court. When we were six or seven, my friends and I would spend the afternoon wandering among the caves, then crawling into the bottom caves through the mounds of earth beneath the locked metal gates. Carrying candles through the dark caves, we would test each other's fortitude, thinking of the dry bones in the lavish stone ossuaries. The thought always sent a pleasant shiver down my spine. My friends seemed fearless, moving freely through the thick darkness, but all the while I saw the souls of the Sanhedrin judges flickering through the condensation that covered the limestone and glowing in the light of the Sabbath candles I had stolen from my mother. Every grotto in those caves conjured up in my mind tales of destruction, exile, and redemption.

When I started studying the book of Genesis, I imagined many of the events in Abraham's life as having taken place in my childhood park. The teachers of Hadar Zion, the religious elementary school I attended, mentioned that the binding of Isaac took place on Mount Moriah, traditionally identified with the Temple Mount in the Old City of Jerusalem. Still, I imagined it taking place in the inviting and threatening park, where the shady pines and carob trees mingled with the thorny bushes. A stone drinking fountain that the municipality installed for the comfort of park visitors and a pile of rocks leaning against a stainless-steel faucet became the altar on which Abraham bound his son. The horns of the ram that became the sacrifice in place of Isaac were tangled in the thicket around the carob tree by the public faucet, while the angel appeared to Abraham from one of the bushes scattered throughout the park.

I loved Abraham then and I love him to this day. But now, as I follow in his footsteps hoping to learn something about journeys and about "Go forth!" I must reconsider that love, particularly when I reflect on my first introduction to biblical Abraham and recall the stories I learned in school that shaped my relationship with him from the outset.

Following the Rabbinic legends, my teachers spoke of young Abraham growing up in Ur of the Chaldees with his father, Terah, the owner of an idol shop. One day Terah left his son to tend the store, but Abraham shattered the idols and, in a precociously wise gesture, placed a stick in the hand of the largest idol. When his father returned, Abraham informed him that the smaller idols had tried to take the large idol's meal, so he shattered them. Terah informed his son that this was impossible, to which Abraham responded that the belief in idols was itself senseless. At the time I took great pleasure in little Abraham's Talmudic dialectic and in his mischief, both of which suited my own personality as a child. The legend continued: Terah, who was very upset at his son's heretical views, marched him to the court of the evil king Nimrod, who sentenced Abraham to be cast into a fiery furnace, but Abraham emerged unscathed.

This legend, and others like it, seeks to justify God's election of Abraham. But the biblical account contains not the slightest hint of these legends. The motivation of the Rabbinic interpreters is clear: they wished to elevate and exalt Abraham, reasoning that there must have been some reason that God chose him over all others. The question of Abraham's election is ultimately the question of Israel's election, of its status as the chosen people, a crucial question throughout the history of the nation that Abraham sires. But what here is so praiseworthy? After all, had I lived then, I too might have recognized the absurdity of idolatry, and God could then have chosen me as His prophet. Why did He choose Abraham?

Generations of interpreters and commentators portray Abraham as a man who acquired wisdom through his own agency and who already as a child sought—and found—his path to God. In essence, they argue, the choice was reciprocal: God chose Abraham because Abraham had already chosen God.

In his *Code of Jewish Law* (*Mishneh Torah*), Maimonides depicts Abraham as a natural philosopher or a scientist, although Maimonides displays a more profound understanding of the nature of idolatry. Ultimately, Abraham is portrayed as a figure much like Aristotle, whom Maimonides so admired. In his introduction to the "Laws of Idolatry," Maimonides describes Abraham lifting his eyes to the night skies, contemplating the moon and the stars and pondering their origin and their purpose. Who created them? Why do they exist? According to Maimonides, Abraham employed a series of syllogisms to reach the conclusion that there is only one God who governs the world. Here is Maimonides's formulation:

> After this mighty man [Abraham] was weaned, he began to explore and think. Though he was a child, he began to think incessantly, day and night, wondering: How is it possible for the sphere to continue to revolve without having anyone controlling it? Who is causing it to revolve? Surely, it does not cause itself to revolve. He had no teacher, nor was there anyone to inform him. Rather, he was mired in Ur of the Chaldees among the foolish idolaters. His father, mother, and all the people around

him were idol worshipers, and he would worship with them. However, his heart was seeking and gaining understanding. Ultimately, he grasped the way of truth and understood the path of righteousness through his precise comprehension. He realized that there was one God who controlled the sphere, that He created everything, and that there is no other God among all other entities. He knew that the entire world was living in error. What caused them to err was their worship of the stars and images, which made them lose sight of the truth. Abraham was forty years old when he became aware of his Creator.[1]

Abraham uncovered the unity that underlies these forces and their dependence upon a single deity that transcends the manifestations of its power in the natural world. Abraham had the intellectual power to arrive at monotheism as a rational conclusion, and then he sought to disseminate this insight as widely as possible.

The Bible certainly does not describe a monotheist philosopher or a child prodigy. The plain sense of the biblical narrative reveals a middle-aged man who chooses to abandon all that is familiar to him and set off on a new path, promising nothing and committing to nothing—Abraham does not need God or other teachers to show him the way. Even before the Bible has God say "Go forth!" to Abraham, it describes Terah, Abraham, and the members of their clan leaving the Chaldean culture they know so well and heading for the land of Canaan (Genesis 11:27–32). Their departure is painted in dark hues: Sarah is barren, and Haran, Abraham's younger brother, dies at a young age. There is no reason to think their departure from Ur was precipitated by a divine epiphany, since the family is clearly struggling with the crisis of death and barrenness. Abraham and his family are not rebelling against anything so much as hoping to change their luck by leaving behind their present circumstances and striking out for greener pastures. It is only subsequently that God appears to Abraham:

> Now the Lord said to Abram, "Go forth from your country and your kindred and your father's house to the land that I will show you. I will make of you a great nation, and I will bless

you, and make your name great, so that you will be a blessing."
(Genesis 12:1–2)

Abraham was not a professional rebel or a card-carrying philosopher. He was not even a prophet who underwent a spectacular, life-altering revelation.

Why, then, does God say, "Go forth!" to a man who has already decided to do so for personal reasons? Why does God promise Abraham so much in return for his going forth? And why did God choose this Abraham character over all the other people wandering in search of a better tomorrow?

The non-heroic Abraham is a more powerful figure. When he feels his home and surroundings have become lifeless and stagnant, he is willing to uproot himself rather than fight against these feelings by shutting himself off in his familiar world. Ultimately, this willingness paves the way for God's revelation. That said, the fruits of this revelation are never really clear. God promises Abraham a vague "blessing" and "abundance." Moreover, God's request from Abraham that he "go forth ... to the land that I will show you" is not explicitly linked to Canaan, since Abraham planned on traveling to Canaan even before God's revelation. The departure from Ur is not the test, since he left of his own accord. How, then, given this new understanding, are we to interpret the divine command "Go forth!"?

The Zohar offers a profound interpretation of these verses:

"They went forth with them from Ur of the Chaldees to go to the land of Canaan": When he came to this place he was met with a baffling obscurity which he could not penetrate. When God, however, perceived his efforts and his desire, He straightway revealed Himself to him and said, "Go forth!," so as to know yourself and prepare yourself; "from your country," from that side of the inhabited world to which you were hitherto attached; "and your kindred," from that wisdom wherewith you did cast your horoscope, noting the hour and second of you birth and star that was then in the ascendant; "and your father's house," that you should not heed your father's house, even if you could hope by virtue of your father's house for some prosperity in the world; therefore, be gone from *this* wisdom and from *this* consideration. That this interpretation is right may be proved thus. They had left Ur of the Chaldees and were in Haran. Why, then, should God say to Abram "Go forth from your country and your kindred"? It must therefore be as we explained. "To the land that I will show you," i.e., I shall show you that which you were not able to discover, the power of that land so recondite and obscure.[2]

This striking interpretation of the famous command "Go forth!" represents the core paradigm of motion toward the Void, beginning with contraction and withdrawal from the familiar world. The crisis the family undergoes in Ur of the Chaldees causes its members to break with their familiar surroundings, even before God calls out to Abraham. The family renounces its culture and homeland and enters into a liminal state—no longer in a permanent place, but not yet knowing where it is headed. When the family is in Haran, a way station between Ur and Canaan, Abraham needs to decide how to proceed. He can either remain in Haran or continue on to the land of Canaan. Canaan, then, becomes the marker of a certain internal "place," a place that Abraham does not fully fathom and that the Zohar characterizes as baffling obscurity. Despite the instinctual urge to flee the difficult, inscrutable places within us, Abraham has the epiphany that it is in this very place that he will find the key to renewing his soul.

The transformation takes place when Abraham is summoned, through the power of his faith, to direct his family's crisis toward a journey of faith, toward *terra incognita*, and thus continue the process of withdrawal "from your country"—from the surrounding culture that remains embedded in his soul; "from your kindred"—from the soil in which he was raised, the childhood memories that make up the landscape of his youth; "from your father's house"—from the customs and mores of his immediate family—and to wander to an unknown land.

Abraham was the father of the believers not because he was the first to believe in a single God—the Bible never mentions this, and today we know of ancient monotheistic cultures that predate the presumed time of Abraham. Abraham is the father of the believers because he supplied the paradigm for the journey of the soul toward the unknown.

Abraham's story is an example of the dangers that attend this type of believer, dangers that find clear and striking expression in the Bible's account of Abraham's life in the years following God's revelation. The Rabbis suggest that these stories constitute ten tests that God puts to Abraham to verify that his religious faith is strong and true. They say he passed all ten.

Alas, the Bible itself does not agree with the sages on this point. How difficult it is to read the Bible's account of Abraham's sojourn in Egypt shortly after hearing the powerful command "Go forth!" that led him to Canaan. Abraham recognizes Sarah's great beauty and asks that she pretend to be his sister, lest he be harmed. He abdicates his responsibility for her and asks her to submit herself to the mercy of the Egyptians. These are difficult verses. A man who turns his back on his previous, barren way of life often seeks to renounce his responsibilities toward the now-abandoned world and perhaps toward the past more generally. Feeling the freedom that accompanies this change, he does not want remnants of the past to impede his movement. Barren Sarah is just such a vestige of the past that he wants to forget, so it is not surprising that he uses the first opportunity that presents itself to dispatch his wife to others. For seeing her great beauty, Pharaoh does indeed take her for a wife and lavishes on Abraham money, gifts, male and female slaves, and more. God then punishes Pharaoh, rebuking him for taking another man's wife, and Pharaoh returns Sarah to Abraham and dismisses them, never wanting to see Abraham again. Abraham keeps the money and gifts and accepts generous reparations to boot. In other words, Abraham makes his first fortune by casting off all responsibility and, in essence, selling wife's services. Is this a test he passes? The biblical account is so straightforward and explicit that it leaves no room for debate. Moreover, God returns Abraham's past to him in the form of Sarah; one does not acquire freedom in the Void by effacing the past.

Abraham is not portrayed as a great philosopher or a man of rare righteousness. He does not even pick up on the heavy hints God drops to guide him along his new path. Though he does erect altars to God, the events following his trip to Egypt with Sarah—separation from Lot, his orphaned nephew whom he had adopted as a son—portray him as oblivious to God's hints. A random dispute between Abraham's and Lot's shepherds is all it takes for Abraham to expel Lot from his camp (Genesis 13:7–12), even though he knows Lot could be heading off for Sodom, whose people "were wicked, great sinners against the Lord" (Genesis 13:13). Lot is immediately taken captive in a regional war. A guilt-ridden Abraham embarks on a commando operation against Lot's captors and frees his nephew. When he is offered part of the booty of the defeated armies, he says, "I have sworn to the Lord, God Most High, maker of heaven and earth, that I would not take a thread or a sandal-thong or anything that is yours, so that you might not say, 'I have made Abram rich'" (Genesis 14:22–23).

Abraham does not pass the tests he comes across in the course of his life. Again and again he seeks to shrug off responsibility for his past. More troubling, this last episode reveals him to be a self-righteous hypocrite. He is willing to pimp his wife out for financial gain but refuses the spoils of the victor in battle. The justification he offers is astoundingly direct—lest anyone say, "I have made Abram rich." He accepts money when none can see, but in public he presents himself as a principled man unwilling to benefit from unearned gains.

2

After reading the Abraham narratives in Genesis, I feel like erasing everything I wrote earlier about his faith within the Void. If this is what happens to a man who sheds his familiar social norms, if, that is, abandoning one's particular culture transforms him into an immoral, boorish human being, what could I possibly want with the whole "Go forth!" business?

I immediately see my own life in light of this process: I too turned my back on the world of my childhood, on my family, on my kindred, on my father's and mother's house. I recall too the fake identity I donned when I left—the antagonistic identity of one who can only say "no," who declares war on his former society, a battle waged by the pen that in my hand became a sword pointed at the world of my childhood. I was not the only one who did so. Hundreds of thousands of Jews traveled this path when they left their homes and their kindred in Europe and set out to raze the old Jewish world in the first half of the twentieth century. Did they, in fact, turn their back on that world and succeed in constructing a new identity based on antagonism? Did they establish a new world? Or perhaps they merely replaced an old identity with one that is newer but no less inauthentic, an identity that yields pretense and hypocrisy. This self-righteous identity ultimately sacrificed the "other," sacrificed all the "Sarahs" and the "Lots" in the world. But they returned to us and relentlessly continue to return; we strike out at them, but they refuse to disappear, refuse to efface the reality of their existence, forcing us to maintain false identities.

I must find the courage to ask myself perhaps the most difficult questions of all: Was it a mistake to leave my father's house? Why did I rush off on the journey of my youth? Why did I hurry and don this borrowed identity that, like some of the identities in the world I left behind, is suffused with hypocrisy and pretense, with lies and deceit, with the stifling air of yet another prison cell? Like Abraham, I too had to cast off responsibility for my immediate family. I did not want to be tied to anyone, preferring solitude. But, like Abraham, my commitments keep reappearing, sneaking in through the back door.

When I turn to the biblical text as it is, stripped of all the midrashim and interpretations, I understand: antagonism is not yet faith. Disparaging a particular cultural world or denying a world-view does not yield faith. Faith is departing on a journey even while knowing that when all is said and done you may find yourself in the same place you left. The journey of faith does not entail the promise of a new truth—you might also encounter the truth you have rejected anew, and it will pulse in your veins like a new creation.

When I read how completely Abraham failed the first tests of his journey, I remind myself how dangerous it is to set out looking for "the new" for its own sake. Suddenly it dawns on me: sometimes it is better to remain in the previous place and search for renewal there.

—

Though the Bible does not connect the two explicitly, immediately following the description of Abraham's hypocrisy we find one of the most lyrical and sublime passages in Genesis:

> After these things the word of the Lord came to Abram in a vision, "Do not be afraid, Abram, I am your shield; your reward shall be very great." But Abram said, "O Lord God, what will you give me, for I continue childless, and the heir of my house is Eliezer of Damascus?" And Abram said, "You have given me no offspring, and so a slave born in my house is to be my heir." (Genesis 15:1–3)

Following his string of failures with Sarah in Egypt and the expulsion of Lot, Abraham finds himself in a deep crisis. Though he has turned his back on his old self, it pursues him mercilessly. Perhaps he questions his decision to travel to a *terra incognita*, to the unknown land within him, and he comes to the agonizing realization that the euphoria of that initial decision is fleeting. He sees the barrenness of his soul and blames it on the people around him who did not choose a new direction for themselves. His relationship with Sarah is strained (as the biblical account later suggests), and his relationship with Lot, his adopted son, has been irreparably damaged. What will you give me? Abraham asks God with biting irony. I did not ask for a reward—I wanted only to change, for my life to look different. But it did not change and is now worse than ever.

In the interpretation I am offering here, God's answer—"This man shall not be your heir; no one but your very own issue shall be your heir" (Genesis 15:4)—is a reminder to Abraham. Your heir cannot be someone external to you, he must issue from you. The desired result, the new way you seek, will not be found by casting off the people around you. The proof? The failed attempts to "get rid" of Sarah and Lot. The change is gestating within you but has not yet been born. "'Look toward heaven and count the stars, if you are able to count them.' Then He said to him, 'So shall your descendants be'" (Genesis 15:5). Return, in other words, to the starting point of the journey, when you gazed at the stars of the firmament and were unable to count them, to define them. Nonetheless you set out on your way, since deep inside you knew that an undefined state is itself a path—a path that cannot be fully set or determined, and it is certainly not a place of respite after your difficult journey. The new path is a direction, a road with more than you can ever anticipate.

A new understanding briefly flashes in Abraham's mind, and he believes—that is, he knows—that this faith is uncountable; it is a wealth of possibilities of paths and directions, too numerous to count. God promises Abraham this land of faith, this promised land of unknowing—not the physical land of Canaan: "I am the Lord who brought you from Ur of the Chaldees, to give you this land to possess" (Genesis 15:7).

But Abraham, having been burned by the elusive chimeras of the Void Space, wants to be sure he is on the right path. For the ultimate problem in the pathless path of the Void Space is the lack of maps or milestones to guide the traveler. What looks like a marker from afar invariably turns out to be a mirage; each time we imagine we have reached safe haven, we must withdraw from the world around us for a time and ask ourselves whether this is not one of the disguises of the false consciousness. So Abraham asks God, "O Lord God [*Elohim*],[3] how am I to know that I shall possess it?" (Genesis 15:8).

How am I to know that I am journeying along the correct path? How am I to know that the Void toward which I have chosen to march will lead me to rebirth? Perhaps I will remain within the abyss from which none return. God's answer is stunningly powerful:

> He said to him, "Bring me a heifer three years old, a female goat three years old, a ram three years old, a turtledove, and a young

pigeon." He brought him all these and cut them in two, laying each half over against the other; but he did not cut the birds in two. And when birds of prey came down on the carcasses, Abram drove them away. (Genesis 15:9–11)

Sundered carcasses? This is God's answer to Abraham? What is the significance of carcasses carved down the middle and set across one another? This was apparently a common covenantal ceremony in the ancient Near East. But if God is establishing a covenant with Abraham, why does Abraham experience an unbearable depression? "As the sun was going down, a deep sleep fell upon Abram, and a deep and terrifying darkness descended upon him" (Genesis 15:12).

Jewish interpreters have labored for centuries to explain this dark encounter, and particularly to cast the "terrifying darkness" that descended on Abraham as a prophetic allusion to the future enslavement of Israel in exile. But if this is a message about things to come, why does terrifying darkness descend on Abraham before anything concerning exile and enslavement is communicated?

To my mind, the so-called Covenant Between the Pieces symbolizes the difficult answer God gives Abraham: there is not now nor will there ever be a secure path to the safe haven you seek. The path will forever pass "between the pieces," between day and night, between here and there. You can never rest on a fixed, established, reality. The path between the pieces must, moreover, be guarded against birds of prey that come to eat the carcasses, against evil spirits that threaten a person when he is most enfeebled.

What, then, can be known? The only clear knowledge we have—cold comfort indeed!—is that each of us must traverse this path alone. Abraham's descendants will have to experience enslavement and redemption in an ongoing cycle that is part of their own path. We cannot redeem others, not even our own children. After all, it does not matter how vigorously I try to guide my children along their path, to educate them. Ultimately, their path will be determined by their own choices.

God's answer is emphatic. You wanted to know? By all means:

> Know this for certain, that your offspring shall be aliens in a
> land that is not theirs, and shall be slaves there, and they shall
> be oppressed for four hundred years; but I will bring judgment
> on the nation that they serve, and afterwards they shall come
> out with great possessions. As for yourself, you shall go to your
> ancestors in peace; you shall be buried in a good old age. And
> they shall come back here in the fourth generation; for the iniq-
> uity of the Amorites is not yet complete. (Genesis 15:13–16)

Like you, your sons will have to traverse the entire circuit from the
beginning. You may reach a ripe old age, confident in the knowledge
of your fate, but I, says God, cannot limit myself to partners who
march only toward what is known. Your sons will have to travel a
long road, first experiencing slavery and then striving for freedom,
crossing the wilderness toward an unknown, unsown land, to receive
an unfamiliar Law at Sinai. In the course of his answer, God also
manages to needle Abraham: Unlike you, I will not cast off my
responsibility; I have previous commitments toward the Amorites,
whose iniquity is not yet complete. I cannot send the Amorites away
the way you sent away the loved ones who so "inconvenienced" you.

⁓

Every day, as I head toward my home, a stone's throw from the West
Bank, I cross a concrete wall between the pieces, between the divisions, that grows ever higher and ever longer. A year earlier, when
they began to build the wall between us and the Palestinian city of
Qalqilyah, I averted my gaze, trying to deny the violent separation
taking place in my own land of "Go forth!" Now my eyes have
grown accustomed to it and I no longer see it. My eyes have grown
accustomed to many things, such as five-year-old children from the
Palestinian Territories driven by poverty to beg for money at busy
intersections, knowing their parents will beat them if they return
home without a good sum in their pocket. My ears too have grown
accustomed to the unmistakable sound of gunfire from over the wall.
My eyes are shut. My heart closed tight. Fear for my children's future
dulls my sensory perceptions.

Abraham too, I rationalize, was in favor of separation. After all, it was he who said to his nephew, Lot, "Separate yourself from me" (Genesis 13:9), thus seeking to distinguish his true progeny from those of his other family members. But that separation was ultimately of no avail, and his relationship with Lot grew more complicated when he was forced to do battle with the four kings to rescue Lot from his captors. We cannot flee our responsibility, I think to myself. God Himself does not believe in separation and informs Abraham that he cannot yet take possession of the land promised to his descendants because "the iniquity of the Amorites is not yet complete" (Genesis 15:16). The Amorite living in Canaan also possesses certain rights, God informs Abraham, and it is not possible to expel them or separate from them.

What, then, is the solution? Again I read God's answer to Abraham in the Covenant Between the Pieces. God promises Abraham a path that passes "between the pieces," winding through a place like no other, between sundry and distinct pieces of reality. God can provide such an enigmatic and mysterious path only because He too has dared to traverse it in the act of creation.

But Abraham is in no rush to pass through the Covenant Between the Pieces. For now, God traverses it alone. Perhaps at this point in his life Abraham's weakness forces him to consciously relinquish the decisions and dreams of his first voyage into the startling realm of the Void. In this dark hour, Abraham regrets the "Go forth!" and wishes to be a weak man standing in front of a great God. He does not want to encounter a God who refuses to provide an absolute truth at the end of the journey.

Many Jewish thinkers and guides, both ancient and modern, speak of the meaning of the covenant—that faith is ultimately a contract made with God to remain committed to a certain way of life—and of the covenant the People of Israel have with the Land of Israel. This, they claim, is true faith: a fixed and thoroughly determined way of life that I must adopt for myself and use as the basis for my children's education. In return, I too will receive a set of promises. It does not matter what I think or feel, they assert; faith is nothing more or less than accepting the covenant. But by this point in my journey I have encountered a different God—a changing and renewing God. A God who passes through the pieces, rather than carving them for others or informing them where truth is located. A God without a fixed truth, and whose constant change is the only possible assurance for my own ongoing renewal, for the full realization of my potential as a creature made in the image of God. The covenant I am making with you, God tells Abraham, is reciprocal: pass through the pieces, and I will pass through as well. A pity Abraham never did pass through them—had he done so his descendants might have been better equipped to negotiate the awesome but also exhilarating complexity of the space between set definitions and fixed categories. Had he done so, he might not have been asked to bind his son.

But Abraham remains silent, frozen in place. Only God's physical manifestation, "a smoking fire-pot and a flaming torch" (Genesis 15:17), passes between the carved carcasses. Abraham is paralyzed with fear, unable to absorb what has been communicated, not daring to walk along this path. Is it possible that even after such a stunning revelation Abraham still does not understand what is occurring? Or perhaps he has been suddenly transformed into one of those believers who are willing to accept any form of religious obligation and suffering—but not the fact that the object of their adoration, God Himself, must travel the same path. Maybe Abraham is a believer who will acknowledge anything but the words that cut him to the bone: God is not as you always imagined Him. God is not the stable rock of salvation upon which to anchor your existence when the life of the flesh becomes unbearable.

I have compassion for Abraham. After all, how can one live with the knowledge that even God is not a reliable support? When Abraham set off on his journey, agreeing to search for a way of life he understood only vaguely at the time, he believed in a God for whom these matters are clear, who knows what He is doing and what He hopes to achieve. And perhaps—most importantly—a God who is not Himself in a constant state of flux and renewal.

3

Abraham is not going between the pieces, which means, in my view, that he refuses to enter into the covenant of the Void and is forced to choose a new way of life for himself, a transformation manifested externally in his name change from Abram to Abraham. From Abram, an elevated father, he becomes "the father of a multitude of nations" (Genesis 17:5), a man who faces forward toward the promise of his own future and the future of his descendants. As part of this identity change, God commands Abraham to mark the covenant in his flesh. No longer the Covenant Between the Pieces, but the covenant of circumcision. Abraham refuses the former but performs the latter. Why?

One possible answer is expressed in the earliest extant work of Kabbalah, *Sefer ha-Bahir*, whose anonymous author lived around the tenth century CE. The *Bahir* is the first work to mention the divine structure of the *sefirot* and also the first to identify the divine *sefirot* in human terms: Abraham represents the *sefirah Hesed*, mercy or compassion; Isaac represents *Din*, harsh judgment; and Jacob represents *Tiferet*, glory. Other biblical figures—Joseph, Moses, Aaron, David—are similarly identified with particular *sefirot*. But now, as I examine the life of Abraham, I find that his association with *Hesed* is more complex than I had recognized.

Before his identification with *Hesed*, Abraham could have been identified with another element altogether:

> Rabbi Meir said: Why is it written "And God said, 'Let there be light,' and there was light"? Why does it not say, "and it was so"? This teaches us that the light was very intense, so that no created thing could gaze upon it.... Abraham came, and He sought a power to give him. He gave him this precious stone, but he did not want it. He was worthy and took *Hesed* as his attribute, as it is written "*Hesed* to Abraham" (Micah 7:20).[4]

Abraham is given the choice of the power named "precious stone," which contains some of the light "that no created thing could gaze upon," the hidden light that is concealed for the righteous in the world to come. On my reading of the Abraham narratives, this is a reference to the divine element, the overflowing power, the divine effluence that precedes God's contraction, teeming with potential, concealed within the deepest abyss of the Void Space. But Abraham is not interested in this precious stone and chooses *Hesed* as his *sefirah*. From this point on, Abraham does not want to make any decision on his own—he loathes the relentless choices of the Void. He yearns for a God who will provide him with clear and unambiguous instructions, a God who does not change. And so, when God nonetheless is revealed to him, "Then Abram fell on his face" (Genesis 17:3).

Abraham sells the God of the Void Space for the stew of the God of *Hesed*.

But why do I write about him so? How dare I disparage a man who wants to secure his future and the future of his children? Perhaps Abraham was simply more self-aware and he recognized that he was incapable of journeying through the Void Space—that he has failed and in so doing has harmed his family and loved ones. After all, I too want a pension, disability insurance, health insurance, home insurance, plumbing insurance, and any other insurance that might cover over the abyss that is my fear of the unknown. Besides, what is wrong with choosing a God of love and compassion? I can think of many worse transgressions. The God of positive thinking is without question one of the more successful gods of my time. Why don't *I* choose the God of compassion as well?

But *Hesed*, "compassion," is a less innocent and a less positive *sefirah* than its name suggests. In the writings of the kabbalists, *Hesed* represents creative force, a power of giving and formation that shoots forth like an arrow with no target, flying unimpeded in all directions. God's birth emerges from the deepest depths of *Keter, Hokhmah*, and *Binah*, moving from them toward an existence of contraction and definition—a process characterized first and foremost by love. *Hesed* is the promise of an infinite effluence of life and blessedness for all creatures great and small, each of which continues, in its own way, the process of birth from the "one." *Hesed*'s divine effluence knows no limits and no proportion. The limitless eruption breaking forth from *Binah* is here distilled into a yearning for a specific form, for every creature that will ever exist. This is the channel of divine effluence, a love that encompasses all.

But after the "breaking of the vessels," God's wisdom recognizes that it requires more than love to give full and tangible expression to the process of creation, that is, to endow it with location and reality. Unbounded love may stun, even paralyze. Exaggerated love may even be transformed into evil. For this reason, *Hesed* enters the space of creation yoked to its opposite, *Din* (or *Gevurah*), a force that limits and checks love, that establishes a fixed framework for the divine effluence of compassion, all according to the needs and capacities of its recipient. *Hesed* is a male *sefirah* in that it wishes to indiscriminately penetrate the space around it—to give, to influence, to bestow. *Din*, on the other hand, checks *Hesed*'s divine effluence, setting limits and borders for it, like a vessel whose shape will determine the contours of *Hesed*'s divine effluence, halting its flow lest it overshoot and cause an "overdose" of compassion.

Abraham experiences *Hesed* in its pure, pre-*Din* form, that is, before it was checked and impeded. In this state, *Hesed* does not know how to keep itself within its proper borders, and over time, the *sefirah* is transformed into a new form of cruelty. But even before this happens, Abraham loses his ability to reach difficult decisions and judge justly, both of which require the borders fixed by *Din*.

Abraham marries another woman, Hagar, his wife's handmaiden. When she becomes pregnant, Sarah is overcome with jealousy, and Abraham again abdicates all responsibility for what takes place in his home, allowing Sarah to torment the handmaiden until Hagar chooses to flee to her death in the desert (Genesis 16:1–6). Abraham finds himself between a rock and a hard place. On the one hand, he cannot endure the suffering of his barren wife, Sarah, as her fertile handmaiden rebels against her. On the other hand, he cannot scold his new wife, Hagar. Abraham chooses *Hesed*, which precludes him from reaching decisions that require *din*, harsh judgment.

Hesed has a very ugly side. The word appears, oddly, in the Levitical prohibition against brother-sister incest:

> If a man takes his sister, a daughter of his father or a daughter of his mother, and sees her nakedness, and she sees his nakedness, it is a *Hesed*, and they shall be cut off in the sight of their people; he has uncovered his sister's nakedness, he shall be subject to punishment. (Leviticus 20:17)

Tikkunei ha-Zohar, a late stratum of the Zohar, tries to explain why *Hesed*, which usually means "kindness" or "compassion," appears in the context of incest: "Whoever combines letters where they should remain separate, it is as though he separated between them, and so the Torah states that the punishment of the brother and sister is that they 'be cut off—measure for measure.'"[5] The brother-sister incest imagery suggests that the fertility of *Hesed* is transformed into death when it grows too powerful.

At this point I understand another core difference between the *sefirot* of abstract thought (*Keter*, *Hokhmah*, and *Binah*), and the *sefirot* that emanate at later stages. Within the Void Space, *Hokhmah* and *Binah* are the supreme *sefirot*, and their interconnected and mutually reinforcing nature plays a vital and necessary role. The more deeply I settle into this site, the more new consequences will become clear to me. But once I have been reborn from within the space of *Binah*, I find myself in an area that requires me to separate and distinguish different essences. This is the space of contraction, the space of the practical *sefirot*.

Of course, *Hesed*, Abraham's chosen *sefirah*, possesses very positive aspects as well. As a child, I always imagined Abraham still in the throes of agony following his self-circumcision at the age of ninety-nine, yet rising to serve the three angels who come to announce the birth of Isaac. At school, we were all taught that Abraham reveals himself to be a generous host. Three strangers show up at his door, and Abraham immediately provides them with a fancy spread. The rabbis who elaborated on these biblical narratives neglected to mention that the situation within Abraham's household was terribly different: the family suffers from a surplus of grace, so much so that it had become warped, distorted into a state of lying and cruelty. Abraham may be a gracious host, but he does not display such generosity toward his own family.

The family continues to grapple with grave events. Reading between the lines of the biblical narrative, we find that an atmosphere of suspicion and distrust hangs between Sarah and Abraham. As a woman, Sarah does not participate in the meal Abraham serves his guests. Instead, she positions herself behind the tent's entrance and eavesdrops on their conversation. After the guests depart, God asks Abraham why Sarah laughed; Abraham approaches Sarah and they debate whether she laughed. The scene typifies the depths of suspicion and hostility at work between Sarah and Abraham. Maybe it is because of Sarah's years of barrenness, but this does not mean that we are free to remove God from the equation—God who never allows the infertility to be forgotten or the elderly couple to make their peace with it. God repeats His promise to provide Abraham with descendants like the sand on the seashore but tarries mightily in fulfilling it. God tests more than just Abraham's faith in a better future—He implicates Abraham and Sarah's marriage over the course of the long waiting period.

The gap between Abraham's foreign relations, so to speak, and his domestic policy is an important leitmotif of the Abraham narratives, starting with his decision to reject the faith of the Void. Angels stop to visit Abraham on their way to destroy Sodom, Gomorrah, and the rest of the cities of the plain. While they are on their journey, the Bible suddenly informs us of God's thoughts: "I am planning a glorious future for Abraham, so I cannot conceal from him my decision to destroy Sodom and the surrounding towns." God wishes to examine Abraham's response to better understand his character, and respond he does: "Then Abraham came near and said, 'Will You indeed sweep away the righteous with the wicked?'" (Genesis 18:23). Abraham argues before God that it is unjust to destroy the good along with the evil, haggling with God, until he is told that there are not even ten righteous men in Sodom. At that point, Abraham despairs and returns to his tent.

How does the Bible represent Abraham in this story? He pleads for the righteous and the wicked alike; he oozes unconditional love for humanity; he seeks to save the cities of the plain from God's wrath. In both our stories, then, Abraham is an exalted and merciful figure: first a caring host, then a man who tries to save the people of Sodom and Gomorrah, even though they are irredeemably evil. But Abraham never suggests that God extract the righteous from the city to save them; he tries to save the righteous *and* the wicked. Why does Abraham want to save the horribly wicked residents of Sodom? Is this a test he passes?

God says that He knows Abraham to be a man of righteousness and justice. What precisely does this mean? Justice usually means condemning the guilty and acquitting the innocent. Does sparing Sodom and the surrounding cities for the sake of ten righteous men constitute justice? Clearly not. This may be an act of *Hesed*, of mercy, but not of justice. As the debate proceeds, Abraham asks God, "Shall not the Judge of all the earth do what is just?" (Genesis 18:25). God responds that He will indeed act justly, which is precisely why He considers it right to punish the wicked, even if a number of righteous men are destroyed along with them. It is odd that neither God nor Abraham considers the possibility of isolating the righteous from the wicked and thus sparing them. Why don't they consider this course of action, when this is the justice shown Lot and his family?

Again I see Abraham opting for boundless mercy, determined to save a city full of wicked men for the sake of ten righteous ones. Mercy here is total and unrestrained. Suffice it to say that there are ten righteous men and an entire city of criminals is to be spared, though the cries of those who suffered at the hands of the Sodomites have pierced the very heavens. What kind of justice is it if a wicked city is spared? What of their future victims? Abraham's *Hesed*, his mercy or compassion, blinds him to their plight—he simply cannot see them.

In the following narrative, the biblical camera zooms in on the city of Sodom. The people Abraham had hosted arrive at the city, and suddenly they are transformed into angels: "The two angels came to Sodom in the evening, and Lot was sitting in the gateway of Sodom" (Genesis 19:1). We soon discover Lot to be a warm and welcoming host as well, and I remind myself that Lot's father, Haran, died at a young age, and Lot was raised in Abraham's house. Lot, then, is Abraham's adopted son and has learned everything from him—thus the similar attitude toward guests. Indeed, the book of Genesis highlights the similarity between the two by employing similar words and phrases in the two hospitality narratives.

But then the extreme depravity of the citizens of Sodom becomes apparent: "But before they lay down, the men of the city, the men of Sodom, both young and old, all the people to the last man, surrounded the house" (Genesis 19:4). The men of the city demand that Lot send out his guests to be raped, but Lot steps out and suggests the townspeople rape his two virgin daughters instead of the guests. Now, with all due respect to Lot's outstanding hospitality, the solution he offers the men of Sodom—to violate his own daughters as compensation—seems incomprehensible.[6]

Comparing the Lot narrative with the story of Abraham's hospitality, a pattern emerges: When the two protagonists deal with the outside world, they show boundless, indiscriminate mercy. But when they look inward, to their own families, extreme mercy engenders extreme cruelty toward those closest to them. Abraham trafficks his own wife and sends Hagar, pregnant, into the wilderness (he will do so again, when he exiles Hagar and his own elder son). As for Lot, the present episode describes an appalling treatment of his young daughters.

There are those who say Abraham and Lot need to be understood against the backdrop of the norms of their day. But according to the later tradition, God chose Abraham precisely because he was born into this broader social context but rebelled against it. The fact that in the ancient world women and children counted as the man's property does not justify cruelty. I am trying to examine the man Abraham, free of all the accretions of later traditions. As he is portrayed in the Bible, I cannot see in Abraham an exemplary figure.

I believe the book of Genesis creates a narrative continuity between the two stories to call our attention to the way in which *Hesed* can be transformed into unmitigated evil. A man who chooses to live his life according to a principle of pure mercy is incapable of setting limits for himself. In this sense, the purpose of the Lot story is not only to show the evil of the men of Sodom and justify their annihilation, but also to demonstrate the cultural heritage that Abraham bequeathed his adopted son.

Happily, Lot's daughters are not violated. The angels intervene, striking the men of Sodom with blinding light and hurrying Lot, his wife, and his daughters out of the city before it is destroyed. God then destroys the cities of the plain, and the narrative shifts to Lot and his daughters, who hide out in a cave in the mountains. Lot's daughters believe the world has come to an end and that there are no other survivors. Wanting children, they give their father wine until he passes out and then rape him on consecutive nights. As a result of this "*Hesed*" intercourse, they are impregnated and give birth to the nations of Amon and Moab.

How does the story of Lot and his daughters fit into the broader narrative theme? I believe the key element of the story is the cave in which these terrible events take place. The cave symbolizes a withdrawal inward, and I read the story as dealing not only with literal incest but with the perversion of family relationships more broadly and the perversion of the biblical protagonists. Lot abused his daughters to the point that he was willing to send them to be gang-raped by the men of Sodom, so it is not surprising that his daughters rape him when given the chance. We see here the perversion of the family dynamic not only in the father's treatment of his wife and children, but as endemic to the entire system—everything in the cave is corrupt, perverted, broken. I hear the Bible crying out between the lines, warning that if we choose mercy exclusively, the greatest perversions will occur in the place of our greatest love.

But Abraham's story is not yet over. Again he sells his wife, Sarah, this time to Abimelech, the king of Gerar. Again he emerges from the exchange a richer man. Again he drives out his relatives—this time Ishmael, his playful and perhaps mocking son, and Hagar—to apparently certain death in the wilderness. And so on and so on.

Hesed becomes a perverting prism through which to view the world. Abraham argued against destroying an utterly corrupt city, but then he obligingly follows God's instructions and sends Hagar and Ishmael into the wilderness:

> So Abraham rose early in the morning, and took bread and a skin of water, and gave it to Hagar, putting it on her shoulder, along with the child, and sent her away. And she departed, and wandered about in the wilderness of Beer Sheba. (Genesis 21:14)

As the Hebrew month of Heshvan draws to an end, the doctors will try to remove my friend's daughter from life support, to see if she can breathe on her own. Though he is under terrible pressure, my friend remains steadfast. The doctors have threatened to seek the court's intervention to secure permission to operate on his daughter, but he refuses. The girl is removed from life support, but her lungs do not respond and she is immediately reconnected. It is a terrible disappointment.

That evening my wife asks me how so many people could be praying fervently for the child to recover, but to no avail? According to the traditional understanding, these prayers ascend to *Binah*, the site of change and transformation—so why don't they manage to effect the desired changes? I add a question of my own: Both the child and her parents find themselves in the Void Space—she in her coma, they in their unbearable pain. Is the attempt to change reality through prayer merely an exercise in futility? Perhaps it is impossible to change course; perhaps once a decree has been issued from the heavens, it can no longer be reversed.

The next morning I skip my customary private prayer and continue reading the Abraham narrative: "After these things God tested Abraham ..." (Genesis 22:1). Here too there are leitmotifs from earlier Abraham narratives. The verse "Take your son, your only son Isaac, whom you love, and go to the land of Moriah, and offer him there as a burnt offering on one of the mountains that I shall indicate" (Genesis 22:2) echoes the earlier command "Go from your country and your kindred and your father's house to the land that I will show you" (Genesis 12:1), which begins the Abraham cycle. Genesis 22 also asserts that "Abraham rose early in the morning" (v. 3), a phrase used a few verses earlier in the banishment of Ishmael narrative (Genesis 21:14). These stories call our attention to the abyss that separates "internal" Abraham from "external" Abraham. Outwardly, Abraham is a man of compassion and mercy, a man of *Hesed*, pursuing peace and justice; inwardly, he is a hard and abusive man.

The most extreme example of the rupture within Abraham's personality is the binding of Isaac. Abraham does not send his son Isaac into the wilderness, where he has a chance—albeit slim—of surviving. Instead, he himself takes a rope, a ceremonial knife, and tinder and prepares to slaughter his son with his own hands. Even setting aside the family relations, the fact that Isaac is his son and his hope for descendants, it is still astounding to see Abraham, the lover of justice, the same man who argued with God over the lives of the wicked men of Sodom, willing to carry out the premeditated murder of an innocent man. I repeat: Abraham is going to commit murder. The fact that the victim is his son adds an obvious emotional resonance, but even we if examine the matter in dispassionate legal terms—as a matter of justice and righteousness—this is first-degree murder.

The story leads to this extreme moment, and the questions must be asked: What is God hoping to achieve? Toward what kind of climax has God directed the Abraham narrative? What's the catch? I believe that since God so loves Abraham, He causes him to confront, again and again, how necessary it is to set limits for the compassion within him, to cause him to finally understand that he must awaken within himself some degree of *Gevurah* before this all leads to disaster. God wants Abraham to stop loving and admiring Him so much, since such love is ultimately transformed into overt cruelty. God is looking for a clear "No!" from Abraham, a clear signal that the latter has discovered the proper balance between *Hesed* and his inner limits.

God does not test Abraham in the sense of trying to ascertain if he will pass or fail, but rather wishes to educate him. God uses extreme and flagrantly unjust demands to lead Abraham toward a new understanding, a new consciousness. The reeducation begins with Ishmael, the less beloved son. But when God sees that Abraham does not make an effort to save him, He tries again, this time adopting a more extreme tack and involving the beloved (and now only) son, Isaac. God does not want the man he has chosen to live in such a state of dissonance between his public and his domestic personae: a man who works to bring grace and compassion to all, while his family experiences serial cruelty—the result of his inability to set boundaries for *Hesed*. God actually wants Abraham to resist these cruel instructions, but Abraham *fails* these tests. Abraham has chosen *Hesed* as his *sefirah* and so cannot break out of his depraved behavior patterns.

God wants to know if Abraham has reached a level of authenticity that will allow him to respond with "No!" Can he think creatively and logically within the ideological framework known as "God"? After all, this is frequently our problem when we leave the Void—we latch onto a particular way of life to the point that we become its captives, even when it leads us to the edge of the abyss. For Abraham, who lives according to the most extreme manifestation of *Hesed*, saying "No!" when God commands him to offer Isaac would constitute a radical break with the most basic principles that guide his life.

In contrast to the received wisdom of the Jewish interpretive tradition that holds that Abraham passed all ten tests God posed, it seems to me that he failed each one. The biblical proof of this view lies in the new relationship God forges with Abraham after the near sacrifice of Isaac. In the chapters thus far, we find God and Abraham in constant conversation, but from the moment that Isaac is unbound, there is not a single verse of dialogue between the two. The Bible itself indicates that Abraham failed his final test, and as a result God despairs of him and ceases all communication. It further follows that God failed in choosing Abraham as the founder of the new nation.

This is a very sad story, since it speaks not only of human failings—it not only bares the weaknesses of the individuals who are seen as the spiritual patriarchs of the Jewish people, the paragons of religious faith—but also of God's pedagogical failure.

Abraham's failure is the failure of the great believers who set out on an unknown path and find it difficult to continue on it over time. Believers who escape the rarified atmosphere of the Void sometimes seek, as a kind of antidote, a rock-solid faith that will never intrude into the mundane grind of their daily life. It is difficult to live without a single, all-encompassing ideological framework that provides an answer for every question, always and at all times. Abraham is an exemplar of the great believers whose commitment to a particular paradigm of faith precludes the possibility of a flexible and dynamic faith, one that is always in a state of growth and evolution. Ultimately, Abraham is addicted to a single paradigm of faith. And even if the faith in question is characterized as "grace" or "mercy," he is psychologically fixated on an absolute sanctification of particular values, camouflaged by a theology of grace and love. Like all faiths, except for the faith of the Void, once Abraham's becomes fixated, it is no longer attentive to life itself and can even cause a person to be willing to sacrifice those dearest to him.

Abraham, then, represents the paradigmatic example of a man who suffers an overdose of a fixed and inflexible faith, of grace poisoning, and as a result he almost murders his own son.

4

Though I broke with the Orthodox way of life at a relatively young age, I never stopped believing in the God of Abraham, Isaac, and Jacob. For many years I tried to repress my faith and exclude God from my life. But even when I rejected the tradition of my forefathers, I never ceased praying to the God of Israel. For a number of years I was not mindful and present in my prayers, which were not always enunciated in words, but in recent years I have developed a daily dialogue with God through prayers I create, based on my feelings each day. I turn to God using my own words, asking for help in times of trouble and offering thanks in times of joy and blessing. Throughout my life, through good times and bad, I used to see Him as a good and beneficent God who watches over all His creatures, great and small, and can redeem every one of them when they deserve it and sometimes when they do not. I never doubted God's salvific powers, as long as I addressed Him from the depths of my soul and tried to mend my ways.

When things went wrong in my life and pain and sorrow were my lot, I understood this as a sign that I had grown distant from God and was on a path that was leading me away from Him. And I would stand by the prayer lectern in the corner of my study, caress the brown wood, and utter a personal prayer to God. I always imagined myself as a son asking for his father's forgiveness, mercy, help, and advice. As odd as this may sound in the skeptical world I inhabit today, I venture to say that as far as my internal life experience is concerned, most of my prayers have been heard and answered.

Over time, my morning prayer became routine. Every morning, before heading off to work or to my daily affairs, I pray. I try very hard to avoid falling into a fixed liturgy—I am not embarrassed to ask for help even in mundane matters, and I try not to forget to give thanks for what I have received. Though I am not always focused enough to express my feelings in new words that have not been repeated to the point of cliché, I nonetheless try to remain true to my inner truth.

But since I set out on my present journey, daring to methodically investigate my relationship with God and what I can know about Him, I feel myself drawing farther and farther from Him. I am filled with emptiness, as though I were losing a parent. Countless doubts keep me from my old prayer lectern: To whom exactly am I praying? With whom am I speaking? How can I address God as a merciful father? Can I in fact hope for divine intervention in my life? Perhaps I am living in some naive fantasy, speaking with no one but myself.

Why am I feeling as if I've been orphaned? I try to examine this question. I do not doubt the existence of the supreme power we refer to as God and that He created our world. I also do not doubt God's ability to intervene in human affairs, though I recognize that I could never prove that what I experienced as God's presence was, in fact, divine intervention. What, then, is the meaning of the existential loneliness, the profound sadness that overtakes more and more of my soul as I continue along this journey?

When I manage to push beyond the sense of being orphaned, the most powerful emotion I experience is an alienation that attends my awareness of my parents' weaknesses and failures. I recall a concrete image: A child enters his parents' bedroom at night and sees them naked, having intercourse. Their startled look washes over him. He sees in it need, yearning, desire, and shame. From then on, his father is no longer an omnipotent object of admiration, and he suddenly grasps his separateness from his parents.

Is this what I was looking for all along in God, the father figure that I so lacked as a child? But I was never as close to my father and mother as I now am to God. Moreover, in recent years I have spent more time with them, and we have found, in our different worlds, a reasonable coexistence. Pain and sorrow have been replaced by mutual acceptance and appreciation. This, then, is not the core issue.

Rather, in my hyper-focus on Jewish theology, I have distanced myself from God, a process so gradual that I was not aware of it until it became a full-fledged alienation. Now I am not sure it was worth the price. Perhaps I am wiser, perhaps I am more erudite, perhaps my analytic skills are sharper—but I've lost my connection to God my father. I am an orphan. Who will come to my aid, now that I am in need of redemption? Only God can be my savior.

Perhaps this is only a temporary state. Hasidic writers often refer to the Baal Shem Tov's assertion that the mystic experiences a great fall immediately after an uplifting spiritual experience,[7] an image analogous to a father's relationship with his young son. When the father tries to teach his child to walk, he first takes his hands and places his son's feet on his own. Later, when the father encourages the child to walk unaided, the boy may feel abandoned.

The Hasidic corpus, with its remarkable sensitivity to the subtleties of the human soul and to the nuances of our relationship with the world that surrounds us, has a number of names for this religious-psychological phenomenon: the states of greatness and smallness, the fall, advance and return, and more. But the fall is always described as a process that God oversees for the benefit of the individual—so he learns to walk on his own, to always yearn for God's presence, to never take that presence for granted, and so on. But in my case, it was I who initiated the process when I flooded myself with knowledge—insufficient knowledge, to be sure, but enough that I could no longer play the same role. But I have not yet learned how to establish a new relationship, on different terms, with God.

I could have opted for the classical solution and turned to God as "king of the universe": to abide by the conditions stipulated in the contract between sovereign and subject, to keep His commandments (as interpreted by the halakhic authorities) to the best of my ability, and to hope for commensurate reward, be it in this world (according to the Bible) or in the next (according to the Talmud and other later sources). What prevents me from choosing this route? Pride and hubris? Perhaps. But I sense this is not the main reason. My heart tells me that if I accept God as "king of the universe," I will forever lose the hope of regaining His intimate presence, and I am not willing to pay such a dear price. I fear that my life will be meaningless without God's intimate presence, without a personal relationship with God.

The more I learn, the more clearly I try to formulate my views of God and my relationship with Him—the further away He seems to draw from me. I sense a new pain in my heart: I have lost the sense of God as a "merciful and beneficent father," but as of yet have no lord, no sovereign in His stead, no one to call to. My heavens have been drained of God in any meaningful sense, a God who is attentive to my idiosyncrasies, who will happily offer support and aid when needed, who will fill me with hope in my dark hours. To whom shall I pray? To the *ayin*, the "nothingness"? Or perhaps to the king who needs to be worshipped and assisted so that he can overcome his failures? I try to open my mouth in prayer, but cannot. After all I have been through, do I really want to return to the starting point of my journey—to the place where people move their lips in prayer, but their hearts and minds and the inner reaches of their soul do not participate in the prayer?

I am slowly beginning to realize that I left the yeshiva and the ultra-Orthodox world precisely when my feeling of intimacy with God was at its peak.

It was just when I saw God as the personal king of my life, when I carefully followed every halakhic stricture, be it major or minor, that I understood I was paying too high a price. The vassal contract that was the basis of my education, which I gladly internalized in my youth, undermined my psychological ability to reside in God's presence without fear, to maintain a real dialogue. The profound contradiction between the God reflected in the laws of the Jewish legal compilations and the God of my prayers became increasingly pronounced. I left the world of unambiguous paths for *religious* reasons, for I understood that without an intimate relationship with God, my life was meaningless.

I fled for my life from the ultra-Orthodox community and immediately found myself struggling in the harsh reality of a demanding, materialistic world. It was then that I returned to the God of the patriarchs, creating for myself an image of God as a loving and beneficent father, who will redeem me from any and all difficulties, even if I, in my foolishness, pervert my own path. I did not blame myself; I blamed my parents. Occasionally I would address God with the words of Psalm 27, "For my father and mother have forsaken me," and the Lord did indeed gather me in. I lived this way for many years and only recently stopped feeling like a son turning to his father. I do not know precisely when this happened—perhaps when I got married, or when my oldest daughter was born, or when I first felt I was financially secure. Apparently it was a gradual process that lasted close to five years, over which time the image of God as a great and merciful father began to gather cobwebs within me. I felt as though God was lost to me, and when I nonetheless addressed him as a father figure, my words rang hollow and my heart was never in it. Still, I refused to admit that things had changed, the fear of being orphaned overpowering any internal truth.

Now that I can finally admit that this paternal God is of no use to me, what am I to do? Shall I again choose God the king and return to living according to Jewish law? It is very tempting. How else can I educate my daughters not to worship the golden calf in a lawless world? Can I teach them the philosophy of the Void? I must find another set of tablets—laws and rules that will prevent my children from stumbling. This is my commitment, my responsibility as a father. There is nothing wrong with adopting a strict halakhic lifestyle if it secures the future of my daughters and keeps them from falling into the trap of modern idolatry: the sanctification of the external (physical attractiveness, money, image)—a trap from which none, it seems, can escape. A halakhic lifestyle is, on the face of it, a good solution, even though in my heart of hearts I know that this is merely another form of flight, the default option for those who find themselves in the world of the golden calf. Still, is there anything wrong with adopting an Orthodox lifestyle accompanied by a secret wink to those in the know? Shouldn't I be willing to sacrifice my own freedom for the freedom of my daughters?

Maybe some day I will reach that conclusion. All options must remain open in this journey. But at this point, having become conscious that the father God within me no longer exists, the desire to experience a new image of God gradually crystallizes within me. God who is neither father nor king but rather a true, intimate friend.

I try to run a cost-benefit analysis of adopting this new image, playfully pretending that I have the freedom to choose. The relationship between father and son has no prerequisites. Genetic forces instill in the father a commitment to work for the well-being of his son, so that even when the child falters or fails, the father will provide help and support. Even if the son lies to his father and disobeys him, even if he hates and curses him, the father's love for the son endures. But the relationship is usually not open and reciprocal: the father generally does not reveal all his emotions to the son, and vice versa. Friendship, in contrast, is reciprocal—I too must give; I too must impart. As with my flesh-and-blood friends, I cannot expect unqualified giving in times of need as much as instruction and advice—someone who will point me in the right direction.

Again I am faced with a choice. I cannot bear the knowing, puerile obfuscation of so many previous generations: to continue playing the game of "our father, our king" even when it has become an empty slogan. When it suits us, God is "our father," and when we want to draw from His strength, we call Him "our king." Nor can I accept the ambiguity of the wonderful poet and kabbalist Elazar Azikri in his work *Yedid Nefesh* ("Beloved of My Soul"), which reflects the poet's inability to decide what God he wants: "Beloved friend, merciful father, draw your servant to your will." In a single sentence, Azikri characterizes God as a friend, a father, and a king. How can these different characterizations of our relationship with God coexist in our thoughts? Perhaps Azikri can pull this off, but for me the title "king" implies a relationship that I simply cannot abide, while "father" brings only orphanhood and mourning. Perhaps I have no choice but to select the path of friendship, be it a superficial friendship that requires no more than an occasional phone call or a visit every two months or a true, deep friendship of constant dialogue. Either way, friendship is the only possible relationship I can maintain with God.

Perhaps the time has come for me to expand my own emotional capacities and learn something about friendship—a relationship I have, in my cowardice, avoided for most of my life.

⟶

chapter five

Gevurah
Isaac's Ashes
Lie Heaped upon the Altar

1

I still do not possess enough of the faith particular to friendship. Perhaps the time has come for me to search for my faith in the most basic, most straightforward place of all—in trust. God the king demands loyalty and constant affirmation (an "amen" for every divine statement), not trust. One can even maintain a relationship with God the father without trust. But there can be no relationship with God the friend not based on a solid foundation of trust, which is why I fled most trust-based relationships.

I do not know when the seeds of mistrust, my profound lack of faith in the world and mankind alike, first took root. Perhaps in my early childhood, when I internalized the lying and dishonesty I observed in my immediate surroundings. Or perhaps later, when I encountered the hypocrisy of my educators. Or perhaps after my closest friends rejected me after I left the yeshiva and set out on a new path.

For many years I refused to bare my heart to another. Every friend and acquaintance would, I thought, turn on me eventually. Even to those closest to me I revealed only fragments of my inner self—never the whole truth. As for other people, my heart was always closed to them; I spoke to others only in empty clichés, incapable of disclosing anything about myself. The joie de vivre that was such an integral part of my childhood was replaced by a studied gravitas designed to keep joy and spontaneity at bay. Even relatively recently, the honesty and freedom evident in my television interview program would not have been possible without the distance that separates the interviewer from his subject—the power of my role as interviewer provided the requisite buffer. I did not consider it possible to have a conversation without a clear hierarchical relationship—it would be too dangerous, too frightening, leading inevitably to failure and pain.

It is easy to describe *Binah* as the *sefirah* that has no fear, but so difficult to attain that level. I can condemn Abraham for turning his back on the faith of the Void and opting for the stable and unambiguous world of *Hesed*; he had a unique sense of *Hesed*. Even if my ambivalence toward *Hesed* and its excesses remains, and even if I maintain that this *sefirah* involves the risk of loss of judgment and even the risk of cruelty, all the same I recognize that it is better than the alternatives. After all, for most of my life I have been in the shadow of *Gevurah*, preferring the devil I know so well to the one I don't, even as the latter held out the promise of redemption.

I have withdrawn into the old patterns of my personality: insatiable greed and unyielding selfishness. I am in a cocoon, closing in on me from all sides. It is sealed and begins to fester, until it is no longer possible to take or give. I do not have the trust I need to accept from another individual or from nature, to say nothing of God or the abundant and beneficent nothingness of *Binah*.

My body knows the truth. My body, for all its clumsiness and infuriating slowness, understands more than the intellectual *sefirot* that dart through my brain, stalking their prey and keeping me awake at nights. The body may be slow, but it is thorough. What the mind has long ago forgotten, the body has internalized in a way that no absentmindedness will ever erase. Again my pains grow stronger, the anguish of undeciphered sorrow, unbearable headaches. I cannot think and I cannot work; I am joyless.

These headaches have been with me since I was seven. I have never found a cure, and now my body intrudes every time I try to return to my writing. Indeed, it is precisely when I try to calm my consciousness, to breathe deeply and nurse from the wisdom of the upper *sefirot*, that my body forces me back to the starting point: a debilitating pain that paralyzes my creative, emotional, and intellectual faculties and brings all practical work to a halt.

Isaac's image—the bound patriarch, the forgotten patriarch—rises up from the Bible. In recent years I have spent a great deal of time dealing with Isaac's faith or, more accurately, his lack of faith, and I have come to identify deeply with the image of Isaac being led to the slaughter and bound, recalling my mother leading me, as a child of twelve and a half, to the yeshiva boarding school. I was not ready for this change. For an entire year I suffered from insomnia, spending the nights awake, terrified and lonely, in a room I shared with three friends. But now I see that I am not bound because of some trauma or other, and there is no need to exaggerate the terrors I experienced in my childhood. I am bound like everyone else. We are all bound and re-bound each and every day by our grinding existence, by the habits we have adopted to escape other habits, exchanging our fear for anxiety, our anxiety for aggression. We are in a constant relay race, passing our old fetters from one stage to the next, from childhood to youth and from youth to adulthood, from ourselves to our partners, and from our partners to our children, and from our children back to us, ad infinitum.

Again I go to visit Isaac, the standard kabbalistic name for *Din*, to see if I can occasionally free myself of the chains that bind me.[1] Did he, the paradigm of all bound figures throughout the generations, manage to exchange fear for hope, anxieties for laughter? Or perhaps I will find out, to my horror, that his Hebrew name, *Yitzhak*—"he shall laugh"—represents an unfulfilled hope. After he was bound by his father, Isaac was never able to trust another person. Am I, like Isaac, incapable of finding my father anew?

2

I was five years old, a student in the ultra-Orthodox elementary school, when I first came across the figure of Isaac. Our teacher skimmed over Jacob's early biography, eager to reach the dramatic moments in his life—his flight from his "wicked" brother Esau to the house of Laban, where he meets Rachel, the "sainted" matriarch of Israel. Despite the hurried reading, two verses impressed themselves in my memory. The first describes the first encounter between Isaac and his intended wife, Rebecca: "Isaac went out in the evening to walk in the field" (Genesis 24:63). The second describes Isaac when he is old and blind, wishing to bless his elder son Esau on his deathbed: "When Isaac was old and his eyes were dim so that he could not see, he called his elder son Esau" (Genesis 27:1).

As a child, I enjoyed strolling through the hills surrounding my parents' house, so I identified with Isaac wandering alone in the field. But I was pained to read about his blindness as an old man, a time when he could no longer see the field in bloom, and was relegated to smelling it on the garments of his son Esau, who had returned that evening from the hunt. He misses this wandering so terribly that his first statement to Jacob, who has donned Esau's goat skins, is, "Ah, the smell of my son is like the smell of a field" (Genesis 27:27). This is the smell that overpowers the voice within him that is shouting out, "The voice is Jacob's voice" (Genesis 27:22), the voice trying to tell him that he is being swindled, the victim of a terrible plot, a betrayal.

The years passed and I no longer wandered through the hills. I forgot about Isaac and I forgot the fields. The heroes of my imagination were the glorious Abraham and Jacob—the divine tests they overcame, their pregnant dialogues with God, their great religious visions. A few years later, I encountered an ancient *piyyut* (religious poem) in the Rosh Hashanah liturgy: "Pay us heed, God of Abraham, pay us heed. Pay us heed, Fear of Isaac, pay us heed. Pay us heed, Mighty One of Jacob, pay us heed."[2] Isaac's image presented itself to me anew, beaten, bruised, and frightened, wafting about like a spirit seeking healing and release during the Rosh Hashanah prayers in the crowded Breslov synagogue, like a baby's muffled cry in the women's section. But I was still too young to fully grasp the meaning of the fear with which the poet crowns Isaac.

More years passed, and I renewed my Bible study and again encountered Isaac. I understood then that he experienced a serious trauma during the binding, and I read the Rabbinic legend that the angels wept in sorrow as they witnessed it. According to the Rabbis, the angels' tears (containing a high concentration of heavenly salt) fell into Isaac's eyes as he gazed heavenward, with his father hunched over him wielding the ceremonial knife.[3] They remained there, seeping into his body and gradually effecting their change over the course of his life until eventually Isaac went blind. But what exactly did Isaac see when he looked up at the torn-open heavens above Mount Moriah? What fearful thing did he see in the heavens, causing his relationship with God to be characterized as "the fear of Isaac"?

Let us, for once, speak of Isaac proper. Not of his father, Abraham, who came to be understood (erroneously) as a symbol of love and intimacy with God, and not of the theological conclusions the Western religious traditions formulated in response to this event. Every time I hear or read some interpretation of this mythic event I feel as though we are binding Isaac to Abraham's altar once again. Isaac is completely forgotten, his perspective neglected, always portrayed as a passive youth being led to the altar, doomed to watch his father's knife raised above him. Indeed, he does not resist his father in word or in deed, even when Abraham is about to slaughter him. He is cast as an extra in this stunning theological drama, dutifully bound on the altar of oblivion. Over millennia of biblical interpretation there have been a few individuals who have tried to gain insight into Isaac's consciousness as he was being led to the altar. But even they did not probe his willingness to be sacrificed for God. Who, then, is this man? Can Isaac's entire personality be reduced to a willingness to stretch his neck out for slaughter? Is that a meaningful description of a man who inhabited the biblical world for 180 years?

It is hard to fault those who neglect Isaac. The Bible divulges very little about him. He is the middle child of the three patriarchs, trapped between his father and his son. The singular figure of

Abraham towers above him, the archetypal father of the nation who looms over the book of Genesis like the Tower of Babel, while below, Isaac is eclipsed by his son Jacob, the father of the twelve tribes—the "tribes of Israel," that is, of Jacob. Jacob is a charismatic and deeply human figure, endowed with an outstanding capacity to sacrifice for the sake of love—a man whose tempestuous and often painful life knows peaks and valleys, and wandering. Ultimately Jacob has the courage to characterize the years of his life as "few and hard" (Genesis 47:9). We can only work with what the Bible provides, those who would relegate Isaac to oblivion say to me. This is the fate of costars. Of the fifty chapters in the book of Genesis, only three are devoted to Isaac, compared with fourteen to his father and eight to his son Jacob. Even those three chapters are concerned less with Isaac himself than with the figures surrounding him—Abraham, Sarah, his wife, Rebecca, and his sons, Jacob and Esau.

But the fact that the Bible marginalizes Isaac strengthens my resolve to discover the true identity of this man who is thrice betrayed—by his father at the binding, by his wife and younger son, and by the Bible and its interpreters. Is the Bible justified in treating Isaac as a transitional figure, an impoverished and uninteresting *dramatis persona* who merely transmits Abraham's genetic code? Or perhaps we face a dark secret buried in the basement of the most famous family in Jewish history.

Again I turn to the Jewish tradition's most profound decoders, the interpreters of the deep structure of biblical symbolism who seek to uncover its subconscious depths, to expose the secrets that mainstream Judaism is afraid to look at. To my mind, the kabbalists are the Bible's psychoanalysts, and in their writings we can understand the enigma that is Isaac. Isaac represents *Din*, the *sefirah* that stands as the polar opposite to *Hesed* (the *sefirah* of divine mercy and compassion).

Din represents God when He withholds His effluence in order to guarantee that it will continue to exist. *Gevurah* is the end, the border, the terminal point of the divine overflow, the *sefirah* that judges and regiments it, since left to its own devices God's effluence will remain in an eternal state of turmoil. There can be no time that does not contain a past, a present, and a future; no life that is not finite; no joy that is not followed by sorrow, by a fall; no union without separation; no creation without clear lines of demarcation. As my studies of Abraham taught me, there can be no expansive mercy without the contraction of harsh justice, *Gevurah*.[4]

Abraham's association with unfettered mercy requires borders, that is, that *Gevurah* serve as a counterbalance. Too much love suffocates—it leaves no space for the existence of the other. Despite the necessary role it plays, many kabbalists view *Gevurah* (part of the left side of the sefirotic structure) as dangerous and the source of evil. The Zohar, for example, writes of *Gevurah*'s growing frustration and dissatisfaction with *Hesed*, unhappy that it has been marginalized for the sake of love. The judging and punishing aspect within me is not satisfied by love alone; it wishes to mete out the punishment that the "other" deserves (usually the other that is within me). Instead of doing the work assigned to it—to control and regulate the flow of mercy—*Gevurah* yearns for a moment of absolute control, so that the flow of mercy and love is stopped completely. *Gevurah*, by its very nature, seeks to fully realize itself so that at the moment of this halting, the divine force is transformed into anger and wrath from which emerge the forces of evil. Darkness is born of the divine light, a shadow hanging over our world that finds expression in the potential we all have to do evil.

According to the kabbalists, this is the power responsible for the genesis of evil in the world, the root of all pain and want and darkness. But more than anything else, it is the power responsible for our resistance to God, for man's ability to refuse God's demands, for the space that separates us from God. Interestingly, one of the main descriptions of *Gevurah* is "Isaac" or "the Fear of Isaac."[5]

My curiosity regarding the phrase "Fear of Isaac" turns to shock and rage. Is it not enough that Isaac suffered a horrific trauma that weighed on him the rest of his life—now the kabbalists use his name as a synonym for evil, impurity, and the forces that oppose God? I would expect that a man whose father nearly sacrificed him to God would receive the opposite treatment.

3

Once again I return to the Bible, but this time to the Bible itself, without the interpretive baggage I have been carrying since my childhood. I prepare for a renewed encounter with Isaac, hoping to see him as I did the first time we met—as an independent figure in the biblical narrative. "Isaac went out in the evening to walk in the field" (Genesis 24:63). The adult Isaac, now forty years old, is taking a walk around the time of the sunset in the Negev wilderness. Is it winter? Does he go out to hear the desert floods crashing terrifyingly through the serpentine Negev wadis? Or perhaps it is spring and yellow wildflowers blossom around his knees. We do not know. All we know is that he sets out alone in the evening. Is someone waiting for him in his tent? Isaac still has his father, and his father has many slaves and servants, almost a tribe unto itself. But Isaac does not live with his father anymore. He is off at a distance, pitching his own tent far from the wealth and the bustle of his father's encampment.

Is he angry at his father for the near sacrifice, or did they fight over something else? On the basis of a few fleeting allusions, we can say this: Abraham's glorious family is in a state of complete and utter disrepair, though here the Bible's famous lapidary style becomes outright stingy. We can assume the binding was a bleeding wound in the family psyche, but what was the nature of that wound?

After *Vayera*, the Torah portion that contains the story of the binding of Isaac, there begins a new pericope, *Hayyei Sarah*, "Sarah's Life," although it opens with her death: "Sarah lived for 127 years ... and Abraham went in to mourn for Sarah and to weep for her" (Genesis 23:1–2). Abraham goes to Kiriath-arba (that is, Hebron), where his wife died. Abraham probably came to Hebron from Beer Sheba, in the Negev, the southern region of Canaan. That is where his tribal encampment was located, and he returned there after the binding of Isaac, as the Bible earlier relates: "So Abraham returned to his young men, and they arose and went together to Beer Sheba; and Abraham lived at Beer Sheba" (Genesis 22:19).

What, then, was Sarah doing in Hebron? After all, she left her entire family east of the Jordan, in Mesopotamia, so she was probably not visiting relations. Perhaps Sarah left Abraham when she learned that he almost sacrificed her beloved son to God. Moreover, why did Abraham come to Sarah's grave alone? Where is Isaac, her only son? Is it possible that he does not feel obliged to attend his mother's funeral—the mother who loved him so but was unable to protect him from his father when, in the wee hours of that fateful morning, they set out for Mount Moriah?[6]

Isaac, orphaned of his living father, is twice orphaned by his mother—once in her life and once in her death. Abraham's family is profoundly altered by the binding, breaking up into three estranged camps: Abraham lives in Beer Sheba, Sarah in Hebron, while Isaac resides in a place known as Beer-lahai-roi.[7] In what state is Isaac, living so very alone in the wilderness of the Negev? Again I scour the biblical text, trying to collect the few hints it provides.

Shortly after Sarah's death and burial in Hebron, Abraham returns to his tent in Beer Sheba and sends Eliezer, his chief servant, to their distant native land to find a wife for Isaac. Why does Abraham need to do this, when he himself takes his third wife, Keturah, from among the native women? Does this mean that Isaac is not capable of finding a wife on his own? That his soul has been so badly scarred that he cannot function? Or perhaps the binding, and the family crisis that followed, are so widely known that no local family is willing to betroth their daughter to Abraham's son.

The oddly halting concerns of the servant Eliezer are telling: "What if the woman is not willing to follow me to this land?" (Genesis 24:5). Perhaps, that is, the intended bride's parents will want to meet the groom before giving their daughter to Eliezer. He follows this question with another: "Must I then take your son back to the land from which you came?" (Genesis 24:5). Abraham, shaken by this possibility, has his servant swear that he will not do so, then sends him off, laden with gifts, to find a wife for his son far from the immediate surroundings and their gossip about bound sons. So Eliezer goes to Aram, finds Rebecca, a beautiful young virgin by the well, and shows her objects of gold and silver and jewelry. Knowing the problematic nature of the potential groom, he lies vigorously to her family.[8] He claims that Abraham sent him specifically to them, and he convinces the bride's family that it was providence that brought him to their daughter. This is followed by still more gifts, until they relent and agree to send their daughter to Canaan.

While Eliezer and Rebecca are making their way through Canaan, they come upon Isaac wandering through the field in the evening hours. What does the intended groom look like—this forty-year-old man who does not even know that his father sent a servant to acquire a wife for him? Unlike the other figures in Genesis, whose physical appearance is described, even if only briefly, we know absolutely nothing about Isaac. But we may infer that he looks frightening:

> And Rebecca looked up, and when she saw Isaac, she slipped quickly from the camel, and said to the servant, "Who is the man over there, walking in the field to meet us?" The servant said, "It is my master." So she took her veil and covered herself. (Genesis 24:64–65)

Such is Rebecca's response upon seeing this man, the prince she has been promised.[9] Isaac accepts his father's gift wordlessly, passively. He does not invite his father to the wedding celebration, nor does he express gratitude. He takes Rebecca for a wife, and "so Isaac was comforted after his mother's death" (Genesis 24:67). Perhaps he hoped that Rebecca would never betray him.

Isaac may have made peace with his mother after his wedding, but not with his father. Abraham may have hoped his son would take Rebecca as a form of compensation, thus paving the way for a renewed relationship between them—but it was not to be. Abraham remains isolated in his tent in Beer Sheba, a woman named Keturah by his side, and forms a new family, siring six children from her. Isaac, for his part, breaks with biblical tradition and does not come to receive a blessing before his father's death. Indeed, he sees his father only once after the binding: on the day Abraham is buried, leaving Isaac all his tremendous wealth.

Now we can begin to grasp the harsh power of *Gevurah*, its tendency to withdraw into itself in a way that makes it impossible for the *sefirah* to receive nourishment from the outside, to say nothing of nourishing others. We can understand what happened to Isaac. What can we expect from someone who saw his father—the man who is supposed to provide him with security as a child—raising high a ceremonial knife to slaughter him? What can we expect from someone who knows that his mother failed to protect him from his father? What can we expect from someone who feels that God is hostile to him?

A person betrayed by his mother, by his father, by his God, is probably lost.

Gevurah, the *sefirah* of Isaac's fear, sees evil in all the foundations of being. It cannot maintain a trusting relationship with anyone, but rather retreats into itself like a clenched fist and so dooms itself to an existence of solitude and want. Worst of all, it loses the will to act, to carve out its own path in the world. Isaac withdraws into depression, losing contact with the vitality that finds expression in a creative engagement with the world. His hope is his son Esau, a man of action and of the field—a hunter blessed with great creative power. Isaac tries to draw some power from his son, since his has dissipated altogether.

The next time we encounter Isaac in the biblical narrative, he is poor and exhausted. Abraham's tremendous wealth has all been lost, apparently as a result of Isaac's passivity and helplessness, or perhaps because he intentionally let his father's wealth go to waste. His younger son, Jacob, is preparing lentil stew. His elder son, Esau, returns from an unsuccessful hunt, so hungry that he is willing to sell his birthright to Jacob for a pitiful bowl of stew. "What good is the birthright to you?" Esau asks Jacob. "Our father is dirt-poor; the birthright will never translate into an inheritance!"[10]

At the very last minute, before he collapses into his own fears and trepidations, an event occurs that forces Isaac to emerge from his shell and take action in the real world. A famine strikes Canaan, and Isaac's family must wander south, to Egypt, where the irrigation farming is resistant to drought. And, as sometimes happens, physical movement—even if undertaken in response to external circumstances—brings about dramatic internal change. On his way to Egypt, Isaac passes through the Philistine territory and its capital Gerar, where, to his surprise, God commands him to remain, without explanation or justification.

Isaac's behaves oddly during his stay at Gerar. The Bible tells us that Abimelech, king of Gerar, was a close friend and ally of Abraham's. According to a well-known Talmudic interpretation, Abimelech was Isaac's biological father, having impregnated Sarah when she was taken into his household during Abraham's visit to Gerar. Either way, once in Gerar, Isaac—shockingly—asks Rebecca to introduce herself as his sister, "for he was afraid to say, 'My wife,' thinking, 'or else the men of the place might kill me for the sake of Rebecca, because she is attractive in appearance'" (Genesis 26:7).

This scene appears similar to one involving Abraham and Sarah. In two instances—when he migrates to Egypt and then to Philistia—Abraham has Sarah present herself as his sister.[11] Both times Sarah is taken to be a concubine of the local ruler, whom God proceeds to punish, whereupon Sarah returns to Abraham.

But a careful reading suggests that it is not a repetition at all; in fact, the Bible emphasizes that we are not dealing with the same event.[12] On the contrary, Isaac is parodying his father's actions and thus highlighting Abraham's hypocrisy, staging, as it were, a modern psychodrama at the local playhouse. Isaac, who is trying to heal the wounds his father inflicted on him, can only reveal the depth of the injury through this biting satire. It is as though he were turning to everyone around him and saying: Remember Abraham, who never missed an opportunity to wave the banner of justice and love? He lied constantly to everyone around him, to Sarah, and particularly to me, his son Isaac, who once asked him while walking toward Mount Moriah, "Where is the lamb for the burnt offering?" and he answered, "God Himself will provide the lamb for the burnt offering, my son" (Genesis 22:7–8).

How do I know this is Isaac's parody of his father's life? From the fact that after he has introduced Rebecca as his sister, he makes every effort for the people of Gerar, and particularly Abimelech, who knows his family well, to uncover the lie: "When Isaac had been there a long time, King Abimelech of the Philistines looked out of a window and saw him fondling his wife Rebecca" (Genesis 26:8). Isaac waits for someone to come take his wife away so that he can remind everyone of his father's wily tricks, but no one comes. So Isaac, who is generally so shy, has sexual relations with his "sister" in public—right beneath Abimelech's window, in fact, in plain sight of the neighbors in the surrounding houses, as though there were no other places in Gerar where he could make love to his wife. This is an intentional provocation aimed at eliciting a harsh response on the part of King Abimelech and the citizens of Gerar, all of whom will then recall the similar lies Abraham told, before he became rich and famous and "a prince of God" (Genesis 23:6).

And indeed, from the moment he confronts his (dead) father[13] and publicly ridicules his memory, Isaac's old wounds begin to heal. The hurt, passive Isaac, who frittered away his father's inheritance, has no job, and has fallen into poverty, is transformed into an active and decisive man. For the first time, he is able to receive the positive aspects of his father's *Hesed*: "Isaac sowed seed in that land and in the same year reaped a hundredfold" (Genesis 26:12). The book of Genesis emphasizes "that land" and that year as turning points in Isaac's life; for the first time he confronts the father who bound him on the altar. Only after this process is Isaac able to make peace with his father. The Bible alludes to this by highlighting Isaac's decision to settle in Beer Sheba, where his father formerly resided, the place from which Abraham set out for Mount Moriah. From that moment on, Isaac begins to grow rich: "And the man became rich; he prospered more and more until he became very wealthy" (Genesis 26:13); and he suddenly has time and energy to tend to his father's failed enterprises: "Isaac dug again the wells of water that had been dug in the days of his father Abraham; for the Philistines had stopped them up after the death of Abraham; and he gave them the names that his father had given them" (Genesis 26:18).

The kabbalist Moshe Hayyim Luzzatto interprets Isaac's self-healing, his *tikkun*, in light of the importance the biblical text attributes to these wells:

Isaac dug again the wells, that is, *Gevurah* willingly accepted the mending of *Hesed*, for if *Gevurah* is not in a mended state it will prevent *Hesed* from making these repairs and will block out the light. But if it is in a mended state then it does accept *Hesed*'s repairs. So God caused matters to proceed such that Isaac dug the water wells a second time, in order to show that Isaac here represents *Gevurah* in a mended state, i.e., having undergone *tikkun*—*Gevurah* that willingly accepted the emendations and emanations of the divine light.[14]

Luzzatto interprets Isaac's *tikkun* in psychological terms, that is, as Isaac agreeing for the first time to receive something from *Hesed*, his father's *sefirah*, even though it had treated him so cruelly in binding him. Up to that moment, Isaac had refused his father's *Hesed*-based *tikkun*, embracing *Gevurah* exclusively, so that it surrounded him on all sides, sealing him off from any other influence. Only after using *Gevurah* to "murder" his father was he able to receive his father's *Hesed*.

How is such a complex *tikkun* possible? It is one thing to forgive his father—a man must forgive his father to avoid remaining bound to the site of trauma. But to adopt the father's characteristics, the same characteristics that caused the father to commit the terrible abuses? Isaac's psychological turn here is hard to fully understand.

Luzzatto does not suggest that Isaac's relationship with his father was mended after he adopted Abraham's *Hesed*, but rather that Isaac drew his *Hesed* from a higher site within the sefirotic structure. He writes:

Since the digging of the wells indicates that he is in a state of mended *Gevurah*, he ascended to Beer Sheba, which is the mother, since the mended *Gevurah* bonds with *Binah*, which is its root. That is where he received the prophetic vision, prophecy being located in the mother.[15]

In other words, Isaac did not forgive his father by being receptive to Abraham's *Hesed*, but rather ascended to the very root of *Hesed*, which is *Binah* (i.e., the mother), where there is as yet no division into good and evil. Isaac dug into his own soul until he reached its deepest roots, from which he was able to transition to the source of his father's soul and try to understand the root cause of his error.

Isaac ascended to *Binah*—the *sefirah* of the Void Space—and observed the common root of *Hesed* and *Gevurah*. His *tikkun* was complex: "patricide," reconciliation with his father, gaining an understanding of the deep sources of his father's error, and, finally, ascent to the very place where his father abandoned him in his youth so that Isaac can renew it as a source of divine effluence.

4

Isaac's story helps me to confront anew my relationship with my own father. After many years when he did not speak to me, there began a slow process of reconciliation. The turning point was my wedding, when my father offered a toast in which he cited the last words of Malachi, the last biblical prophet: "Lo, I will send you the prophet Elijah before the great and terrible day of the Lord comes. He will turn the hearts of parents to their children and the hearts of children to their parents, so that I will not come and strike the land with a curse" (Malachi 3:23).

My father always had a strong messianic mind-set, and he went on to claim that true salvation lies in the repair of the relationship between fathers and sons. When he spoke thus, I loved him as I had never loved him before. I admired his depth, his courage, and the *tikkun* he effected in our relationship. But even now, after my relationship with my father has undergone a real and sustained process of improvement, I know that this is only the first step.

When Isaac effected the *tikkun* with his father, he tapped into elements of *Hesed* within himself, allowing him to identify with Abraham. But my father, despite his explicit *Hesed* statements, is *Gevurah* through and through. Even in reconciliation, I cannot draw from him the *Hesed* I so desperately need these days. I can receive his simplicity, as well as his desire to reach down to the very depths, but I cannot receive the wounds life has inflicted on him that make him so anxious. Time and again I recite the same promise—a promise I am never able to keep—that I will find the time to sit and study with him the following saying from Rabbi Nahman of Breslov:

Some people are embroiled in scholarly controversy because they have no faith in themselves, and they have no faith in the new Torah interpretations they produce, and they think the Holy One blessed be He has greater sources of enjoyment than these interpretations. Because they have no faith in their own interpretations, they are lax interpreters and so become controversial. The scholarly controversy causes them to repent, and their new interpretations once again seem important in their eyes, and they produce new interpretations, and so a book comes into existence. Sometimes the book exists on high, such that one can inquire and challenge, while the other repents and so is able to respond and explain. In this way, the heavenly book is formed, as it is written: "Then those who revered the Lord spoke with one another, and the Lord took note and listened, and a book was written." (Malachi 3:16)[16]

Rabbi Nahman, who also loved the prophet Malachi, considered lack of confidence a religious flaw and a weakness. Only controversy (which draws its power from *Gevurah*) causes us to set out on the arduous and painful journey back to regain our faith in ourselves. Replacing self-doubt with self-faith produces a "heavenly book," that is, an innovative Torah interpretation that has never been proposed even in the divine realms. The power of this faith lies precisely in its previously having been shattered.

But how can a person who does not have faith in himself or in his interpretations, and thus avoids writing for fear of ridicule and rejection, effect a *tikkun* involving the other when he becomes the object of controversy? Perhaps such a person will be healed when he finds someone who will listen to him and accept him unconditionally.

I note that for Rabbi Nahman, the key moment is repentance. Perhaps when all our fears are realized, when reality makes manifest our inner consciousness and other people *do* reject and ridicule them, only then do we realize that there is no sense in trying to please others and curry favor in their eyes. Only then is a person forced to ascend to the site of repentance, kabbalistically identified with *Binah*, the *sefirah* of opposites, where he can grow anew from his own root, still innocent of the division and imprisonment and anxieties characteristic of *Gevurah*. Perhaps there he can write his new interpretation, the interpretation that will become a new heavenly book through which God encounters His words anew.

⏤

Perhaps Rabbi Nahman is not saying that there are people who do not write their new interpretations because they lack faith in themselves. Perhaps he is saying something completely different: "Because they have no faith in their own interpretations, they are lax interpreters and as such become controversial." Rabbi Nahman is not referring to people who do not write their novel interpretations, but to those who "are lax" in doing so, "and as a result they become a matter of controversy." The insight garnered by this close reading may appear negligible, and it may be that its fastidious roots lie in the critical confines of *Gevurah* itself, the very place I wish to flee. But when I examine a certain event that occurred in the past few months I realize how profound Rabbi Nahman's words really are and how the power of *Gevurah*—the sheer force of scholarly controversy—can aid us in overcoming *Gevurah*.

The interpretation I offered above of Rabbi Nahman's words was similarly lax. It was easy to expose myself to the penetrating words that struck the still open wound within me. Sloppiness is antithetical to *Gevurah*'s strict nature, but it serves *Gevurah* indirectly all the same. Rabbi Nahman was not referring to faith in ourselves, but rather a faith that employs the tools of *Gevurah* to overcome the negative aspects of that very *sefirah*. *Gevurah*, literally "valor," received this name because contraction, borders, and judgment are all tools for positive change, able to overcome the evil and opaqueness of the *sefirah* itself. When a person flees criticism and judgment, this does not mean he flees the *Gevurah* within him; sometimes negligence causes evil to grow stronger. If we are the object of polemic, when our own sloppiness nourishes the perplexity of our critics and thus undermines our own position, we may repent, but not as sinners. Rather we come to understand that the transgression of sloppiness stems from our attempt to suppress the forces of *Gevurah* within us.

Like Isaac, I may have to employ the tools of *Gevurah* if I am to overcome the forces of negation and evil within the *sefirah*: to go to Abimelech, king of Gerar, to say what needs to be said, to till and sow with the tools of *Gevurah* to then reap a hundredfold. I must not allow Abimelech's servants to stop up the wells I dig, the fonts of my living waters. Reconciliation with my father for the sole purpose of avoiding his ever-critical gaze is, I know, insufficient. I must try to grasp the more primordial, untainted root within myself and draw from it a deep, permeating self-confidence so that the response of the outside world, even its betrayal, cannot undermine what I have labored to build.

The story of Isaac is always moving, for immediately after his recovery from his past wounds, the Bible again hurls him into a betrayal narrative, this one involving his beloved wife, Rebecca, and their young son Jacob.

In its stylized cruelty, the Bible transports the reader to Isaac's later years. After his recovery from his earlier traumas, we now meet Isaac as a blind and thoroughly exhausted old man: "Isaac was old and his eyes were dim so that he could not see" (Genesis 27:1). Isaac may be blind, but he has not forgotten anything, as the sages note in their profoundly symbolic interpretation of his blindness as caused by the tears of the angels that fell into his eyes when the heavens opened above him during his binding. He may have reconciled with his father, but when he grows old, he again sees himself through the eyes of the weeping angels: weak, bound, helpless. The angels that have been burned into Isaac's memory as figures of mercy and compassion are transformed into destructive angels, reminders of his weakness and helplessness. But precisely what *Gevurah* desires is to increase its power so that we will not be able to overcome it.

In the second act of his life, Isaac almost submits to *Gevurah*.

We might say that Isaac succeeded where the other patriarchs failed; he was able to reach old age without having a single aggressive and difficult dialogue with God. His wife, Rebecca, coerces him into the one monologue he addresses to God (asking Him for children).[17] Between God and Isaac we hear only a vexing silence, as if Isaac is uninterested in God, or perhaps his weakness limits him to muted dialogues. Isaac is the only patriarch not to receive a new, theophoric name. "Abram" receives a new letter—a letter that is part of the name of God—and becomes "Abraham"; "Jacob" becomes "Israel"; but Isaac remains "Isaac" his entire life. The Hebrew *Yitzhak* may mean "he shall laugh," but the laughter remains within him, unrealized.

Blind and ill and completely dependent on others, Isaac tries with his remaining strength to confront the forces of *Gevurah*, defiantly turning his back on the role God has assigned Abraham's family. He chooses not to bless his younger son, Jacob, "a mild man, living in tents," who was perhaps better suited than Esau to serve as the custodian of the delicate part of Abraham's spiritual legacy. Surprisingly, Isaac chooses the antithesis of that legacy, Esau, "a skillful hunter, a man of the field" (Genesis 25:27). The Zohar explains the affinity between Isaac and Esau as based on the elements of *Gevurah*, Isaac's *sefirah*, that exist in Esau, the man of action and hunting. In more contemporary terms, we might say that Isaac and Esau have forged a covenant of the body, of the here and now. The love shared by Isaac and Esau has no room for the spirituality and cloying emotionalism associated with Abraham. This is a love that contains a basic truth of "give and take," a mercantile transaction that requires no emotional intimacy that might lead to betrayal—everything is determined by the price charged and the proceeds generated.

Why does Isaac disregard the links between God and man? Again, the kabbalists represent Isaac as having uncovered the evil within the divine forces manifest in the world. When the heavens opened during the binding, Isaac peered into the "black holes" of the divine cosmos, the dark gaps of the God of the Bible, who had not yet been transformed into the impersonal God of radical monotheism (the philosophers would see to that later). When the heavens opened, Isaac undoubtedly saw the love his father felt for God, but he also saw the darker side of that love, the root of evil within God Himself, and perhaps the seeds of evil buried within all human love of God. His vision, momentarily fragmented within the divine depths of *Binah*, beheld both absolute love and absolute evil, both of which find their purest expression in the moment of the binding.

But instead of fighting against the evil within God, evil that flows from the powers of *Gevurah* required for the positive contraction of the universe, Isaac surrenders. Though on a conscious level he chooses Esau, wishing to absorb the vital forces of *Gevurah* within him, at the moment of truth, his internal doubt makes him careless. Despite his obvious suspicion regarding the identity of the son standing before him—"the voice is Jacob's voice, but the hands are Esau's hands" (Genesis 27:22)—he offers little more than the perfunctory examination of the young man standing before him, Jacob disguised as Esau. Even now, in his heart he is tempted to worship the same shadow side that has plagued him since his childhood. The experience of the binding was never fully overcome, and again it weakens his resolve. Isaac chooses to believe Jacob's claim to be Esau, exhibiting the same naiveté that prevented him from realizing his innermost faith.

Do I want to remain in the place where Isaac's *Gevurah* hovers? Does my critique of the extreme *Hesed* faith of Abraham mean that I must embrace the absolute negation associated with Isaac? I would not wish a life like Isaac's. I know evil exists, even within God Himself. But must I see this evil everywhere I turn? After all, where there is evil, there is also good, and the Void Space contains good, even if it is usually hidden, veiled in a world of contraction that does not recognize true choice. What will I gain by fastening onto *Gevurah*? Truth? Integrity? Have I not learned that truth and integrity do not necessarily lead to good? Have I not learned that truth too can wound and be transformed into unmitigated evil? But if we abandon truth, what is left? The delusional consolation of fools? Cheap romanticism? Perhaps there is another truth, a different truth than Isaac's.

Good and evil coexist simultaneously. Rabbi Nahman quotes a famous Talmudic saying—"Both are the words of the living God"[18]—when he tries to characterize the absence of judgment in the Void Space. I can choose to be bewitched by suspicion, but ultimately the suspicion will be turned back onto me, infiltrating my own being so that I will be untrue even to myself.

⟶

chapter six

Tiferet
Integrity beyond Truth

1

The biblical portrait of Abraham is about the need to leave what is known and familiar; the story of Isaac addresses suffering, fear, suspicion, and the need to overcome the wounds of the past. But it is hard for me to identify with Jacob. I have always seen him as a superficial character who refuses to cope with his life in a meaningful way, and I recoiled from the lack of integrity reflected in so many events in his life. My critique of Jacob was so harsh that I did not notice the changes he underwent over the course of his life.

My reading of the Jacob cycle was first and foremost a reflection of an inability to come to terms with my own faults. One of the great Hasidic masters, Rabbi Joshua Heschel of Apta (1755–1825), was known as the *Ohev Yisrael* ("Lover of Israel") after his most important book. The Apta Rebbe was known for his sharp intelligence and his wide learning, but also for his joy and humor and his love of food and drink. "Man sees every fault except his own"—he would cite the Talmudic ruling that a person cannot decide matters of ritual purity pertaining to a blemish on his own skin. But the Apta Rebbe transformed the Talmudic teaching into a doctrine of the human soul:

And the advice for this matter is to examine those around us. That is, if one sees a person committing an unworthy act, let him think to himself, Why did God cause me to see this? Is it not because this fault affects my own home, but my eyes have been too weak to see it? And then he will repent and the Lord will have mercy on him, and in doing so he will cause the other person to turn his heart toward repentance as well. The root of repentance, then, lies in the action of those around us.[1]

The *Ohev Yisrael* explores the difference between truth and integrity. Like many a Hasidic master, he peppered his teachings with hyperbole and fantastic tales, but he never confused these tales with reality. The Apta Rebbe did not mean that the faults we see in others are unreal, mere projections of our own flawed self; they are real. Rather, when we recognize faults in others, we must possess the integrity to recognize that we do so because we know our own faults.

My life, like Jacob's, could be seen as a paradigm of lack of integrity, false pretenses, phoniness, and deception. This is no empty self-flagellation. As my parents' Benjamin, the ninth child following three girls, I was my mother's pampered. My mother was enslaved to me, eager to entertain my every whimsy, and I, for my part, never granted her the right of refusal. Every morning she would dutifully drag herself out of the house to walk me to kindergarten, but only after a daily excursion to a far-off store to buy me a new toy car; every day she would walk to my kindergarten a second time, carrying a fresh cup of orange juice, wait patiently until our recess, then pass me the juice through the fence surrounding the kindergarten playground; every day she asked my permission when she wanted to leave the house to meet with friends or go shopping.

My father, in contrast, could not stand such solicitousness. But he was incapable of engaging my mother in a meaningful discussion about my upbringing, so he held his tongue and resented me for many years. My mother's pampering corrupted my character and precipitated my prolonged estrangement from my father. Our relationship deteriorated further once I became a bargaining chip in their other arguments.

Jacob is the son of Rebecca, who felt that Abraham's servant cheated her when he paired her with Isaac, the rich heir who managed to fritter away everything he had inherited from Abraham. Apparently Rebecca never does learn to love Isaac, as her relationship with him involves silence and treachery. But Isaac is also incapable of sharing his pains and his thoughts with Rebecca. In their relationship with their children, Esau and Jacob, each parent chooses a different child as the object of their love. Like me, Jacob is the sensitive child who hides behind his mother's apron strings and is disparaged by his father. He learns deception and survival from his mother's interactions with his father and brother.

Two harsh moments of deception are characteristic of Jacob's early years: the purchase of the birthright from Esau for a bowl of stew and the theft of his father's blessing by means of lies and disguise. The Bible prefaces each of these events by recounting the circumstances surrounding Jacob's birth—that he grasped the heel of his twin brother. Esau struggles and pushes forward to exit the womb, but Jacob simply latches onto his brother's heel, unwilling to make any effort to break out into the world, to *earn* the birthright. This tendency will grow stronger over the course of his life.

From the moment of his birth, Jacob lives parasitically off the efforts of others. When the twins grow up, the Bible describes Esau as "a skillful hunter, a man of the field," while Jacob is "a mild man, living in tents" (Genesis 25:27). The biblical adjective *tam*, rendered as "mild" in the New Revised Standard Version of the Bible, does not here imply (as it does elsewhere) innocence or naïveté, since the context suggests the opposite is the case. Rather, it refers to an integral, unblemished body and suggests Jacob's unwillingness to do anything that might blemish him: hunt, work the land, help with domestic chores. He sits in the tent with his tender *yeshiva-bocher* hands.

The birthright story begins, "Once when Jacob was cooking a stew, Esau came in from the field, and he was famished" (Genesis 25:29), with the sound of the Hebrew words for "cooking a stew," *vayazed nazid*, calling to mind *zadon*, "malice." Jacob is stewing maliciously, waiting for Esau to return tired and hungry from the field.

The hunt, it seems, has gone poorly, and Esau, famished, asks Jacob for a helping of stew. Though Esau generally provides for the family's livelihood, today Jacob has prepared the stew and before sharing it with his brother sets a condition: "First sell me your birthright" (Genesis 25:31). Esau comes off as hasty and reckless for agreeing without much reflection to this bad deal, while Jacob is little more than a swindler who takes advantage of the naive seller who does not know the value of his merchandise and, famished, sells it at a loss.

In the second narrative, Jacob, acting in concert with his mother, undertakes a much more blatant and egregious deception. Rebecca concocts a sophisticated operation that will allow her beloved Jacob to don a new persona—his brother's, symbolized by the hairy, calloused hands of the man of the field—to obtain his father's blessing. This is not a sin of omission or even a small lie, but a shocking deception that reaches to the foundations of an individual's personality. Jacob steals his brother's identity and takes it for himself.

People lie out of a desire for easy access to money or property, followed by an aversion to confrontation. Lies of this sort are fairly common. Jacob's second deception, where he does not merely give partial or misleading information but instead adopts an entirely new identity, is carried out for the sake of his deepest desire, his father's love. Such a lie is far more dangerous, since the liar can end up losing his true identity. An individual who reaches such a level of deception loses the root of his soul, the core of his personality. He exchanges his identity for a shadowy chimera, the identity of another, until eventually he forgets who he is. Over time he loses the ability to distinguish truth from lie.

The Bible describes Jacob as Rebecca's "baby" (Genesis 25:27–28) but he is in fact a fully grown man. Shortly before the birthright narrative, we are told that Esau is forty years old, so this is Jacob's age as well. We cannot attribute Jacob's terrible deception to juvenile mischief. Nonetheless, Jacob continues to cower behind his mother's apron, as she advises him to flee to Laban, her brother in Haran. The lies of Jacob and his mother, intended to gain the birthright without confrontation or effort, ultimately cause both parents to fear that Esau will kill Jacob in revenge. And Jacob, who sought to cheat his way to his father's inheritance—the divine promise to inherit the Land of Israel—must flee, empty-handed, traveling a long and arduous path, along which he will have to confront the terrible psychological causes of his own predicament.

At this point in his life, Jacob apparently has never worked but instead has lived off the efforts of his family and the preferential treatment of his mother. He is a pampered, conniving liar. The prophet Jeremiah, who lived in a time of degeneracy and decadence, used Jacob's name to refer to the corruption and mistrust surrounding him:

> O that I had in the desert a traveler's lodging-place, that I might leave my people and go away from them! For they are all adulterers, a band of traitors. They bend their tongues like bows; they have grown strong in the land for falsehood, and not for truth; for they proceed from evil to evil, and they do not know me, says the Lord. Beware of your neighbors, and put no trust in any of your kin; for all your kin are supplanters ['*akov Yakov*—Hebrew for "Jacob"], and every neighbor goes around like a slanderer. (Jeremiah 9:1–3)

The prophet uses Jacob as a shorthand reference for a perverted social state of lies and betrayal that undermines the faith of humanity. Jeremiah meant that there are lies that cause such defects in a person's personality that he can no longer believe even himself, to say nothing of others. And indeed, we find that the Jacob who flees from his father's house is physically whole but psychologically damaged. The pampered man who never worked a day, the man accustomed to dealing with difficulties by means of lies, the man with no core, no center to his personality, who is unable to ask his father for the blessing directly, suddenly must go out into the world, completely alone, without help or support.

For the first time, Jacob must sleep away from home, and he is undoubtedly afraid and anxious. But instead of nightmares, he receives a wonderful, comforting dream:

> And he dreamed that there was a ladder set up on the earth, the
> top of it reaching to heaven; and the angels of God were ascend-
> ing and descending on it. And the Lord stood beside him and
> said, "I am the Lord, the God of Abraham your father and the
> God of Isaac; the land on which you lie I will give to you and to
> your offspring; and your offspring shall be like the dust of the
> earth, and you shall spread abroad to the west and to the east and
> to the north and to the south; and all the families of the earth
> shall be blessed in you and in your offspring. Know that I am
> with you and will keep you wherever you go, and will bring you
> back to this land; for I will not leave you until I have done what
> I have promised you." (Genesis 28:12–15)

God makes Jacob sweeping promises, more than Abraham ever
received. But how does Jacob react? He reacts the only way he
knows. He sets out a series of conditions and leads God into an openly
disrespectful deal:

> Then Jacob made a vow, saying, "If God will be with me, and
> will keep me in this way that I go, and will give me bread to eat
> and clothing to wear, so that I come again to my father's house
> in peace, then the Lord shall be my God, and this stone, which I
> have set up for a pillar, shall be God's house; and of all that You
> give me I will surely give one-tenth to You." (Genesis 28:20–22)

We are dealing with a person whose mistrust runs so deep that he
cannot even believe a vision, a revelation that comes to succor him in
his time of need. Though he has nothing to lose, Jacob continues his
reprehensible negotiations even as God reveals Himself to him.

Jacob's mistrustful and pampered response is flabbergasting, but
we can also understand the Jacob's ladder narrative as leading Jacob
toward his new fate. In this stunning night-vision, Jacob sees a ladder
placed between two axes, heaven and earth, with angels ascending
and descending it. The kabbalistic interpretation sees this as an image
of intermediation between the heavens (the top three *sefirot*, *Keter*,
Hokhmah, and *Binah*) and the earth (the terrestrial *sefirah Malkhut*).
The earth represents the concrete, sometimes painful reality of life, a

world in which the hopes and wishes that originate in our thoughts and imagination can only be realized through labor.

Jacob's ladder can also be understood as a vision in which his soul tries to chart out for itself a path for its self-*tikkun*. Jacob, spurred on by his overriding ambition, may seek shortcuts to his goals, but the ladder shows him that these cannot be attained through lies and distortions, only by dealing with them directly. The path runs from heaven to earth, from the realm of fantastic hopes and wishes downward to their concrete realization, passing through the many rungs of the ladder, reaching down toward earth. Only after dealing in a meaningful way with terrestrial reality can one ascend anew and draw down fresh dreams and hopes.

———

The kabbalists identify Jacob with *Tiferet*, the sixth *sefirah*, following *Hesed* and *Gevurah*. The latter two, each occupying an absolute position within the sefirotic structure, cannot be united in a balanced whole without the aid of a third, independent *sefirah*—*Tiferet*. To properly blend *Hesed* and *Gevurah*, *Tiferet* must determine what positive elements exist in each and, only after separating these from the negative elements, channel the positive from the two higher *sefirot* into a third entity, thereby creating a harmonious new reality. This site of harmony, *Tiferet*, is also known as "truth," *emet*, a word that consists of the first, middle, and last letters of the Hebrew alphabet.

Tiferet's truth is the integrity that lies beyond truth. This is a truth that tries to identify the constructive elements that are embedded within the absolute, unyielding truth of *Gevurah* and are undoubtedly found in abundance in the divine effluence *Hesed*. *Tiferet* is located at the heart of the sefirotic structure, the center of the top-to-bottom axis and also of the right-left division. *Tiferet* is the truth that lies along the center axis of the Tree of the *sefirot*, a truth that spans the length and the breadth of all being; the point of equilibrium for the vertical axis of the *sefirot*, from *Keter* to *Malkhut*, as well as for the horizontal axis of *Hesed* and *Gevurah*.

Though they share a great deal, the two axes are very different. The horizontal represents the unending flow from modes of thought to modes of action and back again; it is not concerned with questions of morality. The manifestation of thought in the world, on the one hand, and the influence of the world of action on that of thought, on the other, can be either good or evil. The vertical axis, by contrast, includes a distinct moral component that distinguishes the thoughts and actions on the side of *Gevurah*-evil from those on the side of *Hesed*-good. *Tiferet* is the central *sefirah* for the two axes, sorting out the good in all the *sefirot* and positioning itself so as to best balance between them, a position identified with Jacob, the third patriarch, who is known as "Israel." This represents the perfect combination of Abraham and Isaac.

The kabbalists teach that it is possible to attain a perfect synthesis that defuses the original tension between *Hesed* and *Gevurah*, the right and left, love and harsh judgment. At the same time, *Tiferet* also is the point of equilibrium between the upper three *sefirot* (the world of divine thought) and the practical power of lower reality—*Malkhut*. Jacob, in this sense, represents an unprecedented occurrence, a perfect human being.

But even Jacob does not understand his visions when they occur. At this point in the biblical narrative, no one has informed Jacob that he represents *Tiferet*, the *sefirah* also known as "truth." After his nocturnal ladder vision, he sets out for Haran, where he meets Rachel, herding the sheep of her father Laban and waiting for the other shepherds to roll a large rock off the opening of the well. Jacob falls in love with beautiful Rachel and impresses her by removing the boulder unaided.

Jacob then meets his uncle Laban, who takes his nephew under his treacherous wing, and the Bible proceeds with the story of Jacob and Laban's daughters: "Now Laban had two daughters; the name of the elder was Leah, and the name of the younger was Rachel. Leah's eyes were soft, but Rachel was graceful and beautiful" (Genesis 29:16–17). This is the only occurrence of the phrase "graceful and beautiful" in the Bible—Scripture reserves it for Rachel, as she is the most beautiful woman in the biblical world. Leah, by contrast, has soft eyes. There is a real disparity between the beauty of Rachel and that of Leah. It is no surprise, then, that Jacob falls in love with Rachel. "Jacob loved Rachel; so he said, 'I will serve you seven years for your younger daughter Rachel'" (Genesis 29:18). For the first time in his life, Jacob is willing to labor. Indeed, he undergoes a complete transformation. Leaving home seems to have done him some good. Laban accepts the deal, and Jacob works for seven years, though the time passes in a flash: "Jacob served seven years for Rachel, and they seemed to him but a few days because of the love he had for her" (Genesis 29:20).

But deception comes back to haunt Jacob:

> Then Jacob said to Laban, "Give me my wife that I may go in to her, for my time is completed." So Laban gathered together all the people of the place, and made a feast. But in the evening he took his daughter Leah and brought her to Jacob; and he went in to her. (Laban gave his maid Zilpah to his daughter Leah to be her maid.) When morning came, it was Leah, not Rachel! And Jacob said to Laban, "What is this you have done to me? Did I not serve with you for Rachel? Why then have you deceived me?" Laban said, "This is not done in our country—giving the younger before the firstborn." (Genesis 29:21–26)

This is the Bible's description of a horrible deceit that would have broken the spirit of any normal man. Jacob gives seven years of hard labor because he so yearns for Rachel. But on the day his labor is to be rewarded, the sisters are switched. Jacob lies with his new wife and only in the morning sees it is Leah. When he confronts the father of the bride, Laban hints to him: in our parts we do not give precedence to the younger over the elder, as you did, Jacob, when you stole the birthright.

It is hard to understand how Jacob managed to confuse the sisters. If a man is in love with a woman, lives in the same house with her for seven years, fantasizing all the while about every curve and contour of her body, how does he fail to notice that the woman he finally sleeps with is not the object of his yearning?

I suggest that the love Jacob feels for Rachel is the love of a man who has no idea what love is, of a narcissist whose entire focus is on his own experience. During the seven years of dreaming and fantasizing, Jacob never really saw Rachel, but only a reflection of himself in her. Ultimately, then, it did not matter that Laban shoved Leah into Jacob's tent instead of Rachel. Before the sun rose, forcing him to recognize he was with another woman, everything was just fine in Jacob's eyes, and his relationship with his own reflection—a relationship that now includes a sexual dimension—continued unabated. This is man who cannot step out of the robust and dynamic relationship he maintains with himself. Moreover, it was not difficult to deceive Jacob, since nothing is easier than deceiving a deceiver. A man whose own identity is false will not recognize the falsity of another.

Jacob's counterfeit love of Rachel yields only deception. True, the Jewish tradition presents Rachel as a compassionate and romantic figure. A thousand poems have been written about her, a thousand songs linked with her image. But the Rachel of the biblical Jacob narrative is a different matter entirely. Though Jacob labors for her for fourteen years, she never really appreciates him. When Leah begins bearing children for Jacob—six sons in a row—barren Rachel expresses her frustration dramatically:

> When Rachel saw that she bore Jacob no children, she envied her sister; and she said to Jacob, "Give me children, or I shall die!" Jacob became very angry with Rachel and said, "Am I in the place of God, who has withheld from you the fruit of the womb?" (Genesis 30:1–2)

Rachel makes the exacting demands of a pampered and impatient woman until Jacob can no longer bear the way she expresses her pain. The torment of the barren woman is not hard to understand, but Rachel's pain is linked to jealousy of her sister. This pain too is understandable, but when we compare Rachel's behavior with that of other barren women in the Bible—Sarah or Hannah, for example— we find that the root *k-n-'* (to be jealous) does not appear in their narratives, but only in connection with Rachel. So terrible is her jealousy that Jacob no longer sleeps with Leah, and she must resort to buying sexual relations with her husband with mandrakes. Rachel trades Jacob's body and sexuality like goods hawked to shoppers at the fair. Jacob, shocked, can only agree to the negotiations being carried out behind his back.

How cruel the Bible can be to its protagonists when it tries to get them to change! After all, from the moment Jacob leaves his father's house, his culture of deception and manipulation exacts retribution against him time and again. Jacob steals his father's blessing by disguising himself as his brother, and Laban the Aramean repays Jacob in kind with a bait-and-switch of his daughters. Jacob purchases the birthright from Esau for a bowl of stew, only to have Rachel, whose personality is very similar to Jacob's, trade his own sexuality for a trifling mandrake plant.

Jacob's worldview, his actions, and his culture are all reflected back at him. He cannot flee the repercussions of his deeds or the falseness of his personality, and one by one they come back to haunt him. Moreover, the woman he so dearly loves, and for whose sake he entered into this adventure to begin with, reflects his own image back to him robustly.

After fourteen years in Laban's house, after his deceptions and lies have been flung back at him by his uncle and by his wives, it is clear that Jacob is psychologically in a different place than when he fled his parents' home. Laban's deception forces him to undertake extravagant labor to realize his love and desire for Rachel. In the house of Laban the deceiver, Jacob discovers the need to confront reality in its most concrete manifestations. The mild man has been transformed into a hunter, a man of the field, exposed to harsh weather and loneliness. This is how he describes the conditions he endured working for Laban: "It was like this with me: by day the heat consumed me, and the cold by night, and my sleep fled from my eyes" (Genesis 31:40). Ultimately, Jacob's *tikkun* transforms him into Esau, whose identity he superficially donned as a young man. Now Jacob understands that to merit the blessing intended for Esau, he needs more than a disguise. He must labor to recognize Esau's positive attributes.

2

Only when Jacob truly becomes Esau does he reach the level of maturity that warrants his return to his mother and father in Canaan. But he does not want to leave empty-handed, so he proposes a partnership with Laban, according to which the newborns of the flock will be divided as follows: all the striped, speckled, and mottled goats belong to Jacob, while the unblemished kids belong to Laban.

Again the Bible tells of one of Jacob's dreams, recounted in a conversation he has with his wives, when he tries to convince them to leave their father's house with him:

> During the mating of the flock I once had a dream in which I looked up and saw that the male goats that leaped upon the flock were striped, speckled, and mottled. Then the angel of God said to me in the dream, "Jacob," and I said, "Here I am!" And he said, "Look up and see that all the goats that leap on the flock are striped, speckled, and mottled; for I have seen all that Laban is doing to you. I am the God of Bethel, where you anointed a pillar and made a vow to me. Now leave this land at once and return to the land of your birth." (Genesis 31:10–13)

To increase his cut of the goat births, Jacob hatches a sophisticated plan of genetic engineering. According to the folk wisdom of the day, when a pregnant woman would stare at something or desired a particular food, this would affect the appearance of the child. Jacob uses this technique to influence the kids born in Laban's herd, placing sticks and poles on which he carved spots by the watering troughs. The herd gathers there to drink, the goats gaze on the sticks during mating, and then the nannies breed many speckled kids.

Here is a wonderful example of Jacob's new pragmatism. He has become a successful man of the field who knows better than anyone else around how to effect changes in the world around him, the result of profound thinking that enriches his newfound practical abilities.

At this point Jacob has achieved the *tikkun* of the most significant fault of his youth, that is, the lacuna between the worlds of thought and action. This is perhaps the first time that Jacob understands his dream of the ladder whose base is on the ground but whose top reaches into the heavens. How surprising to discover that on the eve of his return to the land of his fathers he has a second dream, which contains two main motifs: the mating of the goats and the birth of the striped, speckled, and mottled kids.

We might say that the first dream set Jacob on the path toward a better balance between the world of desire and thought and the world of action and that Jacob ultimately completed this journey successfully. But the second, horizontal axis, where *Tiferet* distinguishes between *Hesed* and *Gevurah*, good and evil, still requires *tikkun*. Since the sought-after balance is not between thought and action, but between good and evil, the process requires a more intensive emotional commitment. Jacob must locate the precise point where the equilibrium of thought and action intersects with the ethical dimension of the struggle between good and evil. These intersecting axes find expression in Jacob's dream of the speckled goats, which is ultimately about the need to mate practical abilities with the moral values of *Hesed* and *Gevurah*, compassion and harsh judgment. The art of breeding requires a kind of "genetic engineering" so that the kids are born striped or mottled. In much the same way, the separation and combination of the good elements within *Hesed* and *Gevurah* are achieved by weaving compassion and judgment in complex and dynamic proportions that change from individual to individual and from one point in time to another.

Rabbi Hayyim Vital, the great disciple of Isaac Luria of Safed, chose odd names—"The Speckled Chapter," "The Striped Chapter," and "The Mottled Chapter"—for his most important kabbalistic work, *Etz Hayyim*. These sections (or "gates," in his terminology) deal with the balance between *Hesed* and *Gevurah*, between the upper *sefirot* and contracted reality, and between male and female. These are the horizontal and vertical equilibria of the sefirotic structure, whose imbalance caused the primordial worlds to be destroyed and the vessels shattered.

But while the new Jacob is indeed able to combine his ambitions and dreams with the hard work needed to realize them, he is not yet ready to deal with the horizontal axis of *Tiferet*. Setting out on his return journey to the land of his fathers, he is unable to gaze squarely at Laban and take proper leave of him. He still does not have the *gevurah*, the courage, needed to confront the dark side of *Gevurah*. He sneaks out of Laban's camp like a thief in the night.

Rachel also behaves like a thief. She steals her father's idols, the pride of the household, very dear in both monetary and sentimental value. Laban chases Jacob and his camp, catches up to them, and asks: Why did you flee, and why did you steal my household idols? Jacob, who does not know of Rachel's theft, swears that no one has stolen the idols and invites Laban to search their clothes and belongings. Rachel hides the stolen items under her camel's saddle and then sits on it. To avoid suspicion, she apologizes to her father for not rising to greet him, saying that she is menstruating. This episode reflects Jacob and Rachel's personalities. Neither is able to confront the person standing before them.

But the Bible never allows its heroes to remain in the same place, and Jacob's great confrontation is drawing near; the fragments of his life are about to be made visible to him, and he will not be able to flee them.

3

As Jacob approaches Canaan, he sees in his mind's eye his brother, Esau, who has been waiting twenty years for his revenge. Frightened, Jacob turns to the elegant art of the Israelite patriarchs—bribery and fawning—and he attempts to curry favor in Esau's eyes. He sends word to his brother: "I have oxen, donkeys, flocks, male and female slaves; and I have sent to tell my lord, in order that I may find favor in your sight" (Genesis 32:6).

He sends Esau messengers bearing gifts, offerings of reconciliation, and awaits word. When his messengers return and tell him that

Esau is headed toward him with four hundred men, Jacob is sure that Esau means to kill him and his family. He grows increasingly anxious. Again he is alone, and again he undergoes a night of visions and torment:

> Jacob was left alone; and a man wrestled with him until day-break. When the man saw that he did not prevail against Jacob, he struck him on the hip socket; and Jacob's hip was put out of joint as he wrestled with him. Then he said, "Let me go, for the day is breaking." But Jacob said, "I will not let you go, unless you bless me." So he said to him, "What is your name?" And he said, "Jacob." Then the man said, "You shall no longer be called Jacob, but Israel, for you have striven with God and with humans, and have prevailed." (Genesis 32:25–29)

Jacob transfers his family and property to the far bank of the Yab-bok River, but he remains alone on the near bank all night. That night a man appears and struggles with him until dawn. Who is this mysterious figure? The scene is mythic through and through: Jacob struggles, prevails, and does not allow the man to leave until he blesses him.

Though Maimonides composed his commentary to the Mishnah at an early age, he managed to cut through the fog of Jacob's personality and see that the "man" in question is none other than Jacob himself:

> According to the Mishnah, "The empty man does not fear sin, the ignorant man cannot be saintly, the diffident man cannot learn, and the impatient man cannot teach, and not all who engage much in commerce become wise. In a situation where there are no men, *hishtadel*, strive to be a man." The meaning of *hishtadel*, "strive": habituate your soul and draw it to acquire the virtues. Since there are no wise men there who may instruct you, you be the one who instructs yourself. The Aramaic translation renders "and a man wrestled with him" as *veyishtadel gavra*, "a man strove."[2]

Maimonides only alludes to this psychological interpretation, but centuries later Rabbi Moshe Hayyim Efraim of Sadilkov (1748–1800;

the grandson of the Baal Shem Tov and a favorite of the great Hasidic masters and Rabbi Nahman of Breslov's uncle) interprets these verses in a similar spirit, focusing explicitly on the internal struggle that raged in Jacob's soul on that dark night:

> "And a man wrestled with him until daybreak." This means that there are two inclinations in every man, a good inclination and an evil inclination, and they constitute two thoughts, and from this it follows that even an absolutely evil man will have occasional thoughts of repentance, but that the evil inclination overpowers him. Most Jews, however, possess sacred souls unless he invites into his heart falsehood and flattery for the sake of his livelihood. And the Hebrew word *shahar*, "daybreak," is an acronym for *sheker*, "falsehood," *hanupah*, "flattery," and *ro'a*, "evil." And it increases the evil and decreases the good, and this is the meaning of "And a man wrestled with him," this being the evil inclination, "until *shahar* [daybreak]," that is, until he elevates the qualities alluded to by the acronym *shahar*. Meditate on this matter.[3]

Rabbi Efraim of Sadilkov, a great Hasidic thinker, states explicitly that on that night Jacob struggled with the falsehood, flattery, and evil within his own soul. There is something stunning about this devout Jew's willingness to broach this possibility, which shatters the idealized image of Jacob, the father of the tribes of Israel, and that all this occurred more than two hundred years ago. Jacob suddenly understands, on that fateful night by the Yabbok ford, that the blessing he extracted from his father through lies and deception is valueless. He wants the angel to bless him anew. For Jacob, the blessing consists of changing his name from Jacob, *Yaakov*, to Israel, *Yisra'el*. The name Jacob, which symbolized his inability to confront and negotiate challenges, his deceptive and manipulative self, is replaced by Israel.

The new name expresses a new and radically different personality, one that struggles with both God and man. Jacob's curious struggle with the enigmatic figure apparently is the outward manifestation of the internal struggles taking place in his soul. For the first time in his life he is headed for a confrontation from which he cannot flee. He knows that Esau, who no doubt remembers Jacob's deception, is traveling toward him with four hundred of his men, and so he must bravely face up to his past. Ultimately, Jacob succeeds in confronting the dark elements of his personality and receives the name Israel.

Does Jacob truly become Israel? Several biblical figures undergo name change: Sarai becomes Sarah, Abram becomes Abraham, and in each case the Bible announces the change and from that point on does not repeat the old name. But Jacob continues to be called by both names, sometimes in the very same verse.[4] A striking example is found in another of Jacob's night visions: "God spoke to Israel in visions of the night, and said, 'Jacob, Jacob.' And he said, 'Here I am'" (Genesis 46:2). God speaks these words to Jacob shortly before he sets out with all his descendants to exile in Egypt, when he is encamped in Beer Sheba, where his grandfather Abraham and his father Isaac (in the second stage of his life) once resided. Jacob struggles with his dark memories and dark aspects of his personality throughout his life, and the Bible names him according to the dominant side of his personality at that moment.[5] He bravely confronts his flaws and will continue to do so for the rest of his life. Jacob cannot wipe out his dark sides or unburden the heavy weight of his past in one startling, bitter night. Jacob's struggle with himself will continue until his final day.

Even when Jacob is calmed, realizing there was no real reason for his fears and anxieties, for his defensive strategies and fear of impending violence (Esau has forgiven him and, in fact, set out to greet him), he still cannot accept his brother's love. When Esau invites Jacob to join him, Jacob rebuffs him with various excuses, preferring to continue the journey alone, but promises that once he has recovered from his travels, he and his family will join Esau's camp. This, of course, is just another lie; Jacob will never join his brother. Thus, even after a night of struggle and confrontation at the Yabbok ford, Jacob, with his fear and guilt, remains incapable of dealing with his brother.

Such are the fluctuations of *Tiferet*, Jacob's *sefirah*: swinging from truth to falsehood, from brave confrontation to cowardly flight. This is a fundamental fluctuation that never ends, the result of *Tiferet*'s lack of a clear and distinct identity. The *sefirah* that resides in Jacob does not know that boundless, unconflicted love of Abraham's *Hesed*, nor the judging and confrontational nature of Isaac's *Gevurah*, at times driven to turn its back on the divine effluence as such. *Tiferet*, both as a divine entity and a psychological state, is a patchwork of the marks *Gevurah* leaves on the body of *Hesed*, superimposed on the point of equilibrium between thought and action. *Tiferet*'s greatness is its lack of authenticity, but its identity is not always clear to itself, and so it darts among many different identities, an eternal flame flickering in every direction. After the struggle with the mysterious man, Jacob was "limping because of his hip," and he continues limping to this very day: "Therefore to this day the Israelites do not eat the thigh muscle that is on the hip socket, because he struck Jacob on the hip socket at the thigh muscle" (Genesis 32:33).

"Few and hard have been the years of my life" (Genesis 47:9), says Jacob, but how lovely to see that in his latter days, now in Egypt under the auspices of his son Joseph, who has risen to the position of Pharaoh's viceroy, Jacob is aware of the different aspects warring within him. Before he blesses his children he says to them, "Gather around, that I may tell you what will happen to you in days to come. Assemble and hear, O sons of Jacob; listen to Israel your father" (Genesis 49:1–2). Jacob speaks of his children as "sons of Jacob," implicitly recognizing that his children have been raised in a distinctly "Jacobite" environment—surrounded by deceit, an aversion to confrontation, and flight—and that this has left its mark on them. But when he gathers them round to bless them, he says, "Listen to Israel your father"—the words that follow issue from Israel's world. This approach is anchored in the Bible's profound understanding that the most difficult struggle of all occurs between a parent and his children, the struggle to speak openly and directly with them.

It is only from this space that Jacob could say to Reuben, "Unstable as water, you shall no longer excel because you went up on to your father's bed; then you defiled it—you went up on to my couch!" (Genesis 49:4), and to Simon and Levi, "Cursed be their anger, for it is fierce, and their wrath, for it is cruel! I will divide them in Jacob, and scatter them in Israel" (Genesis 49:7). Only at the very end of his life can Jacob admit to himself that he has failed in his children's education, failed to properly resolve the conflict between his love for his children and his desire to rebuke them. Only when he overcomes his inhibitions and rebukes his elder son Reuben for his rash and lustful behavior toward Bilhah, Jacob's wife, only when he curses the murderous anger of Simon and Levi, and so on with the other children, only then is he Israel once again and his sons can be called, "the Tribes of Israel."

There is a verse in the High Holy Day and Sabbath liturgy: "You will show truth to Jacob and unswerving loyalty to Abraham, as You have sworn to our ancestors from the days of old" (Micah 7:20). Why do the congregants petition "truth" for Jacob? Because Jacob is a liar, and the same logic explains why Abraham requires *Hesed*, compassion, in his soul. The verse teaches that when we observe the Israelite patriarchs, and through them ourselves, we should not expect to find whole or perfect individuals. The patriarchs, like everyone else, need to undergo a process of *tikkun*, self-improvement and perfection.

The Bible's patriarch narratives do not seek to elevate and glorify their protagonists or portray them as perfect or exemplary figures. They are called the patriarchs so that we may live our lives through the processes they undergo in the course of theirs. If we plumb the depths of these narratives, accompanying each figure in his psychological evolution, we too can experience similar change in ourselves.

Each of the patriarchs did not become a patriarch until he rebelled against the ways of his fathers, and each represents a distinct psychological type. Just as each of the ten *sefirot* represents a crisis in the divine process of revelation, so too each of the three patriarchs carries within him a core rupture that has shaped his life, and though he spends his life trying to dress this wound, ultimately he must bear it until his death.

The first book of the Bible is called Genesis not only because it recounts the origins of the world, but also because the characters in the book manage to find their way back to the genesis of their soul and, once there, to transform and reshape themselves. The patriarchs do indeed leave their fathers, but they return to them at a later time.

4

For the first time since my bris, I return to the hospital synagogue and its Chagall windows, which formerly inspired my convoluted name. This time I am here for afternoon prayers with my close friend who has been by his unconscious daughter's side for so long. My friend, who by now knows well the subterranean corridors of the hospital, leads me out from the bowels of the earth directly to the door of the synagogue. The light streaming through the Chagall windows cuts through the gloom of the hospital corridors. I put on a yarmulke and try to look like I am participating in the service, but my gaze wanders to the windows, and in my imagination I am speaking with Chagall himself. Thousands of years had to pass for Jewish art to descend from the rigid glory of Jewish law to the earthy warmth of Chagall's Hasidic mysticism, to a God that speaks in colors and symbols, to a dreamscape, reaching out like a mesh of colorful arteries.[6]

chapter seven

Netzah
Miriam, Prophetess of Water

1

I have managed to unburden myself of three names: *ha-katan*, *medzinik*, and *der kleyner*. The remaining two, Israel and Dov, are still with me.

My present tendency to revive my forgotten name, "Israel," is not just the result of my struggle with the duplicitous elements in "Jacob," but also of a struggle with my body. All the educational institutions I attended as a child and a youth blatantly denigrated the body. True, this never became an ideological tenet; Ashkenazi Judaism did not, as a whole, follow the more extreme trends within medieval European Christianity and attempt to suppress the body by all means possible. But still, the Jewish tradition I grew up in did not accord the body the respect it deserves. My schools never had gym class, nor was there any discussion of physical fitness. During puberty, and the onset of sexual desire, our bodies were portrayed as disruptive elements, a hindrance to our spiritual and intellectual development.

In the yeshiva, different rabbis treated the body differently. One rabbi, who had grown up in the more moderate Orthodox Zionist institutions, frowned on students' ascetic practices and fasts, while another recommended them wholeheartedly. My natural tendency was to side with the latter; I understood the love of God as starkly opposed to honoring the body. When a physical altercation would

153

break out among the students, the teachers would condemn the use of physical strength by repeating the words from Genesis 27:22, so familiar to us all: "the hands are Esau's hands," blind Isaac's words to Jacob disguised in Esau's clothes. Following the Talmudic tradition, "the voice of Jacob" was employed as praise, in contrast to Esau's hairy arms. "'The voice is Jacob's voice,'—this teaches that Jacob has no authority except over the voice; 'but the hands are Esau's hands'—this teaches that Esau has no authority except over the hands."[1]

Rabbi Akiva, the letters of whose Hebrew name are similar to those of Yaakov (i.e., Jacob), represents the paradigm of the ideal Talmudic sage, capable of finding biblical proof texts for any halakhic ruling. This is the sage whom even Moses cannot understand, the greatest mystic of all who "entered the *pardes*,"[2] the mystical orchard, and emerged unscathed. But Rabbi Akiva was, above all, an example of self-sacrifice in the service of Jewish law and Torah study. The following midrash tells of Rabbi Akiva's torture and death as a result of his insistence on Torah study:

> Once the wicked Roman government issued a decree forbidding the Jews to study and practice the Torah. Pappus ben Judah came by and, upon finding Rabbi Akiva publicly holding session in which he occupied himself with Torah, Pappus asked him: Akiva, are you not afraid of the government? Rabbi Akiva replied: You, Pappus, who are said to be wise, are in fact a fool. I can explain what I am doing by means of a parable: A fox was walking on a riverbank and, seeing fishes hastening here and there, asked them, "From whom are you fleeing?" They replied, "From the nets and traps set for us by men." So the fox said to them, "How would you like to come up on dry land, so that you and I may live together the way my ancestors lived with yours?" They replied, "You—the one they call the cleverest of animals—are in fact a fool. If we are fearful in the place where we stay alive, how much more fearful should we be in a place where we are sure to die!" So it is with us. If we are fearful when we sit and study the Torah, of which it is written, "For that is your life and the length of your days" (Deuteronomy 30:20), how

much more fearful ought we be should we cease to study the words of Torah![3]

The midrash goes on to recount that shortly thereafter the Romans captured and jailed Rabbi Akiva. One of his students, Rabbi Yehoshua of Gerasa, was allowed to bring him a small amount of water every day. One day, the Roman guard suspected the water was being used to burrow a tunnel out of Rabbi Akiva's cell, so he spilled out half the amount. Upon receiving the deficient jug, Rabbi Akiva promptly washed his hands with the entire amount. His student, Yehoshua, wondered, "Rabbi, the water does not suffice for drinking, but for washing it does?" To which Rabbi Akiva replied, "But what else am I to do? For the sages state that 'whoever belittles the commandment of hand washing is uprooted from the world'; better I should die and not die two deaths." It was Yom Kippur that day, so Rabbi Yehoshua of Gerasa took leave of Rabbi Akiva and went home.

That same day, Rabbi Akiva was called before the Roman governor, the wicked Tyranus Rufus. He ordered his soldiers to rake Rabbi Akiva's flesh with metal combs, but Rabbi Akiva joyously recited the *Shema*. Tyranus Rufus said to him, "Old man, you are either insane or you disregard suffering." Rabbi Akiva replied, "May your soul depart! I am neither a fool nor do I disregard suffering. Rather, all my days I recited the verse 'You shall love the Lord your God with all your heart, with all your soul, and with all your might' (Deuteronomy 6:5). I loved God with all my heart, and I loved God with all my might, but I have not proven that I love God with all my soul. Since I have now received an opportunity to fulfill the commandment 'with all your soul' and the time of the *Shema* has arrived—I did not let it pass. So I recite and am overjoyed." His disciples too said, "Our master, even to this point?" He said, "All my life I was pained by the verse 'and with all your soul'—even if God takes your soul. I wondered, when will I have the opportunity to fulfill this commandment? Now that I have it, will I not do so?" His soul departed as he was reciting the word "one." A heavenly voice was heard saying, "Blessed are you Rabbi Akiva, for your soul departed on the word 'one.'"[4]

The story of Rabbi Akiva's death is the story of many generations of Talmudists. In the yeshiva, we revered the exemplary behavior of one who was willing to die on account of a relatively minor religious obligation such as washing hands. Generations of scholars yearned, "were pained," and waited their whole life for the moment they could manifest their love of God by martyring themselves. Rabbi Akiva's death was the death of the body for the salvation of the soul, an event motivated by a love of the soul that cannot coexist with the love of the body. True life, then, is not found in this world but in the next, and Rabbi Akiva's death bespeaks a willingness to abandon all reality and dive headlong into the "Void." This much is clear from God's response to Moses's perplexity at Rabbi Akiva's death:

> He [Moses] said, "You've shown me his greatness in Torah, now show me his reward." He [God] said, "Return." He went back and saw that they [the Romans] were raking his [Akiva's] flesh. He said [to God], "Such is Torah and such is its reward?" God said, "Be silent, thus it arose in my thought."[5]

This is the death of the martyrs that sanctifies thought and spirit over the body.

But things are not so simple. This is not, after all, an extreme, monastic asceticism in which one is called upon to weaken the body and its desires. Rabbi Akiva, like many of his contemporary disciples, believed that the body possesses value, though only as a vehicle for the spirit. Even those who provide proper care for the body do so only so that the spirit's activity will not be disturbed by pain or disease. But if a conflict between the two emerges, the spirit is invariably accorded primacy. Such was Rabbi Akiva's love for God, a love that contained within it a drive toward the destruction of the body and the negation of marital love.

Even when Rabbi Akiva spoke of loving one's neighbor "as yourself: this is a great rule in the Torah,"[6] he was motivated not by his love of mankind so much as his love of the spiritual image of God hidden within mankind. This approach finds clear expression in Rabbi Tanhuma's explanation of Rabbi Akiva's saying:

Rabbi Akiva says, "You shall love your neighbor as yourself (Leviticus 19:18): this is a great rule in the Torah," that is, lest you say since I was degraded, let my neighbor be degraded along with me; since I was cursed, let my neighbor be cursed along with me. Rabbi Tanhuma says: If you say thus, know who it is you are degrading—"in the image of God made He man."[7]

Rabbi Tanhuma's interpretation of Rabbi Akiva's injunction is that the obligation to love and respect our neighbors derives from the respect due God, whose image is reflected in that of man. Yes, man is the image of God, but only a distant image. God is the sun around which we all revolve.

There are those who refer to Rabbi Akiva as "the sage of love," noting his particular fondness for the Song of Songs, which the sages once wanted to suppress on account of its open eroticism, until Rabbi Akiva stood up and declared, "All the writings of Scripture are holy, but the Song of Songs is the holy of holies"—thus preserving the scroll's canonic status.[8] One might understand this statement to mean that, unlike some of his colleagues, Rabbi Akiva raised love to the level of holiness. But a broader examination of Rabbinic sources reveals Rabbi Akiva's disparaging attitude toward marriage, due in part, no doubt, to how poorly marital love compares with the love of God one encounters in the ever-changing "Void."

Unlike his colleagues, Rabbi Akiva held that divorce could be granted without cause; it is enough that the husband has met a more attractive woman. Here is a ruling from the Mishnah tractate *Gittin*, which deals with divorce and the grounds for divorce: "The School of Shammai say: a man may not divorce his wife unless he has found unchastity in her, for it is written 'For he has found in her indecency' (Deuteronomy 24:1)." In other words, according to the School of Shammai, a man may divorce his wife if he discovers she has behaved immodestly. "But the School of Hillel say: even if she spoiled a dish for him."[9]

Along comes Rabbi Akiva. And bear in mind this is the sage who famously was an ignorant and impoverished shepherd until he met Rachel, the daughter of Kalba Sabua, a wealthy landowner and aristocrat. She fell in love with Akiva and agreed to live in poverty with him for many years, allowing him to set off to study Torah far off, even selling her own hair to provide for his livelihood. Lo and behold, the same Rabbi Akiva, who was fortunate to find such a loving and devoted wife, states in the Mishnah passage (and this is a statement of law, not a Rabbinic legend), "Even if he finds a prettier woman than she." In other words, no grounds are required for divorce! If the man finds a more attractive woman, he is free to divorce his wife, for Scripture states, "Suppose a man enters into marriage with a woman, but she does not please him because he finds something objectionable about her" (Deuteronomy 24:1).

There is a correlation between Rabbi Akiva's opposition of the body to the soul and intellect, on the one hand, and of human versus divine love, on the other. The love of one's body, like a man's love of a woman, is not justified if it does not lead to an elevation of the soul and the love of God. The body is the chariot of the soul, nothing more. Just as the love of our fellow man is a springboard for our love of God, so too the body and human love—inherently limited and inevitably given to peaks and valleys—are of no inherent value.

Since I experienced a strong bond with God first and only later with people, I was openly and arrogantly dismissive of the possibility of deep emotional ties between individuals. I viewed the powerful emotions I experienced as a youth in my relationship with God as a peak that could never again be scaled, something I would never know in the mundane world. How could I love a man or a woman, whose faults soon become apparent, when I compare them with the infinite perfection of God—the object of my youthful love and desire? As beautiful and exciting and wise as a woman may be, how can she not pale in comparison to my youthful, forever unsatisfied love of God?

Many important classical Jewish sources center around the notion that romantic love is ultimately ancillary, a mere propaedeutic for true love—the love of God. Even the great Rabbi Akiva, whose love for his wife Rachel turned his life around completely and became the basis for one of the great love stories of Rabbinic literature—even Rabbi Akiva forsook worldly love for the love of God. Indeed, he asserted, with unbelievable self-cruelty, that he had yearned his whole life to die in agony to more fully manifest his love of God.

Maimonides, the rationalist, asks:

> What is the proper degree of love? That a person should love God with a very great and exceeding love until his soul is bound up in the love of God. Thus, he will always be obsessed with this love as if he is lovesick. A lovesick person's thoughts are never diverted from the love of that woman. He is always obsessed with her, when he sits down, when he gets up, when he eats and drinks. With an even greater love should the love of God be in the hearts of those who love Him and are obsessed with Him at all times, as we are commanded: "Love God ... with all your heart and with all your soul" (Deuteronomy 6:5). This concept was implied by Solomon when he said, metaphorically, "I am lovesick" (Song of Songs 2:5). Indeed, the totality of the Song of Songs is a parable describing this love.[10]

Maimonides apparently considered himself the heir to the biblical Moses, the master of the prophets. Like Moses, Maimonides sought to establish legal traditions for the masses who cannot see God face-to-face. It is not for naught that many generations have praised Maimonides with the saying "From Moses to Moses—none were like Moses." The man was a doctor and surely knew what he was talking about when he wrote:

> Semen is the strength of the body, its life force, and the light of the eyes; the greater the emission of sperm, the greater the damage to the body, to its strength and the greater the loss to one's life span. This was implied by Solomon in his wisdom: "Do not give your strength to women" (Proverbs 31:3). Whoever is steeped in sexual relations, old age springs upon him before its time, his strength is depleted, his eyes become dim, and a foul odor emanates from his mouth and his armpits, the hair of his head, his eyebrows, and

eyelashes fall out, the hair of his beard, armpits, and legs grows in abundance, his teeth fall out and he suffers many pains beyond these. The wise of the doctors have said: One of a thousand dies from other illnesses and a thousand from excessive intercourse.[11]

Perhaps this was Maimonides's objective medical opinion, a common enough medieval view. But it seems to me there is a more substantial link between the Jewish conception of the body and the Jewish conception of romantic love, beginning with Moses, through Rabbi Akiva, and up to Maimonides. Indeed, it may be that ascetic Christianity was born of a powerful and authentically Jewish tradition that can be found in the Bible, in Rabbinic literature, and in many exemplary Jewish figures throughout the generations. We are told that Judaism is not a religion of asceticism or monasticism. Simon the Righteous, an important priest and sage from the time of the Mishnah, refused to eat the sacrificial meat of the offering he made upon completing his Nazirite period, because he considered Nazirite abstinence a sin he did not want to encourage.[12] But sometimes a more ambiguous picture emerges.

The sages of the Second Temple period criticized disciples who chose not to raise families, but were it not for the profound crisis of the Jewish world of the day, presumably they would have recommended asceticism and total devotion to Torah study. Talmudic sages were absent from home for years. Rabbi Akiva was away from his home for twenty-four years.

The longer I remain in the wordlessness of the body, the more I learn from it things my forefathers could never have imagined. The most important lesson the body has taught me is the contrast between the speed of the spirit and the sluggishness of the body. Like Rabbi Akiva, most of the traditional Jewish sources have become enamored of the spirit's speed, of the mind's ability to dart about at the speed of light, to link one matter to another, building glorious and imposing skyscrapers of ideas. But the body is as slow as a turtle compared with the speed of thoughts.

For the past several months I have been practicing a basic sitting position in my weekly yoga classes. The process is laborious, frustrating, and very, very slow. I find that it is precisely when I do not employ my intellect and consciousness—so eager are they to reach their desired destination—that my body responds and I slowly but surely advance. The mind is fast, it but tends to forget; the body is slow, but it forgets nothing of what it has learned. Attending to the sensations of the body, I discover a new and wondrous world.

2

Love too has its own language and requires a continuous, patient dialogue if it is to survive over time. I begin to investigate the figure of Moses, the master of the prophets and perhaps the master of Jewish asceticism. One of the oddest passages in the Bible concerns the heroes Moses and Aaron and their older sister, Miriam: "Miriam and Aaron spoke with Moses because of the woman of Cush whom he had married (for he had indeed married a Cushite woman)" (Numbers 12:1).

What did Miriam and Aaron say to Moses? The Bible is silent on this point. Perhaps they said a man of Moses's status should not marry a Cushite, that is, an Ethiopian woman. But from what follows it is clear that their complaint is not based on despicable racism, but on another claim: "They said, 'Has the Lord spoken only through Moses? Has he not spoken through us also?'" (Numbers 12:2).

Moses's brother and sister are saying to him: God does not speak with you alone, but rather with us as well. We are a prophetess and the high priest, and both of us come in contact with God. God's reaction is anger:

> Suddenly the Lord said to Moses, Aaron, and Miriam, "Come out, you three, to the Tent of Meeting." So the three of them came out. Then the Lord came down in a pillar of cloud, and stood at the entrance of the tent, and called Aaron and Miriam; and they both came forward. And He said, "Hear my words: When there are prophets among you, I the Lord make Myself known to them in visions; I speak to them in dreams. Not so with My servant Moses; he is entrusted with all My house. With

him I speak face-to-face—clearly, not in riddles; and he beholds the form of the Lord. Why then were you not afraid to speak against my servant Moses?" And the anger of the Lord was kindled against them, and he departed. (Numbers 12:4–9)

God afflicts Miriam with leprosy. Aaron turns to Moses, pleading that he not take such offense to their words. Moses agrees to his brother's request and beseeches God to heal Miriam, but God tells Moses that Miriam must be treated like a girl who has angered her father. Miriam will be excluded from the encampment for seven days:

When the cloud went away from over the tent, Miriam had become leprous, as white as snow. And Aaron turned toward Miriam and saw that she was leprous. Then Aaron said to Moses, "Oh, my lord, do not punish us for a sin that we have so foolishly committed. Do not let her be like one stillborn, whose flesh is half consumed when it comes out of its mother's womb." And Moses cried to the Lord, "O God, please heal her." But the Lord said to Moses, "If her father had but spat in her face, would she not bear her shame for seven days? Let her be shut out of the camp for seven days, and after that she may be brought in again." (Numbers 12:10–14)

In the penultimate verse of the chapter we find a stunning plot twist: "So Miriam was shut out of the camp for seven days; and the people did not set out on the march until Miriam had been brought in again" (Numbers 12:15). What is going on? The cloud departs from above the Tent of Meeting before Miriam's leprosy is known. During the Israelites' wandering in the desert, the cloud functions as a kind of semaphore, signaling when to camp and when to decamp. When it descends onto the Tent of Meeting the Israelites know it is time to pitch camp, even if they have not reached a place of water or food; when it lifts up, it is an indication for them to break camp, pack up their possessions, and continue on their journey. Here, however, the Bible recounts that the cloud lifted, signaling it was time to decamp, but the Israelites were unwilling to resume the journey until Miriam rejoined them.

Are the Israelites rebelling against God's instruction to break camp, and if so, why? What concern is it of theirs what happens within Miriam, Aaron, and Moses's family? The Talmudic sages provide the information missing in the biblical narrative:

> "Miriam and Aaron spoke with Moses" ... What did they say? They said: When the elders were appointed, all Israel lit candles and celebrated the elders' taking office. When Miriam saw the candles she said, "Blessed are they and blessed are their wives." Hearing this, Zipporah said to her, "Do not say 'blessed are their wives,' but rather 'woe to their wives'! From the day the Holy One blessed be He spoke to your brother Moses he has not attended to my needs." Miriam immediately went to speak with Aaron and they were debating the matter, as it written: "Miriam and Aaron spoke with Moses because of the woman"—that is, because of his separation from the woman. They said, "Moses has grown proud. Has the Holy One blessed be He spoken with him alone? No, He has spoken with many prophets and with us as well, and none of us have separated from our wives that way he has."[13]

The midrash recounts a heartbreaking drama within Israel's leading family. The background of our narrative is the great desert festivities held in honor of the seventy judicial appointments Moses made after deciding to delegate authority. We can imagine the great bonfires crackling in the desert night, the dances, the food and the drink. Miriam and Zipporah are standing at a distance, watching the festivities, when Miriam makes an offhand comment: How great is the happiness of the judges and their wives. But Zipporah says she pities their wives. Moses has not had intercourse with her even once since the day he was ordained a prophet, that is, from the time of God's revelation to Moses at the burning bush.

Miriam, Moses's older sister, is surprised and immediately goes to speak with Aaron, and the two set out to confront Moses. In other words, Miriam and Aaron are concerned with their little brother's marital harmony. He may be the national leader of Israel, but his family is in crisis. Miriam and Aaron tell Moses that he is not the only person called to prophecy—they themselves are prophets, yet have not discontinued sexual activity with their partners. Why is he doing what other prophets feel no need to do?

According to this midrash, Miriam and Aaron have no complaints concerning Zipporah's origin. On the contrary, they are trying to defend her, scolding Moses for abandoning his proselyte wife whom he invited into a nation foreign to her: instead of helping her find her place, he has consigned her to terrible loneliness. But Miriam and Aaron's main complaint against Moses is theological, involving the very nature of prophecy. What does it mean to be a prophet, that is, to act as God's representative to human society? In this debate, Moses exemplifies the view that links prophecy to a radical repudiation of his personal life. He does not see his wife and children anymore, so deeply ensconced is he in the Tent of Meeting. Can a prophet, a mediator between God and the nation, avoid living in contact with the people and with his family? Moses lives in the Tent of Meeting, alienated from his immediate environment, and has now appointed a council of seventy elders who will relieve him of any daily contact with the public. Can an ascetic function as a prophet and as a leader?

God answers this question, for the biblical language indicates that God affirms Miriam and Aaron's claims as far as "regular" prophets are concerned—only to assert that the situation with Moses is different. God speaks of Moses in very intimate terms, as if he is a partner or companion: "Not so with my servant Moses; he is entrusted with all my house. With him I speak face-to-face—clearly, not in riddles; and he beholds the form of the Lord" (Numbers 12:7–8). God portrays Moses as a family member; the two inhabit the same house and hold face-to-face conversations. Moses encounters God in real life, not merely in a dream or a vision. Yes, God says to Miriam and Aaron, it is generally inappropriate for a prophet or a leader to avoid physical and intellectual contact with other people, but Moses is unique.

Still, even if Miriam and Aaron accepted God's argument, the Israelites were unwilling to do so, voting with their feet by refusing to budge even after the cloud lifted from the Tent of Meeting. In so doing, the people effectively said to God: With all due respect, we are not interested in such a leader. We want Miriam.

This enigmatic episode paves the way for an in-depth examination of the nature of biblical prophets. Moses is one such figure, a prophet who towers above the people, transcending the mundane world. But there is another image, of Miriam, who tells Moses that she is not pleased with his form of prophecy.

After the golden calf episode, Moses's prophetic pronouncements are introduced by a phrase that remains constant throughout the course of the desert wanderings: "God spoke with Moses in the Tent of Meeting and said, 'Command the Israelites [to do such and such].'" Moses, in other words, meets God in the solitary confines of the Tent of Meeting, where he receives his instructions and passes them on, with the expectation that the Israelites will follow them faithfully. There is no dialogue between the Israelites and Moses or between Moses and God. This is a model of inattentive and inflexible leadership: the mind decides, and the body executes.

In our first encounter with Miriam the prophetess, she already holds public office as the leader of the Israelite women at the parting of the Red Sea. After Pharaoh and his troops have drowned in the sea, Moses begins the Song at the Sea: "Then Moses and the Israelites sang this song to the Lord" (Exodus 15:1). After the singing by the men, the Bible recounts, "Then the prophet Miriam, Aaron's sister, took a tambourine in her hand; and all the women went out after her with tambourines and with dancing. And Miriam responded to them in song" (Exodus 15:20–21). Is the account of Miriam and the women who follow her part of the Song at the Sea, or is it a separate episode? The narrative opens with the statement that Moses began the song and the people joined in. And then we find this additional account about Miriam, here referred to as a prophetess, who sets out dancing with her tambourine and responds to the women in song. What qualifies a woman as a prophetess who causes the masses to break out in dance and sings her response?

Miriam's role was tied to the terrible water shortage that plagued the people over the course of their journey to Canaan. When they reach Marah (the Hebrew word for "bitterness," so named for the bitter waters found there), God instructs Moses to toss a piece of wood into the waters to sweeten them. The Israelites then wander to Rephidim and encounter the same problem. There is no potable water, so they quarrel with Moses, who responds angrily, "Why do you quarrel with me? Why do you test the Lord?" (Exodus 17:2). But the people do not want to quarrel; they thirst for water to drink: "Why did you bring us out of Egypt, to kill us and our children and livestock with thirst?" (Exodus 17:3). The argument heats up: "So Moses cried out to the Lord, 'What shall I do with this people? They are almost ready to stone me'" (Exodus 17:4). At that point, God instructs Moses to strike a rock with his staff until water flows from it.

While Moses must strike a rock with his staff to produce water, his sister Miriam has another method. The Talmudic legend tells of Miriam's overflowing well, which moved with the Israelites in all their journeys in the desert. The sages concluded that the well provided water as long as Miriam was alive, but it ran dry following her death. An early Rabbinic passage describes the miraculous well as follows:

> Miriam's well, which accompanied Israel through their desert wanderings, was like a large boulder bubbling up as though from this jar. It would ascend with them to the mountains and descend with them into the valleys. Wherever the Israelites resided, the well resided with them in an elevated place by the entrance to the Tent of Meeting. The tribal chiefs of Israel would surround it with their staffs and recite the verses "Spring up, O well!—Sing to it! Spring up, O well!—Sing to it!" and the waters bubbled up like a standing column. Then each of the tribal chiefs would draw water with his staff, each to his tribe and to his clan, as it is written, "the well that the leaders sank."[14]

Unlike Moses and his blows against the rock, Miriam's well gives its water when it is seduced with song. This legend seems to represent an attempt to contrast the prophetic practices of Moses and of Miriam. The tribal chiefs bring their staffs to the well, carrying, like Moses, a symbol of their power, but they do not strike it, opting instead for music. Moreover, the well flows up for each tribal chief individually; the chief must serenade the water if he wants it to flow to his tribe or clan, and each chief draws the water to his tent using his staff. Authority is individual. In the Moses narrative, it is only he who can extract water from the rock, while Miriam's well gives water to all.

The well is located across from the Tent of Meeting, a symbolic indication that Miriam's well is the antithesis of the Tent of Meeting, the institution most closely linked with Moses. The water and the different modes of extracting it are, then, metaphors for different modes of leadership, of prophecy, and of communication with God. Does divine-human communication require a designated third party, a mediator that can speak directly with God, or can anyone perform the miracle of the water? Is prophecy a form of dialogue, or is it a directive from on high that we have no choice but to obey? Should the prophet "respond" to the people, breaking out in timbreled dance like Miriam, or does he lead a monastic life?

What does God say to Miriam after she scolds Moses for his ascetic seclusion? God does not tell her she is wrong. On the contrary, God validates her position but says that Moses represents a special case. Were it any other prophet over the centuries, Miriam would be correct. But Moses is no ordinary prophet. He enjoys a unique intimacy with God. In later kabbalistic sources, Moses is often associated with the *Shekhinah*, God's immanent presence in the world, which is also understood as God's feminine aspect. (Sometimes Moses is associated with the male aspect of this union, which implies that God represents the female aspect). If Miriam is correct, why is she punished so severely? The answer would appear to lie in the intimate relationship between God and Moses: God is offended that she has misunderstood His relationship with Moses.

In the Rabbinic legend, Miriam's well ran dry after her death but continued to wander with the Israelites even after they reached Canaan and crossed the Jordan, ultimately establishing itself on the Temple Mount, beneath the Holy of Holies. Whatever the true nature of this well, the narrative presents us with two paradigms of prophecy. Miriam's prophecy is open, free, more individualistic, and much less violent and imperious than Moses's. The legend also says that the waters of Miriam's well will flow again at the end of days. In other words, the Rabbinic sages recognized that the paradigm of Mosaic prophecy is not the only possible one, and may not even be the best one. Indeed, God Himself states that this prophecy is only suited for the particular individual known as Moses, living in a particular era. In future times, Miriam's well will once again supply Israel with its waters. The paradigm of Miriam's prophecy—prophecy based on dialogue, on a personal connection between God and man, in stark contrast to the prophecy of the Tent of Meeting—will again predominate.

Miriam's prophecy will be the prophecy of the body. When Miriam wants to prophesy, she takes her tambourine and leads the women in dance. Her prophecy is closer to the body than that of Moses, so evidently divorced from his own corporeality, a merely verbal prophecy of laws and commandments. Miriam's prophecy, in other words, is more fully integrated in the world and finds expression through nonverbal means, through flowing water, music, dance. And it is Miriam's prophecy that is associated with the end of days, with redemption. Hers is the paradigm the sages hope for in the messianic age. When God tells Moses he will not be allowed to enter Canaan, he cites the quarrel at the bitter waters as justification.[15] But it may be that the true referent is the quarrel discussed here. God does not want the Mosaic model of prophecy to reign in Canaan. It is suited for the birth of the nation and its maturation during the desert wanderings. But once people establish permanent settlements and begin to draw sustenance from the earth, a new model of prophecy is called for.

How do Moses and Miriam differ as prophets? Moses prefers the white clouds of glory to the Ethiopian woman he married. He prefers the intimate prophecy of the cave at Mount Sinai, face-to-face communication, without riddles or dreams or symbols; direct speech that knows nothing of the complexity and the chaotic fluctuations of our earthly lives.

Miriam, by contrast, stands in the center of the encampment and prophesies with her whole body, surrounded by men and women alike. Perhaps this is the deep meaning of the Rabbinic saying "A handmaiden at the Red Sea saw what Ezekiel ben Buzi the priest never saw."[16] Not because she is a handmaiden and Ezekiel was a priest, but because she is a woman and he is a man. It was Miriam's female prophecy that beheld the epiphany at the Red Sea. Immediately upon crossing the Red Sea, "the prophet Miriam, Aaron's sister, took a tambourine in her hand; and all the women went out after her with tambourines and with dancing" (Exodus 15:20). Miriam prophesies in the fashion of a true midwife, moving her own feet as she draws the feet of the women into the dance, helping the Israelite tribal chiefs birth their own personal prophecies as they sing their songs before her well. She does not enter into a dark room, light a candle, and labor away until she produces the precise meter of the Song at the Sea; she goes out with the women, dancing and shaking her tambourine.

chapter eight

Hod

Bar Yohai, the New Interpreter of the Body

1

Rabbi Shimon bar Yohai challenges his companions: "How long will we remain on a single path? It is time for transformation, even if it means annulling other elements found in the Torah, for it is written: "It is time for the Lord to act, for Your law has been violated" (Psalm 119:126). Rabbi Shimon here cites an oft-interpreted verse, which, due to Hebrew's flexible word order, can be understood as a divine injunction to violate the Torah: "They have violated Your Torah *because* it is time to act for the Lord." Sometimes we act to build anew the image of God, even if in so doing we destroy other parts of God's Torah, of God's teachings.[1]

Rabbi Shimon continues, "Time is short, and the creditor is impatient. A herald cries out every day. But the reapers in the field are few, and they are on the edges of the vineyard. They do not look, nor do they know fully where they are going."[2] There is no point in waiting for someone else to do this work for us, says Rabbi Shimon bar Yohai. We, the harvesters in the field, are few, and we find ourselves on the margins of the vineyard ("vineyard" is commonly used to refer to the world of Torah scholarship, a reference to the "Yavne

[or, Jamnia] Vineyard," where Rabbinic Judaism was established).[3]
Rabbi Shimon urges:

> Assemble, friends, at the meeting place, garbed in mail, with
> swords and lances in your hands. Look to your equipment:
> counsel, wisdom, understanding, knowledge, sight, power of
> hands and legs. Appoint a king over you who has the power
> of life and death and who can utter words of truth, words that
> the holy ones above will heed, and that they will rejoice to hear
> and know.

Rabbi Shimon asks everyone to employ all their powers, of the spirit
and of the body, of the brain and of the feet, yet still he hesitates:

> Rabbi Shimon sat down and wept. He said: "Alas if I reveal!
> Alas if I do not reveal!" The companions who were there were
> silent. Rabbi Abba arose and said to him: "If it pleases you,
> master, to reveal, you know it is written, 'The Lord's secret is
> for those who fear him' (Psalm 25:14), and these companions do
> fear the Lord, and they have already entered the assembly of
> the tabernacle. Some of them have entered, and some have also
> emerged."[4]

Rabbi Abba, the most senior figure in the assembly (after Rabbi Shimon himself) does not understand why he and his friends require
such extensive introductions. You have nothing to worry about
on our account, he says to Rabbi Shimon, we are all God-fearers.
We all know that we are not seeking to reinterpret the tradition
we have received in order to obtain some external good such as
honor or financial gain, or even to justify our actions and calm our
conscience.

Rabbi Shimon is apparently assuaged and begins with, of all
things, a ritual of the body:

> They stretched out their hands to Rabbi Shimon, and extended
> their fingers toward the heavens, and they went into the field
> among the trees and sat down. Rabbi Shimon arose and prayed.

> He then sat down among them and said: "'Put your hands in my
> lap.'" They put out their hands and he grasped them."

Rabbi Shimon and his companions form a circle among the trees of
the field, outside the walls of the *beit midrash*. There they establish
a sense of intimacy, an interiority within an outdoor setting, holding each other's hands and providing one another with strength as
they approach the great moment in which they will break with the
tradition of Rabbi Akiva. Rabbi Shimon begins with a sharp warning: "He began by quoting: 'Cursed be the man who makes a graven
or molten image ... the work of the hands of the craftsman, and that
sets it up in secret' (Deuteronomy 27:15). And they all responded by
saying, Amen."

Why begin this exciting assembly with such a severe warning,
execrating anyone who fashions an idol or an image? This verse, part
of the curse and blessing ritual in Deuteronomy, is generally interpreted as a straightforward warning not to anthropomorphize God.
But the Zohar in general and the Great Assembly passages in particular contain many plastic depictions of God's limbs and so pose a
risk of an anthropomorphic conception of God that could degenerate
into idolatry. Many Jewish sages have, over the generations, distanced
themselves from Jewish esotericism and Kabbalah, fearing that readers would engage the kabbalistic texts literally and become idolaters.[5]
We may wonder why Rabbi Shimon does not cite the explicit inter-
diction in the Decalogue not to worship graven gods of silver and
gold and instead turns to a relatively obscure verse from the blessings
and the execrations on Mounts Gerizim and Ebal.

Perhaps because Rabbi Shimon sought to emphasize an element
present in that passage but not in the other biblical interdictions—the
words *vesam ba-seter*, "he set it up in secret." Rabbi Shimon is not
concerned that someone would associate vulgar images of bodies and
limbs with God. He seems more concerned with the possibility that
one of his companions will make his (Rabbi Shimon's) imagery of the
Divine into an esoteric doctrine. The issue, then, is not so much his
God imagery finding broader circulation among a general public and
being understood as a graven God of silver and gold. Rather, Rabbi

Shimon fears that some will understand God as a graven image and then transform this theology into an esoteric doctrine. Public opinions can be contested, not so esoteric doctrines.

Ultimately, Rabbi Shimon is justifying his entire argument, the anthropomorphic images of the Divine, the emphasis on the body, along with the public dissemination of esoteric doctrines precisely so that they not become idolatrous. For it is they who try to pass off their visions of God as "hidden wisdom" who run the risk of transforming them into idolatry. Transparency poses the greatest danger for those who dare not expose their theological views to public scrutiny and to the challenge of competing views. Rabbi Shimon warns his companions not to turn the secret kabbalistic doctrines ("he set it up in secret") into the object of idolatrous worship, that is, into a fixed halakhic doctrine unto itself.

> Rabbi Shimon began by quoting: "It is time to act for the Lord."
> Why is it time to act for the Lord? Because they have violated
> Your Law. What does this phrase mean? It refers to the heav-
> enly Torah, which is annulled if this Name is not treated as it
> should be.... It is written: "Happy are you, O Israel! Who is like
> you?" (Deuteronomy 33:29), and it is also written: "Who is like
> You, O Lord, among the gods?" (Exodus 15:11). He called to his
> son, Rabbi Elazar, and he sat him down before him, and Rabbi
> Abba he seated on the other side. And he said: We comprise the
> whole. Thus far are the pillars set right. They were silent. They
> heard a noise and their knees knocked together. What sound
> was it? The sound made by the entry of the assembly of heaven.[6]

Rabbi Shimon states that Judaism is in such poor shape that there is a risk that "the heavenly Torah," that is, the corpus of divine knowledge, will be lost. According to this view, God's knowledge cannot be sustained without human beings who constantly produce and renew it. The Zohar's scholars shoulder a weighty task: to save the heavenly Torah by apprehending it in novel ways. That is why Rabbi Ishmael cites the two verses, with their implicit comparison of God and Israel.

The Bible asks, "Who is like you?" of both. God no longer stands at the center, with mankind revolving around Him; rather both are on equal footing, exerting a reciprocal influence on one another.

This is the Copernican Revolution Rabbi Shimon effects in the Zohar: to love God and relate to God out of a position of equality and reciprocal influence, the body and the spirit enjoying equal prominence.

No wonder the initial reaction of the Zohar companions to the idea that they influence "the heavenly congregation" is fear. They shake so violently their knees knock. But he immediately reassures them:

> Rabbi Shimon was glad, and said: "O Lord, I have heard Your sound, and I stand in trepidation" (Habakkuk 3:2). There, fear was the appropriate response. For us, the matter depends on love. As it is written: "You shall love the Lord your God" (Deuteronomy 6:5), and it is written: "It was because the Lord loved you" (Deuteronomy 7:8), and it is written: "I have loved you, says the Lord" (Malachi 1:2), etc.

Rabbi Shimon cites the verse from Habakkuk, which originally refers to the theophany at Sinai: "O Lord, I have heard Your sound, and I stand in trepidation." But Rabbi Shimon employs the verse as paradigmatic of a state of fear. Fear was the appropriate response at Sinai, but times have changed: "For us, the matter depends on love." With this passage, Rabbi Shimon reverses the conventional relationship between God and man and the doctrine of love espoused by earlier sages, first and foremost by his great master, Rabbi Akiva.

Rabbi Shimon does not deny the mystical tradition of Rabbi Akiva, his master, but rather reverses its direction, radically transforming its significance. Up to this point, we have dealt with the human love of God, which tends to lead man into a state of self-effacement, neglecting himself, his body, and his romantic love. Rabbi Shimon seeks to transfer God to our own human terms. Everything we know about God can be applied to ourselves. In speaking of God, let us draw upon the images rooted in our lives and our bodies;

in speaking of our love of God, let us first speak of the love we feel for our lovers. Let us sanctify our selves, our bodies, our loves, transforming our very being into a sacred act that is superior to any love we could direct outward at God, love that inevitably contains an element of fear and self-negation.

The Great Assembly passages deal almost exclusively with the corporeality of God, which leads us to recognize the paramount importance of our own bodies, even down to their most minor details. Perhaps Rabbi Shimon is arguing that if we are unable to understand the importance of our bodies directly, we may succeed by foisting a body onto God and trying to grasp God through the sanctity of our own embodied state.

It would be hard to overstate the radical transformation that Rabbi Shimon bar Yohai underwent. Like Rabbi Akiva, he too was hostile to Roman rule and belittled the culture of the body that Rome represented in those days. Rabbi Shimon and his son Elazar hid in a cave for thirteen years because the Roman authorities were threatening to kill them. But why was Rabbi Shimon persecuted? The Talmud tells of a meeting of four sages, each of whom expressed his view regarding the practical and corporeal culture of Rome:

> On one occasion, while Rabbi Judah, Rabbi Yose, and Rabbi Shimon were sitting together, Judah the son of proselytes happened to sit with them. Rabbi Judah began the discussion by observing: "How noble are the works of this [Roman] nation! They laid out streets, they built bridges, they erected baths." Rabbi Yose remained silent, but Rabbi Shimon bar Yohai spoke up and said: "All that they made, they made to serve themselves: they laid out streets to settle harlots in them; baths, to pamper themselves; bridges, to levy tolls." Now, Judah the son of proselytes went off and kept retelling the sages' words, until they were heard by the [Roman] government, which decreed: Judah, who acclaimed, shall be acclaimed; Yose, who remained silent, shall be exiled to Sepphoris; Shimon, who vilified, shall be put to death.[7]

The Babylonian Talmud describes how, in their cave, Rabbi Shimon and his son Rabbi Elazar would bury themselves in the dirt every day so that their clothing would not fray, donning their clothes only at the appointed times of prayer. After twelve years Elijah comes and announces that the death sentence against them has been lifted. When they emerge from their hiding place, they see farmers tending to their crops and cannot understand how people can be working for their livelihood when they could be studying Torah: "These men forsake life eternal and engage in life temporal!" Whatever they cast their eyes upon was immediately incinerated. At that, a divine voice went forth and said, "Have you come out to destroy My world? Return to your cave!"[8] This time, the punishment is meted out by God, and the two are sent back to the cave for an additional year, to mend their ways.

When the year of punishment has passed, Rabbi Shimon and Rabbi Elazar again emerge from the cave, their bodies covered with running sores. According to the Talmud, the tears they shed "hopped" into their sores, causing them to scream and writhe in pain.

Perhaps it was the physical agony Rabbi Shimon suffered in the cave that so radically changed his attitude toward human physicality. According to the Talmud, Rabbi Shimon and Rabbi Elazar's first act after healing themselves and emerging once again from the cave has to do with the *tikkun* of the physical condition of others. They labor to establish—*letakken*, the same Hebrew root as *tikkun*—a public place that is suspected of being ritually unclean. Rabbi Shimon justifies this act with the claim that he learned it from no less an authority than Jacob:

> Since a miracle occurred for me, I will go and establish that which requires establishment. As it is written, "And Jacob arrived whole [*shalem*]" (Genesis 33:18), whole with regard to his body, whole with regard to his property, whole with regard to his Torah. "And he camped before the city," Rav said: He minted coins for them. Shmuel said: He established markets for them. Rabbi Yohanan said: He established bathhouses for them.[9]

Rabbi Shimon suddenly understands the biblical phrase "the voice is Jacob's voice" in a completely new way. "The voice is Jacob's voice" is no longer intended as a compliment, the way Rabbi Akiva and his companions interpret it, but rather as a psychological flaw in need of transformation. Only after his struggle with the angel was Jacob able to overcome his psychological afflictions and understand that his task was to establish markets and bathhouses for the residents of Shechem. Perhaps Rabbi Shimon understands that it was only after Jacob struggled with the angel of his own weaknesses and began to limp, that is, became handicapped, that he become "whole with regard to his body."

Many centuries pass from the biblical days of Jacob until Rabbi Shimon bar Yohai of the Zohar is able to understand something else concerning the body. In addition to its role as the carriage of the soul, the body is vital to our spiritual development. The spirit has much to learn from the body. How does Moses differ from the other prophets? asks Rabbi Shimon bar Yohai in the Zohar, and answers:

> Moses gazed into a speculum that shines, whereas the other prophets gazed into one that does not. Moses received the divine message standing and with all his senses unimpaired, and he comprehended it fully ... whereas other prophets fell on their faces in a state of exhaustion and did not obtain a perfectly clear message.[10]

In other words, Moses's prophecy was more vital and more lucid because his body participated in it. Moreover, Moses's body grew exceptionally strong as his spirit gained power. The rest of the prophets, says the Zohar, toil under the effects of what Jacob underwent during his struggle with the angel at Yabbok ford, an angel traditionally associated with Esau—"the hands are Esau's hands." According to the Zohar, the cryptic statement that Jacob began limping on his thigh after the struggle with the angel offers a clue to the weakness of the other prophets:

> The reason why all the prophets except Moses were weak was that "he touched the hollow of Jacob's thigh through the sinew"

that draws to the thigh all its energy; the energy of the thigh was broken, and Jacob remained "limping on his thigh," and hence the rest of the prophets, with the exception of Moses, could not retain their faculties during a vision and grasp it fully.[11]

Rabbi Shimon of the Talmud and the Zohar is trying, I think, to effect a *tikkun* that comes in response to the anti-corporeal doctrines of Moses, and of the Talmudic Moses, that is, Rabbi Akiva. Our body is not merely an instrument for spiritual worship, he suggests, for only by integrating our physical being with our spiritual worship can we attain lucid and immediate prophecy. The Talmudic sages described the quality of Moses's prophecy as "shining aspeclaria," meaning that the light of prophecy was coming from within him. Moses beheld God face-to-face, the gaze of partners. The true redemption of the Children of Israel, teaches the Zohar, is tied to the *tikkun* of Jacob's infirm leg. Historically, Israel's infirmity has been its inability to integrate spiritual worship and physical might.

The kabbalists describe the *sefirot Netzah* and *Hod* as the two legs of *Tiferet*, that is, of Jacob's *sefirah*. Along with the *tikkun* of his lies, and his practical and moral bankruptcy, Jacob must undergo yet another *tikkun* for the infirmity of his leg: to integrate body and spirit and combine the insights of each; to yoke together the *sefirot* of the legs with the *sefirot* of thought located in the Void Space.[12] Rabbi Yehudah Leib of Gur interprets the change of Jacob's name to Israel as follows:

> "You shall no longer be called Jacob, but Israel" (Genesis 32:29): The Children of Israel merited both these names that correspond to the body and the soul. For every person must effect a *tikkun* of the body until he becomes governed by the force of his soul; at that point he becomes known as Israel. And regarding Jacob's struggle with the angel, the soul of a man enjoys a higher status than an angel, but only *as* soul, while the angelic body enjoys a higher status than the human. For the human body subsists in the world of action, but Jacob the Patriarch, of blessed memory, effected a *tikkun* in his body such that he

became the chariot of the Lord, may He be praised, and his body became like a soul. As a result, he was able to struggle with the angel on the material level of his body as well, as it is written, "You shall no longer be called Jacob." That is, that the body that is known as Jacob is no longer in the aspect of the body, but rather has been transformed into spirit, like the soul. And thus it is written, "And Jacob arrived whole [*shalem*]" (Genesis 33:18), which refers to the equality of his body and soul, a state known as *shalom*. There is strife between the body and the soul of every Jew, and the wholeness of the person is determined by the *tikkun* of the body.[13]

But Rabbi Yehudah Leib of Gur argues that the strife between the body and the soul is to be resolved by endowing the body with spiritual powers like those of the soul. Apparently Rabbi Yehudah Leib of Gur did not suffer the physical anguish of Rabbi Shimon bar Yohai, and certainly not of Rabbi Nahman of Breslov, who spent his youth in asceticism, until he finally fell ill and died at a young age. Upon falling ill, Rabbi Nahman recognized the folly of his youth, and even though he had missed the chance to alter his situation, he tried to effect a *tikkun* by means of his writings:

And every person must show great compassion for the flesh of the body, illuminating it with every insight and perception that the soul perceives. The body should also be informed of this perception as in "Hide not from your own flesh" (Isaiah 58:7). Specifically, "from your own flesh." Do not hide your eyes from showing compassion for your flesh—the flesh of your body. For it is necessary to show great compassion for the body, to see to purify it, so as to be able to inform it of all the insights and perceptions that the soul perceives. This is because the soul of every human being is continuously seeing and comprehending very exalted things. But the body knows nothing of them. Therefore, every person must show great compassion for the flesh of the body. He should see to purify the body so that the soul will be able to inform it of all that she is always seeing and comprehending.[14]

Up to this point, Rabbi Nahman's position would doubtless garner the support of Rabbi Yehudah Leib of Gur, but later in his discussion Rabbi Nahman offers a more detailed account of the body: yes, the spiritual overflow should be channeled into the body, but there are also times when the spirit must turn to the body for guidance. Sometimes, Rabbi Nahman teaches, when the spirit is diminished and at its nadir, the pleasures of the body—the phrase itself bordered on profanity for the young Rabbi Nahman!—can remind the spirit of its own greatness:

> Now, when the body is in this category, it benefits the soul. For there are times when the latter falls from her level. However, if the body is clear and illuminated, the soul is capable of picking herself up and returning to her level because of the body. That is, through the pleasures of the body, she will be able to recall and ascend to her own pleasures. For now that the body is also good and right, it does not get trapped in the pleasures. Thus the soul is capable of returning by means of the pleasures of the body, to her position and her pleasures.[15]

The body, Rabbi Nahman teaches us, is also positive; it is also kosher. But how many centuries of Jewish thought had to elapse before someone dared utter this simple truth! Not only is the body good and kosher, it is also endowed with a quality the spirit will never possess: long-term memory. The spirit's alacrity, its ability to flit about and dart in any direction with incomparable speed, can at times be a handicap, since it forgets just as quickly. In periods of weakness, when it is laid low, the spirit forgets its moments of power and greatness. If, during such times, I succeed in strengthening the body and passing on to it the spiritual knowledge I have gained, I can use the body's long-term memory to help the spirit recall its own power. It may be clumsy and slow, but the body is much more thorough than the spirit. Once it internalizes a particular state, it almost never forgets it—for better or for worse.

Similarly, when I focus on my physical well-being and try to reverse the damage I have caused over the years, I cannot expect the kind of speedy *tikkun* I know from my psychological and intellectual processes. The physical process is slow compared to the speed of the mind, and I must travel great distances and generate many new memories if I am to repair or erase the sadness embedded in the body. The body teaches patience and perseverance in ways the spirit never could. But this is the only path to authentic prophecy, as the Zohar teaches, and as Rabbi Nahman adds: "This corresponds to 'From my flesh I will behold God'—specifically from 'my flesh.' In other words, by means of the flesh of the body he will behold God, that is, perceptions of godliness."[16] Elsewhere in *Likkute Moharan* Rabbi Nahman asserts that as long as spiritual knowledge has not been assimilated into the body, it is impossible to attain new spiritual insights.

I wish I could read myself through my body, like a dancer or a yogi, rather than reading myself through the teachings of the biblical fathers and the Talmudic sages. What is nearer to me than my own body? What conveys my selfhood to me more immediately?

I console myself with the thought that mine is the authentically Jewish path, reading myself through the prism of classical Jewish culture—through the texts of all the generations that preceded me. This, after all, is precisely what the sages of the Talmud did in their glorious readings of the Bible, as did generations upon generations of later interpreters and thinkers, including the sages of the Zohar, Isaac Luria, and Rabbi Nahman. I have become a link in a chain that stretches across the generations.

2

Just as the body needs a new interpretation, I must find a new interpretation of love. I will never experience the love of God without first experiencing human, romantic love. Only the simultaneous experience of the two will allow me to truly understand the full continuum of faith, without illusions.

For all its various genres and styles, kabbalistic literature tends to couch the core relationships underlying reality—between the different elements of the Divine, between God and man, between different individuals, and between different parts within us—in terms drawn from the union of male and female. Why did this binary opposition become the central symbol of all reality? There is one intuitive answer, namely, that male and the female are complementary categories and their union produces something new. But why do they complement each other? What is it about this union?

The relationship between male and female aspects is often explored in the context of the *sefirot Hesed* and *Gevurah*. *Hesed* is the power of unceasing divine effluence, while *Gevurah* is the vessel that establishes borders, delimits, and ultimately contains this divine effluence, thus making it finite. Only *Hesed* contained in *Gevurah*—only, that is, the union of the two—produces *Tiferet*, the balanced and calibrated synthesis of the opposing forces. We first encounter a tangible influence on the material world within *Tiferet*, making it an example of the importance of the union between male and female. Male here symbolizes a raging, unbridled force, a will that yearns to be manifested, fully realized, while female represents the delimiting and containing element. The female consists of two distinct elements: on the one hand, cessation and delimitation—an act of harsh judgment, or *din*; on the other hand, surrounding and enclosure, giving form and existence to the divine effluence stored within her, for desire and drive cannot subsist outside of the female vessel. In the language of Greek philosophy, the female is the "matter," while the male is the "form."

But there is another dimension to male-female union that transcends the relations between the *sefirot*, a dimension that is arguably the basis for the symbolic force of sexual union in the kabbalistic system as a whole. The union between male and female is dynamic and contains within it the potential for both transformation and ongoing reciprocal influence. But in order for the union to maintain this dynamism, two conditions must be met: it must be continuous, that is, uninterrupted, and it must evolve. In other words, this is an ongoing, ever-flowering relationship, not a circle that forever leads us back to the same point, but rather a spiral advancing from one level to the next, dynamic and evolving and constantly empowering itself.

The secret to this process lies in the male and female's ability to reverse roles while in a state of union. As soon as the matter receives its form and is sealed within the vessel, the vessel begins to influence it, thus taking on male characteristics. The dynamism lies in a constant reciprocity between the sexes so that at no time is one defined solely and invariably as male or female. Symbolically, the sexes are forever in flux, forever being transposed, and this role reversal engenders a state of dynamism. When the divine effluence, understood as will or drive, is delineated and defined within the sefirotic world, this new definition is transformed into a power or force that overflows into a new vessel and so is transformed from female to male. Every person is called "male" when they influence another, but when they are receptive to another and can contain what they have received within them, they are called "female."

The constant fluctuations between male and female teach me the secret of the twin dynamisms of bursting into, on the one hand, and of containing what bursts me into, on the other. I ought to be in a constant state of transformation from male to female and back again, and sometimes to be both simultaneously.

The Zohar regularly presents its sages delivering their homilies to small groups of scholars. It is rare to find in the Zohar an individual sitting in solitary contemplation. The same is true of Rabbinic literature as a whole. The Talmud and the midrashic collections were produced collectively, the result of collaboration.

One of the most beautiful passages in the Zohar is an exposition of the esoteric meaning of the kiss.[17] The discussion begins with a midrash on the second verse of the Song of Songs, the scroll that Rabbi Akiva saved by claiming that it deals with the love of God and Israel. Rabbi Shimon and the Zohar companions, as is their wont, understand Rabbi Akiva's teaching in corporeal, human terms:

> "Let him kiss me with the kisses of his mouth" (Song of Songs 1:2). What did King Solomon mean by introducing words of love between the upper world and the lower world, and by beginning the praise of love, which he has introduced between them, with "Let him kiss me"?

Following an interpretive tradition that dates back to the Mishnah and Talmud, according to which the Song of Songs bears witness to

the love between God and Israel, the Zohar asks why the Bible uses
erotic imagery to describe this relationship. And why, moreover,
should this erotically charged text begin with a kiss, which the Zohar
companions understand as extraneous to the act of intercourse:

> They have already given an explanation for this, and it is that
> inseparable love of spirit, for spirit can be expressed only by a
> kiss, and a kiss is with the mouth, for that is the source and
> outlet of the spirit. And when they kiss one another, the spirits
> cling to each other, and they are one, and then there is one love.[18]

The first and broadest response the Zohar offers is to assert that kisses
are the expression of the spiritual cleaving of the couple, transforming their bond into "one love." But what does this phrase mean?
After all, when a couple kisses there are two loves involved—the love
each feels for the other. But the Zohar continues its interpretation,
citing the Book of Hamnuna Saba, apparently the product of the
fertile imagination of the Zohar authors:

> In the Book of the Ancient Rav Hamnuna Saba, he says on the
> verse: The kiss of love extends into four spirits, and the four
> spirits cling together, and they are within the mystery of the
> faith, and they ascend by four letters, and these are the letters
> upon which the Holy Name depends, and upon which the upper
> and the lower realms depend, and upon which the praise in the
> Song of Songs depends. And which are they? *Alef, he, bet, he*—
> the letters that spell out the Hebrew *ahavah*, "love." They are
> the supernal chariot, and they are the companionship, unison,
> and wholeness of all. These letters are four spirits; they are the
> spirits of love and delight, for all the limbs of the body are with-
> out any pain at all. There are four spirits in the kiss, and each
> one is comprised within its companion. And since one spirit is
> comprised within another, and this other is comprised within
> the former, the two spirits become one, and then the four are
> wholly joined, flowing into one another and contained within
> one another. And when they spread abroad a single fruit is made
> from these four spirits, one spirit comprised of four spirits, and

this ascends and splits firmaments until it ascends and dwells by a palace called "the palace of love," a palace upon which love depends, and the spirit is similarly called "love."[19]

Just as *ahavah*, the Hebrew word for "love," is made up of four Hebrew letters, so the union of male and female involves four distinct aspects. The Zohar holds that every individual contains both a male and a female aspect, so the union of a man and a woman is fourfold. The kiss does not occur only between the male and the female—the male within the male unites with the female within the female, while the male within the female unites with the female within the male. Intercourse is not a one-way activity that the male imparts to the woman; it is reciprocal. As soon as the man enters the woman and is contained within her, the female imparts the divine effluence within her and thus becomes male.

Why does the kiss symbolize reciprocal intercourse? Because of the *ruach*, the spirit or breath, of life, that is commingled when one mouth is placed on the other. As we saw above, male and female are not fixed attributes: every male becomes a female and every female becomes a male, and this reversal occurs at the moment of the kiss, which is called *ahavah*, love. In union, then, body is absorbed into the spirit and the spirit into the body.

"And then the four are wholly joined together in one single unison, flowing into one another and being contained within one another." The Zohar does not speak of one power flowing into another, rather they are flowing "into one another." Along with the continuous dynamism, the union of these powers creates unity, a single, complete essence. From the moment of union on, there no longer exists a separation between the powers and they become one. Intercourse creates a single essence, and this is the esoteric meaning of the "palace of love," the constant dynamism characteristic of these relations. They are also "the supernal chariot," shifting interrelations manifested not only in the terrestrial world below, but also cosmically, among the divine creative potencies. Here, then, is the genesis and the constitution of the divine world itself.

chapter nine

Yesod
All the Dreams

1

We now come to the Joseph cycle:

> This is the story of the family of Jacob. Joseph, being seventeen years old, was shepherding the flock with his brothers; he was a lad with the sons of Bilhah and Zilpah, his father's wives; and Joseph brought a bad report of them to their father. Now Israel loved Joseph more than any other of his children, because he was the son of his old age; and he had made him a long cloak with sleeves. (Genesis 37:2–3)

How is young Joseph portrayed in this opening passage? He is the pampered favorite who tattles on his own brothers. But there is more. The greatest Jewish biblical commentator, Rabbi Shlomo Yitzhaki (Rashi), interprets the phrase "he was a lad" as follows: "This teaches us that he would perform juvenile acts—fixing his hair and painting his eyes."[1] In other words, Joseph is very concerned with his physical appearance, tending to his hair and coloring his eyes. The emphasis here is on Joseph's external appearance, which Genesis later describes as "fair and comely" (Genesis 39:6), adjectives that are not applied to any other man in the Bible. Indeed, only one woman is described in these terms: Rachel, Joseph's mother. A late Talmudic interpretation teaches that Joseph was so beautiful that Egyptian women would march along the city walls throwing jewelry at him so that he might look up at them.[2] Another midrash tells that the female friends of Potiphar's wife would come over to her house claiming they wanted to help her in the kitchen, only to gaze at Joseph. In the presence of his beauty, they would lose their concentration and not notice as they cut their own fingers.

Beautiful Joseph, seventeen years old at the time, is aware of his beauty and works diligently to maintain it. Moreover, Jacob makes sure that he will stand out among his brothers, dressing him in a radiant cloak that further highlights his unique beauty and inflames his brothers' envy. Joseph, for his part, adds fuel to the fires of jealousy by freely sharing his dreams with them:

> But when his brothers saw that their father loved him more than all his brothers, they hated him, and could not speak peaceably to him. Once Joseph had a dream, and when he told it to his brothers, they hated him even more. He said to them, "Listen to this dream that I dreamed. There we were, binding sheaves in the field. Suddenly my sheaf rose and stood upright; then your sheaves gathered around it, and bowed down to my sheaf." His brothers said to him, "Are you indeed to reign over us? Are you indeed to have dominion over us?" So they hated him even more because of his dreams and his words. He had another dream, and told it to his brothers, saying, "Look, I have had another dream: the sun, the moon, and eleven stars were bowing down to me." But when he told it to his father and to his brothers, his father rebuked him, and said to him, "What kind of dream is this that you have had? Shall we indeed come, I and your mother and your brothers, and bow to the ground before you?" So his brothers were jealous of him, but his father kept the matter in mind. Now his brothers went to pasture their father's flock near Shechem. And Israel said to Joseph, "Are not your brothers pasturing the flock at Shechem? Come, I will send you to them." He answered, "Here I am." So he said to him, "Go now, see if it is well with your brothers and with the flock;

and bring word back to me." So he sent him from the valley of Hebron and he came to Shechem. (Genesis 37:4–14)

Joseph's brothers hate him so bitterly that they cannot even greet him, but Joseph continues recounting his dreams, which further infuriates his brothers. Genesis emphasizes this fact through the word *vayosefu*, "[they hated him] even more" (Genesis 37:8), which is linked to Joseph's Hebrew name, *Yosef*, both in its sound and in its meaning. The brothers' hatred for Joseph grows, but Joseph pays no heed. His self-aggrandizing dreams grow more extreme. In the first dream he sees himself as the choice sheaf, a fine stalk of wheat that symbolizes economic success and financial control, that is, worldly power. The second dream is more far-reaching, as it includes cosmic and superhuman, almost divine, motifs: all the heavenly bodies prostrate themselves before Joseph, suggesting that he sees himself as the sovereign of the heavens and the earth.

How could Joseph remain oblivious to his brothers' hatred? He herds sheep with them, but they will not so much as greet him. Why, then, does he continue to tell them his annoying dreams? Why does he taunt his brothers so?

Joseph's behavior will remain an enigma unless we assume he is narcissistic and given to delusions of grandeur. He is completely oblivious to what is transpiring between his brothers and him, blind to their smoldering hatred and to the imminent crisis—irrespective of how clear it may be for those with eyes to see. True, the biblical narrative marks Joseph as a heroic figure from the very outset, and he does indeed become one of the key figures of Genesis and the beginning of Exodus. Here, however, he elicits little sympathy. It is Jacob, his father, who sees clearly what is occurring.

The Bible tells us that when Jacob saw the brothers' jealousy of Joseph he "kept the matter in mind," that is, he understood the problem and sought to resolve it. When the brothers set off to herd their father's flocks in Shechem, Jacob sees this as an opportunity to have Joseph spend time in their company. Jacob hopes that the distance from home and the time spent in his brothers' midst will cause Joseph to step back from his narcissism and delusions of grandeur and improve his relationship with them. But the moment for reconciliation has already passed. When the brothers see Joseph approaching, they plot to kill him. Reuben, the eldest brother, manages to convince the group not to kill him immediately, but rather to hurl him into a pit. Ultimately, the brothers decide to sell Joseph as a slave to a passing caravan of Ishmaelites. They dip Joseph's cloak of many colors in blood so that Jacob will think that "Joseph is without doubt torn to pieces" (Genesis 37:33).

The motif of the garment is one of the more beautiful literary themes in the Joseph cycle. Early on, the narrative speaks of the many-colored cloak that Jacob has made for Joseph. Now Joseph's brothers strip him of his cloak, tear it, and stain it with blood, so they can tell their father they found it and must assume that Joseph has been mauled to death. In the beginning of the story, the cloak symbolizes Joseph's remarkable physical appearance, but now he is stripped of it both physically and metaphorically.

The Ishmaelites sell the now cloakless Joseph to the Midianites, and they in turn sell him to the Egyptians, and thus Joseph finds himself in the house of Potiphar, an officer of Pharaoh. Joseph earns his master's trust and eventually is given oversight of the entire household. Potiphar's wife begs Joseph to sleep with her, but he refuses, arguing that Potiphar has shown him such kindness that he cannot betray his trust:

> Look, with me here, my master has no concern about anything
> in the house, and he has put everything that he has in my hand.
> There is no one greater in this house than I am, nor has he kept
> back anything from me except yourself, because you are his
> wife. (Genesis 39:8–9)

It is difficult to understand how a young man, in his sexual prime, lonely and betrayed by his family, is able to refuse an invitation to lie with a woman, all the more so a woman who wields authority over him. The steadfast refusal perhaps is part of Joseph's realization that it was his beauty that brought this calamitous state (and the murderous jealousy of his brothers) upon him. A person betrayed by his beauty, as the pampered child of elderly parents, wants others to appreciate him for his talents and his labors, as Potiphar clearly does, and not for the striking physical beauty that attracts Potiphar's wife.

This is the first step in Joseph's gradual break with the self-consciousness that characterized him as a youth. But the process of maturation is not yet complete, for his refusal was not clear and unambiguous:

> And although she spoke to Joseph day after day, he would not consent to lie beside her or to be with her. One day, however, when he went into the house to do his work, while no one else was in the house, she caught hold of his garment, saying, "Lie with me!" But he left his garment in her hand, and fled and ran outside. (Genesis 39:10–12)

The Talmudic sages dwelled at length on the phrase "when he went into the house to do his work, while no one else was in the house," trying to understand the Bible's emphasis on the absence of other people in the house. What exactly took place there?

> "One day, however, when he went into the house to do his work, and while no one else was in the house"—Rabbi Yohanan says, this indicates both intended to transgress; "to do his work"— Rav and Shmuel [debated the matter]: one said the verse refers literally to his work, the other that he went into the house to tend to his needs; "no one else was in the house"—could it be that an estate as grand as that evildoer's was completely empty? It was taught in the School of Rabbi Ishmael: That day was a holiday for them, and everyone had gone to their idolatrous worship, but she told them she was sick. She thought to herself, Joseph will need me more today than any ever.[3]

In other words, Rabbi Yohanan claims that Joseph arrived at the house knowing no one was present because he planned on sleeping with Potiphar's wife. Additional comments about the logistics of the act are provided by the School of Rabbi Ishmael, which explains that the house was empty because it was a holiday and the entire household had gone to celebrate at the local Egyptian temple. This midrash portrays Potiphar's wife as psychologically astute: she wants to take advantage of Joseph's loneliness during the holiday to seduce him, so she pretends to be sick and remains at home in the hope that Joseph's holiday depression will drive him to seek comfort in her arms.

The Talmud goes on:

> "She caught hold of his garment"—at that precise moment, the image of his father appeared at the window, saying: "Joseph, the names of your brothers will one day be engraved on the stones of the priestly breastplate, and you will be among them. Should your name be erased from among them as you are patronizing a prostitute?"

According to the Talmudic sages, Joseph had already submitted to her demands and was about to lie with her when the image of his father appeared at the window, warning Joseph that he would lose everything through this one act. What squandered future does Joseph's father set forth before him? A future in which fraternal love is permanently engraved on the gems that adorn the breastplate of the high priest. It is, then, Joseph's status as an equal among his brothers that is at stake here. This is the same Joseph who at the age of seventeen cared for nothing less than being his brothers' equal, but now, deliberating whether to lie with Potiphar's wife, he is swayed by the fear that he *not* be counted among his brothers:

> "Yet his bow remained taut"—Rabbi Yohanan said, in the name of Rabbi Meir, that his bow regained its strength; "and his arms grew agile"—he dug his hands into the earth, and ejaculated semen through his nails; "by the hands of the mighty one, Jacob"—who caused him to be engraved on the precious stones of the priestly breastplate? None other than the mighty one, Jacob; "by the name of the shepherd, the rock of Israel"— on account of this he merited becoming a shepherd, as it is written "Shepherd of Israel, you who lead a flock like Joseph" (Psalm 80:1). It is taught: Joseph was worthy of having twelve tribes descend from him, just as they descended from Jacob,

his father, as it is written, "These are the generations of Jacob Joseph" (Genesis 37:2), but he ejaculated the semen through his fingernails.

The midrash quotes a verse from Jacob's blessing to Joseph, "Yet his bow remained taut, and his arms were made agile by the hands of the mighty one Jacob, by the name of the Shepherd, the Rock of Israel"[4] (Genesis 49:24), interpreting it as referring to Joseph's erect penis, ready to have intercourse with Potiphar's wife, but at the very last moment Joseph pulls back and ejaculates through his fingernails; at the last possible minute, when the two are lying naked in bed, Joseph sees the image of his father warning him lest he consummate the act that will banish him from among his brothers, and he is able to change course.

Clearly, Joseph understands himself very differently now than he did prior to this event. The first time Potiphar's wife tried to seduce him, he told her he could not inflict such an injustice on another man, on Potiphar. But here he finds strength to resist because he cannot inflict such an injustice on himself, that is, to sever himself from his brothers. Joseph is undergoing a powerful transformation: from a person who saw himself as superior to everyone else, in essence seeing only himself, to one who appreciates his master's trust, and finally, to one who appreciates his family and wants to be one of the brothers.

Despite the profound change in Joseph's personality, the story ends badly. Potiphar's wife is offended by Joseph's refusal to sleep with her, and when he flees the room, she keeps his garment in her hand. Again the garment motif: no one tears it from Joseph, as his brothers did earlier, but rather Joseph leaves it in Potiphar's wife's hand of his own volition; he casts off his external garment and flees. At that moment, Potiphar's wife cries out that the servant Joseph tried to rape her, and Joseph is imprisoned and thrown, for a second time, into a pit. He is in despair. Who will save a servant who tried to rape his mistress?

The dark pit into which we fall from time to time in our lives may be the beginning of a new future and a corrective experience for a difficult past. The first pit into which his brothers hurled him did not yield a corrective experience because Joseph did not descend into it by choice. Not so the second pit, which he enters following his refusal to lay with Potiphar's wife. This was the result of a mature, considered moral choice. In more traditional terms we might say that Joseph has done *teshuvah*, he has repented, avoiding a possible sin and regretting a committed sin. But what good is God's forgiveness to Joseph in the pit? His life appears to have reached a dead end, and there seems to be no hope that he will emerge from the darkness.

2

The Hebrew term *hazarah bi-teshuvah*, "repentance," represents one of the most convoluted conceptual developments in the history of Jewish thought and the Hebrew language. In modern Hebrew, someone has "repented" (*hazar bi-teshuvah*) when he becomes religiously observant according to the norms of the Orthodox community. Fortunately for me, kabbalistic and Hasidic authors effect a "repentance" of sorts in the phrase itself, turning it away from its semantic errors by reversing its meaning. The profound process of repentance that emerges from these writings does not seek God's (or anyone else's) forgiveness for past sins. This is, to be sure, a necessary condition, but it is not sufficient.

The deeper sense of repentance hinges on a person's capacity to transform the root cause of his error, to return to the point in time when he misinterpreted his life, and to begin a new life narrative, a new life interpretation, from that point on. Shimon ben Lakish, also known as Resh Lakish, a violent bandit who transformed himself and became a Talmudic sage and scholar, asserted that repentance transforms our transgressions into merits.[5] Many kabbalistic traditions have understood these words as expressing an idea that goes far beyond God's relationship with the sins of our youth. Rather, at its most profound, the process of repentance effects real, substantive change in the biography of the individual in question: his transgressions are blotted out from the heavenly ledger and will not be counted when, released of this mortal coil, he stands in judgment before God.

Moreover, the transformation reverses the valence of past transgressions, so that their qualitative and quantitative force is transported to the side of merit, even in the physical world. It is as if a person had gone back to a particular point in his past and altered his life from then on. According to these kabbalistic authors, we can travel through time in our own consciousness and alter physical reality itself.

By the rules of the kabbalistic system, this is a completely rational notion. Since the creation of the world is an ongoing process effected by the *sefirot*, if a person descends deeply enough into his own soul, to the *Binah* within himself, where there is not yet the temporal division into past, present, and future, he can transform his own past. Contrary to the penitent's natural inclination to want to forget his past deeds, to detach himself from his past, the descent into the *Binah* within requires that he confront the chaos of good and bad within him. He must integrate this turbulent reality into his own being, until he is eventually able to emerge from it, reborn.

The course of our lives is made up of a narrative that exists in our own consciousness and in the consciousness of others, an invisible line we draw between our experiences, by means of which we outline a *curriculum*, a course of events. If I wish to reinvent myself, I must narrate my life anew, interpret it in a new way, renouncing the narrative I have recited thus far. But how can I tell my own life story anew? This is not a matter of facades. Time travel through *Binah* means I must identify the point in time when the error began. Returning to an earlier or a later point might make things worse. I do not think I need to return to my early childhood or even to my youth, but rather to the moment when I began to experience pains in my face, but I cannot recall any grave errors from this period, only run-of-the-mill mistakes. My memory plays tricks on me, blocking any further progress.

I return to Joseph in the Egyptian prison. His prospects are bleak, and he must be trying to recall when his life narrative took a turn for the worse. He knows that it was when he ignored his brothers' feelings and slandered them in front of their father; when he flaunted his looks and turned a blind eye to his brothers' murderous hatred. But he asks himself when this all began. Was it the moment that his father gave him the colored cloak, which he did not refuse? The Void Space within *Binah*, the dark womb of the *sefirah*, projects before his eyes various images from his life, and Joseph is unable to decide which of them is the most important.

At some point, between one recollection and the next, Joseph meets two distinguished guests in prison: Pharaoh's chief cupbearer and chief baker. Both are suspected of abusing their office and have been thrown into the pit pending further investigation. Joseph's prison status is so low that he now functions as the other prisoners' servant. One morning he approaches them "and he saw that they were troubled" (Genesis 40:6). The same Joseph who in his youth was oblivious to the feelings of those around him has become so attentive that he senses that the two senior prisoners awoke in a foul mood. "So he asked Pharaoh's officers, who were with him in custody in his master's house, 'Why are your faces downcast today?'" (Genesis 40:7). This is not the same old Joseph.

The two officers recount their dreams, and Joseph interprets them:

> So the chief cupbearer told his dream to Joseph, and said to him, "In my dream there was a vine before me, and on the vine there were three branches. As soon as it budded, its blossoms came out and the clusters ripened into grapes. Pharaoh's cup was in my hand; and I took the grapes and pressed them into Pharaoh's cup, and placed the cup in Pharaoh's hand." Then Joseph said to him, "This is its interpretation: the three branches are three days; within three days Pharaoh will lift up your head and restore you to your office; and you shall place Pharaoh's cup in his hand, just as you used to do when you were his cupbearer. But remember me when it is well with you; please do me the kindness to make mention of me to Pharaoh, and so get me out of this place. For in fact I was stolen out of the land of the Hebrews; and here also I have done nothing that they should have put me into the dungeon." When the chief baker saw that

the interpretation was favorable, he said to Joseph, "I also had a dream: there were three cake baskets on my head, and in the uppermost basket there were all sorts of baked food for Pharaoh, but the birds were eating it out of the basket on my head." And Joseph answered, "This is its interpretation: the three baskets are three days; within three days Pharaoh will lift up your head—from you—and hang you on a pole; and the birds will eat the flesh from you." (Genesis 40:9–19)

Joseph interprets the dreams quickly and decisively. He does not hesitate to ask the chief cupbearer for a favor, nor does he sugarcoat the news of the chief baker's imminent demise. Whence the courage for such a show of determination? And whence the ability to interpret dreams? He has, up to this point, been more a dreamer of dreams. Had he erred in his interpretation, there is little doubt the chief baker would have sent this Hebrew slave accused of rape to his death. How can Joseph allow himself to speak so boldly to the two officers of Pharaoh, who are only imprisoned for interrogation?

The entire episode reflects Joseph's emotional evolution, a process that lies at the heart of this biblical narrative. He has become able to see his fellow man and is attentive to (and able to interpret) nuances in the psychological state of others. Joseph has undergone a profound transformation.

The biblical interpreter Nehama Leibowitz closely examines each dream.[6] The chief cupbearer's dream bespeaks a developed sense of service: he presses grapes into Pharaoh's cup, faithfully fulfilling his task. The chief baker, in contrast, carries three baskets of baked goods on his head, while birds swoop from the sky and eat the contents of the top basket. This is a dream about negligence: the chief baker disclaims responsibility for the content of the third basket, breaching Pharaoh's trust. Leibowitz explains that Joseph was endowed with a profound perspicuity with regard to the dreamers themselves and thus was able to conclude that the chief cupbearer, with his proper understanding of his office and desire to serve his master dutifully and lovingly, was innocent. Even if the chief cupbearer stumbled at some point and was sent to prison, Joseph reasons, he will likely be forgiven. The chief baker's dream, in contrast, reveals a man who is lazy and negligent, so it stands to reason that he was sent to prison for good reason and will ultimately be hanged.

But this answer is not satisfying. Yes, Joseph displays great subtlety in interpreting the dreams of the two officers of Pharaoh's court, but that does not explain his courage. Where did he find the decisiveness and the acuity so evident in his uncompromising interpretation? Did he gamble his life on the slim chance that his interpretation would come true and the chief cupbearer would save him from the pit?

Here again the Zohar is a brilliant reader of the Bible, and specifically the encounter between Joseph and Pharaoh's two officers:

> Come and see: As has been said, all dreams follow the mouth. Now, when Joseph interpreted their dreams, why did he offer one a good interpretation and the other a bad interpretation? Because actually, those dreams concerned Joseph himself, and since he knew the essential root of the matter, he interpreted their dreams as required; to each one he offered an interpretation, to restore the matter to its place.[7]

In this the sages of the Zohar allude to the Talmudic tradition that "all dreams follow the mouth." In other words, the dream is only raw material; it is the interpretation that imbues it with form and meaning. Many Talmudic passages recommend that dreams be interpreted in a positive manner, even if their content is apparently negative, since the interpretation is the key element. This is why the Zohar poses the following question: Since he knows dreams tend to follow their interpretation, why does Joseph offer these interpretations? Why, in other words, does he offer one officer a positive interpretation, the other a negative interpretation? Perhaps he should have interpreted both dreams positively, optimistically. The Zohar's answer is striking: he acts thus because both dreams are ultimately about him.

Joseph has become such a subtle "listener" that he is able to frame the dreams of the chief cupbearer and baker not only in the context of their fates but also as they relate to his own, and it is this discovery that allows him to interpret the dreams. What do the sages of the Zohar mean? How are the officers' dreams related to Joseph's own life?

The two dreams he hears in prison return him to a time when he would wake up in the morning brimming with enthusiasm, ready to recount his dreams to his brothers. At the time, Joseph understood his dreams as signs or omens of his future greatness, of his status as the greatest of the brothers. But these dreams were followed by the very opposite. He was hurled into a pit, sold as a slave, and put in prison. Since Joseph's dream nights, he has suffered through many tribulations that have broken down his earlier self and helped to shape him anew. At the end of this process, he finds himself transformed into a new person, attentive and sensitive, capable of understanding that the officers' dreams were actually about him. He understands, in other words, that these dreams are about him as a youth, dreams he has up to now misinterpreted, thinking they represented him as a king worshipped by all. But he did not understand what kingship entails. Only now does he see that holding such a high office involves responsibility for the subjects of your realm; that the king serves his people, tends to his nation. The leader works harder than all his subordinates.

Joseph was right; his dreams meant he was destined for greatness, but only now does he understand their true meaning. The dreams of the chief cupbearer and the chief baker remind him of his own dreams and of the difference between a mistaken interpretation of political power (which costs the chief baker his life) and a proper one (which saves the chief cupbearer's life). Greatness that produces self-absorption results in aloofness and, ultimately, disaster; greatness that instills a commitment to service and aid toward subordinates results in self-fulfillment. Suddenly, Joseph's dreams rushed back at him, and he altered the interpretation he had given them thus far.

We are witnessing the psychological development of a man who begins as a narcissist dreaming of his own rise to greatness, passes through many dark stages, and finally understands that political power means care and service to others. The motif of Joseph in the pit, first by his brothers' hand and then by Potiphar's, is common in transformation and rebirth narratives. Joseph enters the pit (or cave) and is reborn, emerging armed with new insights and understandings. Joseph's path, in other words, leads him to the Void (involuntarily, at first), where he encounters chaos, gestation, and a malleable reality beyond space and time where evil turns to good and good to evil. He reaches the very root of reality, its source, and there undergoes his astounding transformation. He learns to truly listen to the dreams of the chief cupbearer and the chief baker, and he interprets them brilliantly, producing insights relevant both to their lives and to his own. Having grasped the true meaning of leadership, he is ready for the next stage of his life: to realize his dream.

Two long years pass from the moment Joseph solved the chief cupbearer's dream until the latter returns the favor and mentions to Pharaoh that Joseph is a dream interpreter. During this time, Joseph continues to process the embryonic intuition that flashed through his mind while interpreting the dreams of Pharaoh's officers. He is now ready to ascend another rung in his dream insights and interpret Pharaoh's dreams, dreams that have confounded all the sorcerers of the court.

In Pharaoh's first dream, seven fat and beautiful cows rise up from the Nile, followed by seven emaciated cows that proceed to swallow the fat cows. In the second dream, seven thin stalks of wheat swallow seven ripe and heavy stalks. Pharaoh wakes up alarmed and summons his sorcerers. The Talmud provides a number of interpretations offered by the sorcerers—for example, you will have seven daughters and bury seven daughters[8]—interpretations that are structurally similar to the correct solution offered by Joseph of seven years of drought that will erase the memory of the seven years of plenty that preceded them.

Why does Pharaoh deem Joseph's interpretation correct and embrace it? Because the psychological process Joseph has undergone allows him to avoid interpreting Pharaoh's dreams as personal messages; Joseph has such a developed sense of leadership that he understands that when a king is troubled by his dreams, it is because they touch on his responsibility for the people. Joseph understands

Pharaoh's dreams as heavenly gifts that allow Pharaoh to better serve his kingdom, and it is in this spirit that he interprets them: seven years of plenty and prosperity are approaching, followed by seven years of hunger, but now he is also prepared to offer practical advice. Pharaoh should collect and store grain during the years of plenty to sustain Egypt during the hunger that follows. Pharaoh's heart tells him that this is the correct interpretation; he is impressed by Joseph and repays him by appointing him viceroy.

Again we encounter the motif of the garment: Pharaoh dresses Joseph in opulent clothing, as befit the viceroy (Genesis 41:42), on account of his innovative dream interpretation. And so Joseph becomes the chief provider for Egypt and the surrounding lands in the years of drought. The dreams of his youth have come true.

The Joseph cycle represents the Bible's treatment of our dreams. The resolution of our dreams comes as a result of very long processes; sometimes we need an entire lifetime to understand the true meaning of the dreams of our youth. Even if we interpret a dream correctly, we must understand the deeper meaning of the interpretation. A dream whose interpretation is not fully understood will never come true; only when I understand my own dreams is there a chance they will come true.

3

Just as Abraham, Isaac, and Jacob are identified with *Hesed, Din*, and *Tiferet*, respectively, Joseph is identified with *Yesod*. Topographically, *Yesod* is located along the central axis of *Keter, Tiferet, Yesod*, and *Malkhut* and so channels the divine effluence of the other *sefirot* into *Malkhut*, that is, into the material reality that surrounds us. *Yesod* is the funnel of divine plenty, through which the supernal forces connect and flow into God's feminine aspect, *Malkhut*. The inflow from *Yesod* to *Malkhut* sustains the cosmic union of male and female, of effluence and vessel, and so, in effect, sustains reality itself.

In kabbalistic literature, *Yesod* is associated with the penis. On the face of it, the connection between *Yesod* and Joseph is rooted in his ability to restrain himself and not commit adultery with Potiphar's wife; by resisting such a mighty sexual temptation, Joseph reveals himself as the biblical figure that governs *Yesod*. But this is an incomplete explanation. To grasp the full meaning of *Yesod*, we must dig deeper into the Joseph narrative.

At the end of his rebirth, Joseph emerges from his Void as a provider, a man who nourishes and sustains Egypt and the entire region. Now, *Yesod* is the key *sefirah* in sustaining all reality. Without it, the effluence of the *sefirot* could not flow into the world. As the focus of such great power, *Yesod* might begin to think of itself in narcissistic terms and withhold the effluence, storing it up for itself. But here *Yesod*'s greatness is revealed, namely, its ability to gather into itself the effluence of all the *sefirot* and pass it along to *Malkhut*. *Yesod* has one principal function: its ability to provide for *Malkhut*. It collects power not for its own ends, but rather to sustain our worldly reality.

Through its interpretation of the Joseph narrative, and particularly the identification of Joseph with *Yesod*, the Zohar is able to illustrate the workings of divine power in the world. God created the world not in order to be worshipped or served or obeyed. God, rather, effects His presence in the world through service, a ministering divinity. In Lurianic Kabbalah, Joseph serves as a metonymy for the Divine.[9] The figure of Joseph manifests God's very essence: to minister to the world, that is, to nourish physical reality as a whole and mankind specifically.

But *Yesod* (and Joseph as a symbol of that *sefirah*) is much more than a divine "funnel" that pours the effluence of *Tiferet* into the terrestrial reality known as *Malkhut*. Joseph is the recipient of the very complex and finely balanced admixture of good and evil, thought and action, spirit and body, found in his father, Jacob (*Tiferet*). Joseph is capable of storing these powers within himself for an extended period (seven years), while they undergo a silent transformation, so that in due time he will pour them out into the vessels of reality.

This is Joseph's second essence in both the Bible and Kabbalah: first to contain the different forces, then to wait until they can be "translated," like dreams converted into living speech, and manifested within our physical reality. Dreams cannot pass from the subterranean regions of the soul to be realized in a heartbeat, not only because the path is long and arduous but also because dreams require decoding and processing before we can separate the good they contain from the bad. When in the abyss of dreams, one must master the art of waiting, of biding one's time, until thought may be properly translated into action. This is necessary if we are to preserve the vessels of reality so they do not break and damage the individual or his surroundings. Sometimes it is necessary to gather in the content of a dream slowly, over many years, so it can be distributed in the lean years of hunger and drought.

During the time of his rebirth, in the pit, Joseph knew to wait until he could make manifest his physical beauty without focusing only on how it affects him. When Jacob, Joseph's father, blesses his sons on his deathbed, he crowns Joseph with a special blessing: "Joseph is a fruitful bough, a fruitful bough by a spring" (Genesis 49:22). We are no longer dealing with merely external beauty but a beauty that opens the eyes of all who see it. It transforms the eyes of the viewer, not through jealousy or admiration, but through its power to reflect the beauty or ugliness of the viewer himself. It is of this type of beauty that the psalmist says, "Beautiful to view; the joy of all the earth" (Psalm 48:3).

Rabbi Nahman wrote:

> There exists a righteous man who is the beauty and the glory and grace of the entire world, as in the case of "Joseph was fair and comely" (Genesis 39:6), and "beautiful to view; the joy of all the earth" (Psalm 48:3), for this is the true righteous man, the true *tzaddik*, who is in the aspect of Joseph, being the beautification and the pulchritude of the entire world; for when beauty and glory are revealed in the world, that is, when the *tzaddik* who *is* the beauty of the world becomes renowned and elevated in the world, then the eyes of the world open. For whoever is included in the grace and truth of the *tzaddik*, that is, whoever draws near him and is included within him, his eyes are opened to see, and in particular to examine himself ... as a result, when the *tzaddik* is revealed, the one who is the grace and beauty of

the world, anyone who draws near him and is included in this grace and truth, his eyes are opened and he can see and examine himself ... and he is also able to examine the greatness of God and of the world, since his eyes have been opened.[10]

Judaism associates Joseph not with physical beauty, but rather with righteousness. He is called *Yosef ha-Tzaddik*, Joseph the Righteous. The righteous man's beauty opens the divine eye within us, the eye of the world. Joseph's beauty is intended not for him alone, but for whoever sees him and feels his eyes opening to see his own beauty (and thus be able to interpret his own dreams) in a new light. Rabbi Nahman devotes an entire chapter to Joseph's ability to interpret dreams and to the meaning of translation.

> For one must purify his face to the point that everyone can see his own face in the face of the *tzaddik*, as he could in a mirror. As a result, even without rebuke and without reproof, his friend will feel remorse for his deeds just by having looked into the *tzaddik*'s face. This is because by looking into his face, a person will see himself as if in a mirror and, realizing he is immersed in darkness, will feel remorse.[11]

When Joseph's brothers arrive asking to purchase grain in Egypt,[12] Joseph does not exact his revenge on them; he seeks only to reflect to them their own deeds and lead them down the path of recollection to the moment of their error, lowering their own lives and the life of their father into the pit of deepest despair. He sees them prostrating themselves before him, and superficially his dream has been realized. The sheaves and stars are bowing down to Joseph. But here again he must interpret the dreams of his youth anew, and his brothers too must interpret Joseph's dreams anew if there is to be a corrective experience to the moment they hardened their hearts and ignored his cries from the pit. For now he must maintain his distance: "Joseph also remembered the dreams that he had dreamed for them. He said to them, 'You are spies; you have come to see the nakedness of the land!'" (Genesis 42:9). Joseph leads them through the path of dark pits, until they can make their own way to the moment they erred.

Only then can he share with them the new narrative of his and their history. The book of Genesis emphasizes, "Joseph also remembered the dreams that he had dreamed *for them*." The dreams are also for them, a corrective for the hatred they felt toward him in their youth.

From the darkest recesses of their hearts they conjure up the vivid memory of their deed: "They said to one another, 'Alas, we are paying the penalty for what we did to our brother; we saw his anguish when he pleaded with us, but we would not listen. That is why this anguish has come upon us'" (Genesis 42:21). Only then can Joseph provide them, and himself, with a new narrative; only then can the past take on a different meaning: "And now do not be distressed, or angry with yourselves, because you sold me here; for God sent me before you to preserve life.... So it was not you who sent me here, but God; he has made me a father to Pharaoh, and lord of all his house and ruler over all the land of Egypt" (Genesis 45:5, 45:8). Joseph chooses to couch his tale not in terms of his individual accomplishments, not as the story of a person who began at the lowest depths and managed to reach the highest peak, but rather as God's messenger, who grew and evolved into a leader who provides for others.

4

Though still in the heart of the Joseph cycle, the book of Genesis breaks the narrative flow and introduces the tale of Judah and Tamar. Judah, Joseph's brother, marries his eldest son, Er, to a woman named Tamar. When Er dies childless, Judah marries his second son, Onan, to her, so that their son will be named for Onan's dead brother. Onan is not interested in siring a child for his dead older brother, so he spills his seed to the earth, "so that he would not give offspring to his brother" (Genesis 38:9). God punishes him for this deed and he dies a young man. Having lost two sons already, Judah refuses to marry his youngest, Shelah, to Tamar, fearing she is somehow lethal to her husbands. In response, Tamar dresses as a prostitute and positions herself at the crossroads where Judah passes on his way to shear his herd. Judah sees Tamar and sleeps with her without knowing her true identity. As it happens, Judah had no money to pay the anonymous prostitute for her services, so he leaves his staff, his signet, and his tunic as a pledge for future payment. When Tamar's pregnancy becomes visible, the locals set off to burn her alive, the punishment for an adulterous woman, since by law Tamar belongs to Judah's youngest son. But as she is led out to be burned, she secretly sends Judah the pledge items he left with her, telling him that she is big with his son and reminding him that she is not to blame for his failure to give her to Shelah, his third son. At the last moment, just before she is burned, Judah finds the courage to confess his paternity and his responsibility, saving Tamar from the flames.

Judah is no Joseph, and certainly not the biblical character blessed with the most formidable sexual restraint. Nonetheless, he has the courage to expose his failings in public and right the wrong he did to Tamar. In so doing, he stumbles upon his true destiny, the true interpretation of his dreams. For Judah always wanted to be considered the elder, in place of Reuben, his ne'er-do-well older brother, and now has found his true partner, the woman whose lineage ultimately extends down to no less a figure than King David, the same David that the kabbalists associate with *Malkhut*.

chapter ten

Malkhut
All the Fears

1

There are wonderful interpretations of the Void Space as a place of renewal and regrowth, a site of new beginning. Some describe it as the place of those who have achieved complete repentance, and so attained a higher spiritual level than even the most righteous; a place of favor and power so great that the Talmud states that whoever repents out of love "their transgressions are accounted for them as merits."[1] These same sources teach me that we can alter our narratives while in the Void and literally transform our personal history: change the course of events, annul occurrences that took place, creating in their stead a new narrative. But no one has entrusted me with the key or even divulged to me the location of the gate into this wondrous realm. And if ever I were to find it, I still have not located the precise moment in my past to which the *Binah* time-tunnel must transport me if I am to alter the course of my life from that point on.

Over the centuries, many kabbalists have claimed to have found the gate and the keys to open it. Some provide detailed descriptions of mental exercises and meditation techniques based on letter combinations, with the promise that those who practice them regularly will eventually be able to ascend to a place free of the constraints of space

and time. Others, including great halakhic authorities such as Joseph
Karo (the author of the most important halakhic compendium, the
Shulhan Arukh) and the kabbalist Abraham Abulafia, wrote entire
books documenting their dialogues with divine entities.[2] There were
also Hasidic masters who reached such a point of ecstatic prayer that
they would temporarily lose consciousness and return with descriptions of the divine world.[3]

I have not been blessed with even a fraction of these mystical
abilities, not only because I am not worthy and have not mastered
the kabbalists' entry instructions, but largely because I do not entirely
believe the whole thing is possible. Perhaps I should have tried all the
same. I might have fasted on certain days (as the kabbalists instruct),
meditated on the Hebrew alphabet, and hoped for some form of
enlightenment. But, alas, I cannot believe it. Perhaps my lack of faith
is itself an indication that I am hopelessly trapped in the opaque world
of contraction. But if so, from where will my help come? From where
will all our help come when we feel the contraction closing in on us
from all sides and we are unable to escape for even a moment?

I could have chosen to ignore reality altogether, like Rabbi Akiva.
To leave my home, my wife, my daughters, to close my eyes and
recite "Hear O Israel" while my flesh is raked with steel combs. I
could have said that everything comes from love and that everything
God does in our world is for the best. I could have told people I
entered the orchard, the *pardes*, emerged unscathed and that nothing
changed—that I still love the Almighty just as I loved Him in my
youth. If anyone were to challenge this narrative and confront me
with the flawed reality in which we live—in which I live—I would
simply brush him off with the kabbalistic arguments that prove our
world and everything within it are mere illusions. Ours is the world
of lies, a world of mere appearances, all predicated on the foundation
of God's beneficent oneness. And if my interlocutor were still not
swayed, I would demonstrate that all of our sufferings result from
flaws we have willingly created in ourselves.

Sitting by his daughter's bed, my friend is telling me about
acquaintances and family members who decided to use the crisis as an

opportunity to reprimand him. "Some"—he speaks with restrained anger—"said I need to take stock of my life and my decisions, to better understand why God visited such a punishment upon me. They told me to repent, to ask for forgiveness from anyone I had wronged. But when I examined my actions, I did not find anything that would warrant such punishment for either my daughter or for me."

I was startled; I probably would have rushed to examine my own deeds following such a disaster. I envied his ability to avoid blaming himself. His conclusion was not that no heavenly judge guards over us, but to the contrary: "Since I do not deserve this," he said, "God has no choice but to heal my daughter and bring her back to life." I was afraid; what would become of his faith if his daughter did not recover?

Many traditional believers might not respond as he did. Rather, they would most likely be forced to adopt the view that the world is controlled by the Other Side, by the forces of evil, whose dominance over our lives is not a cause for panic, but rather motivation to live according to God's law and so receive our just reward in the world to come or with the advent of the messianic age.

Another way to deal with evil is to try to repair the world we inhabit. Not to give up, not to hum lullabies to ourselves, but at the same time not to accept pain and suffering as an immutable decree. I must try to redeem myself while I yet live. So I am looking for a path within the traditional Jewish sources that allows us to recall the evil in our lives without averting our gaze, but at the same time provides a way to minimize it.

In the spirit of Purim, which is approaching, I seek answers in a biblical command that appears at first glance wholly unrelated to daily concerns. I am referring to an event that took place during Israel's desert travels, when the Amalekites attack them and battle is waged at Rephidim:

> Remember what Amalek did to you on your journey out of Egypt, how he happened upon you on the way, when you were faint and weary, and struck down all who lagged behind you; he did not fear God. Therefore when the Lord your God has given

you rest from all your enemies on every hand, in the land that
the Lord your God is giving you as an inheritance to possess, you
shall blot out the remembrance of Amalek from under heaven;
do not forget." (Deuteronomy 25:17–19)

This is practical memory, remembering in order to extinguish memory. But the command to remember the Amalekites and blot them out is odd. Why does the Bible attribute such importance to a nation that attacked Israel in the desert? They are not the only nation to have done so. And why should Israel not be commanded to first remember and then destroy all the generations of Egypt? Amalek remains such an open wound in Israel's history that centuries later, the prophet Samuel tears the throne away from King Saul because he failed to kill the Amalekite king and destroy that nation, including women and children and livestock.

The biblical text can be read as a simple demand for revenge. But Jewish authors have revisited the Amalek affair for many years, even after the memory of the original Amalek had been lost without a trace. It was the Jewish insistence that Amalek's memory be a command for all generations that sustained the life and memory of Amalek, providing it with historic longevity and vitality. In the synagogue I attended with my father, when, just before Purim, we would reach the Torah portion *Zakhor*, all the congregants stomped their feet and pounded on the tables, symbolically blotting out Amalek. But since the Amalek portion is the only part of the Bible that Jews are commanded to hear, the Torah chanter had to wait for the noise to die down and then repeat the name Amalek loudly and clearly, so that the congregation would fulfill the commandment. Precisely the attempt to blot out the memory of Amalek, to leave no recollection of this nation, created a new memory, fresher and more penetrating with each passing year.

But it is memory that chains me to my past, to my set patterns of behavior. How can I break through to still-hidden elements if I cannot first forget and blot out evil? The Jewish tradition excels at creating ceremonies and institutions of memory: we are constantly recalling what we suffered at the hands of Amalek, the Exodus from Egypt, and the destruction of the First and Second Temples, ever aware of anti-Jewish riots and pogroms, and of course of the Holocaust and Israel's fallen soldiers. The constant inculcation of memory is like a promise we make to ourselves, that we will not allow these events to recur in the present or the future.

To grasp the Amalek memory ritual, I must account for the later Jewish tendency to transform Amalek from a nation to a comprehensive symbol for evil and impurity as such. It is in this context that traditional sources generally cite another set of biblical verses that deal with the blotting out of Amalek:

> Then the Lord said to Moses, "Write this as a reminder in a book and recite it in the hearing of Joshua: I will utterly blot out the remembrance of Amalek from under heaven." And Moses built an altar and called it "The Lord is my banner." He said, "A hand upon the banner of the Lord! The Lord will have war with Amalek from generation to generation." (Exodus 17:14–16)

These verses intensify the desert battle and Israel's call to take revenge on Amalek, transforming them into a cosmic struggle. Though the portrait is sketchy, these verses hint at a fundamental struggle waged by God against a dark opponent capable of reaching across the generations, an opponent who retains the name Amalek long after the eponymous nation is no more. No victory is possible without simultaneous recollection and forgetting, eternal memory and eternal blotting out.

Jewish texts identify Amalek with an array of evil forces, manifesting themselves anew in every generation. According to the widely held kabbalistic view, all these forces ultimately emanate from one divine source. But closer examination reveals the existence of a parallel world of *sefirot* of impurity and evil. In the kabbalistic corpus, this view is attested to in the writing of Rabbi Yitzhak ben Yaakov ha-Kohen, who wandered through twelfth-century Spain with his brother, Jacob. They collaborated on a series of fascinating treatises. One of them, "An Essay on the Emanation of the Left Side,"[4] provides a detailed description of a *sefirot* structure, almost identical with the familiar set of *sefirot*, that forms intricate worlds populated by the forces of evil.

The Zohar too offers an outline (but no more than that) of the structure of the evil *sefirot*, describing the levels of impurity, their internal organization and structure, as precise parallels to the sacred *sefirot*. There too we find a male side and a female side, a side from which power emanates and flows, and another that delimits and contains this power, naming it and fixing its meaning. The kabbalistic authors assign each of the evil *sefirot* (known collectively as the *Sitra Ahra*, "the Other Side") their own name, with Samael and Lilith marking the male and female aspects of these *sefirot*, respectively.

So similar are the two sefirotic systems that at times it is difficult to tell them apart. The *Sitra Ahra* can scarcely be distinguished from the *sefirot* of life and holiness; the evil *sefirot* camouflage themselves, disguise themselves as the holy *sefirot*, "like a monkey imitating a man."[5] They are the antithesis, the evil negative, of the forces of holiness. Evil terrifies first and foremost for its ability to invisibly permeate everything, for its camouflaged, masked presence. It is no wonder the forces of the *Sitra Ahra* are called *kelippot*, "peels" or "husks," that block the fruit that lies within.

God's form, the structure of the holy *sefirot*, is man's image, which is in God's image, and so too the *sefirot* of impurity constitute an image of their own, a deathly image, which leads to perdition and death. These *sefirot* have no independent selfhood; they are wholly dependent on their ability to emulate the true *sefirot*, as only the latter generate life-sustaining forces.[6]

"The Other God is castrated,"[7] writes the Zohar in reference to the *sefirot* of impurity. That is, even though these *sefirot* contain both male and female aspects, this Other God is emasculated, incapable of producing viable progeny, without any generative power. The *Sitra Ahra*'s impotence is described in Lurianic Kabbalah as an absence of marrow, that is, of internal substance, of interiority; it exists in a state of pure exteriority.[8] The worlds governed by the *Sitra Ahra* are forever "siphoning" the original, creative forces within the world and using them to duplicate themselves and become a graven, masked image. The vital kernel that they require for their subsistence is immediately transformed into a fixed pattern of castration, disguise, fixation, and destruction.

The clearest and most straightforward example of this process is the way technological society appropriates great scientific discoveries and harnesses them for the needs of a culture of war and destruction. The secrets of the atom, germs, and viruses are transformed into instruments of death, whose specter hangs over mankind every day. Physics, biology, computer science, all created to advance human life, metamorphosed into instruments of enslavement.

In this sense, the commandment to remember Amalek takes on existential importance. Most people can resist visible Amaleks, can fight back against Amaleks in plain sight, but when the most diabolical Amalek of all lies in wait, hidden in his disguise, some people will mistake it for a force of good. We must continually recognize the existence of dark powers forever disguised as positive, vital forces. Recollection is the first and most important step in this process; memory is a necessary condition for eradicating those powers of the *Sitra Ahra* disguised as holiness and creativity.

How do the forces of the *Sitra Ahra* come to be? Are there really evil beings named Samael and Lilith who go about seizing positive, creative elements and corrupting them? Are these external forces, or perhaps something that we ourselves create? Is there, in fact, an evil god, like the god who revealed himself to me on that Sabbath eve when I was in such pain, or is the image of the evil god merely the by-product of a psychological *Sitra Ahra* that I have constructed? This is a critical question, for if it is an internal entity, something I myself have created, there exists a chance, however slim, of destroying it. Not so if I must confront an ontologically independent entity over which I have no control.

Certain kabbalistic schools do hold that the powers of evil are independent entities and offer various defenses against them, barriers between them and mankind, and ways to escape their grasp.

This was generally my view as well, so I steered clear of those kabbalistic doctrines and largely ignored the topic; I have no emotional or intellectual stake in mythological creatures, the ghosts and goblins and angels of destruction that were forced into my imagination as a boy. (I always imagined the angels of destruction galloping in the dense black soot curling up from the giant bonfires that dotted my neighborhood during Lag ba-Omer.) I have long since left behind the notion that every human sin produces thousands of destroying angels that swoop down to harm the sinner.

But stripped of their literary trappings, the *Sitra Ahra* discussions undoubtedly refer to real forces in our world. Everywhere and in every society, they work according to fixed and well-wrought models of force and antagonism, competition and gratuitous aggression, preying on the weak and helpless.

These systems all appear to run smoothly, they provide us with "progress" and "abundance," the competition bringing out the "best" in everyone; we are all familiar with the idolatrous worship of "success." But when these systems become the be-all and end-all, when they are held up as the only legitimate course of action in the world, at that moment they become the *Sitra Ahra* within.

This worldview contains all the elements that kabbalists attribute to the *Sitra Ahra*: a highly dynamic, active, vital operation, with all the trappings of authentic creativity. But this system creates distance from the sources that are deepest and most authentic. At a certain point, it assumes control of my consciousness, so that I cannot even visualize a different reality. Even if I grow weary of it and understand that this worldview does not speak to my deeper needs or that I do not want to raise my children into such a reality, I will eventually despair and continue worshipping these idols.

But there is another *Sitra Ahra*, one that we construct within ourselves, that perhaps can be undone. All this is hinted at by the great expert on the *Sitra Ahra*, the Talmudic sage Elisha ben Abuyah. He was part of a group of four sages, Rabbi Akiva among them, who entered the mystical orchard, the *pardes*, but unlike his companions, Elisha ben Abuyah "cut the shoots [became a heretic]."

Why did he "cut the shoots"? According to later Talmudic authorities,[9] he did so because in the course of his heavenly journey he met an angel named Metatron, who was seated in judgment on a heavenly throne, deciding the fate of mankind. This led Elisha to conclude that "there are two heavenly authorities," that is, a good god and an evil god. These same sages called Elisha *Aher*, "the Other," because he become other than who he had been, and moreover he had discovered, as it were, the other side of the divinity and declared it an independent god.

After recounting Elisha's sin and the fact that he began to frequent prostitutes, the Talmud has him meet his most important disciple, one of the greatest sages from the time of the Mishnah, Rabbi Meir. The two discuss the interpretation of "[On the day of prosperity be joyful, and on the day of adversity consider;] God has made the one as well as the other" (Ecclesiastes 7:14), a verse that many generations of kabbalists have interpreted as a reference to the dualism of the holy *sefirot* versus those of the *Sitra Ahra*. Elisha ben Abuyah asks Rabbi Meir how he interprets the verse, and Rabbi Meir's response is superficial and simplistic: "Everything the Holy One blessed be He created in His world—He created a counterpart for it: He created mountains—and He created valleys; He created seas—and He created rivers." In other words, the created world is complete and harmonious, free of meaningful tensions. Ben Abuyah's response is surprisingly vehement: "Rabbi Akiva your master would not have said thus, but rather: He created the righteous—He created the wicked; He created heaven—He created Hell. Each and every one is made up of two parts."

Elisha ben Abuyah is here teaching Rabbi Meir a mystical lesson he may himself no longer believe, but his intellectual integrity compels him to mention it nonetheless: every person contains both a heaven and a hell. These are the two worlds that are available to a person over the course of his life; we are free to choose our own private heaven or hell, which are unlike the heavens and hells of others.

The Zohar too, despite its detailed and complex descriptions of the destructive forces that make up the *Sitra Ahra*, locates the entire structure within the human soul. The Zohar devotes a long discussion to the development of the evil *sefirot*, describing their primordial formation as emerging from smoke, obscuring man's ability to gaze at *Binah*, the *sefirah* from which the *sefirot* of building and creation emanate. The Hebrew word for smoke, *ashan*, is interpreted as an acronym for *olam* (world), *shanah* (year), and *nefesh* (soul), three terms that express the *Ein Sof*'s contraction into the limits of space, time, and man, a process whose genesis lies in *Binah*, and which continues down to the other "active" *sefirot*.

Here is the beginning of the Zohar's description of the *Sitra Ahra*:

> The first grade is a darkness that displays three hues: that of smoke, of fire, and that of blackness. The smoky hue is the apparition of the evil seducer who seduces mankind to stray from the path and to be rebellious. In reference to such it is written, "There shall be no strange god within you; you shall not bow down to a foreign god" (Psalm 81:9). The first half of the verse refers to the male, the second to the female. This refers to the anger [*rogez*] that gathers influence and dominion in the world, and presses humanity to do evil.[10]

It seems surprising that the Zohar locates the genesis of the *Sitra Ahra* in the human soul, and it is odd that it identifies the primordial, core element of this evil construct as *rogez*. This term, translated as "anger" above, generally refers to umbrage, and this interpretation makes sense in the context of the origin of hatred and evil as the Zohar describes it. But why would anger be the root of all evil? After all, sometimes anger is justified. More generally, why does the Zohar employ the term *rogez* rather than its more common synonym *ka'as*, which is quite common throughout the Zohar? In the Hebrew Bible the different occurrences of *rogez* generally refer to the *cause* of anger, rather than to the emotion itself, that is, the word means "fear" or "anxiety," not "anger."[11]

But if fear lies at the origin of the *Sitra Ahra*, how can it be countered? Is it even possible not to be afraid in the face of evil? The Zohar teaches that fear is the foundation of the *Sitra Ahra* and asserts that fear "spreads throughout the world, causing people to twist their behavior in anger and strengthening their anger." The Zohar quotes a peculiar biblical verse, "There shall be no strange god within you" (Psalm 81:10), likening the fear that is "within you" to a strange god rooted in us. It then cites the end of the verse, "you shall not bow down to a foreign god," that is, do not surrender to the foreign fear that enters us from the outside world.[12]

But why am I responsible for my fears? After all, fear is the result of God's contraction, for that is the source of our time-bound lives, our corruptible bodily existence, and innumerable other difficulties. What is the source of this fear, then? None other than the holy *sefirah Binah*, the starting point of divine infinity's contraction, the contraction of the three highest *sefirot*, which produces harsh judgment, that is, limitation, and from this point on our lives cannot but be governed by fear. But here lies the great confusion of the *Sitra Ahra*. The contraction of *Binah* is a positive transformation aimed at building up our material world. Yet at times, or perhaps as a rule, finitude and limitation are erroneously inscribed as forms of fear.

There is no real difficulty, as long as one can see finitude as part and parcel of a broader constructive process of infinite effluence. The root of evil begins to present itself when finitude disguises itself as the exclusive representative of all reality as such. When my eyes see nothing but finitude, corruption, and harsh judgment (the foundations of divine contraction), that is when fear takes root in my heart and begins to flourish. Finally, at the peak of its strength, it becomes a full-fledged complex of forces, branching out of that first, primordial fear, and I begin to think that this complex makes up the sum total of my existence. Such is reality and such are its laws, I say to myself, and whoever is unwilling to submit to the laws of fear is either foolish or deluded. This, of course, is precisely the goal of the *Sitra Ahra*, to be seen as the sole representative of reality.

Here is a question that has occupied many traditional Bible interpreters. Deuteronomy states that Israel is to blot out the memory of Amalek who "happened upon you on the way" (Deuteronomy 25:17). What does this mean? "Happened upon" sounds like a chance encounter.[13] The commentators suggest that Amalek symbolizes a worldview that submits to the influence of chance, of blind fate. In this interpretation, the Amalek that Israel encountered during the Exodus from Egypt was not a physical horde but rather a worldview that states that we do not control our lives but rather are subject only to external circumstances. It should be remembered that the battle the Israelites waged against Amalek following the miracles they witnessed in Egypt may have caused them to lose sight of the contingent, random forces that govern the world. If so, this battle represents the first, painful cut of the reality of power relations, a cut intended to renew the reign of fear and violence. Amalek, then, is a symbol of the painful scars we experience when we free ourselves from a state of blessed naiveté.

As always, I am able to make good progress while under the illusion that I can overcome all difficulties, but Amalek happens upon me on the way when I am faint and weary, my self-confidence at an ebb, and then I forget the original impetus that set me on this path: "Remember what Amalek did to you on your journey out of Egypt, how he happened upon you on the way, when you were faint and weary, and struck down all who lagged behind you; he did not fear God" (Deuteronomy 25:17–18). After examining some event that hurt me deeply, I tend to blame my innocence, my naive belief that I can change myself and the world, and I quickly replace it with a more "mature" and "hardened" and "realistic" view, lest I be hurt again in the future. "Amalek," according to the ancient interpreters, is a force that covers our faces, blocking our vision from the vital, creative powers capable of resisting it.[14]

The view enunciated in most kabbalistic texts states that man is responsible for his own fate, is the creator of his world, and has the power to alter fate through his actions. The kabbalists do not deny the existence of fate, but they characterize it as evil; fate is the *Sitra Ahra*. Things that occur for no apparent reason are the true essence of the *Sitra Ahra*. Amalek may be meaningless as a physical nation, but it is highly significant once we understand it as contingent fate that seeks to dominate our lives.

If I am limited by the old scars, if I worship fate and circumstance, I am worshipping the *Sitra Ahra*. Just as I am commanded to remember the Exodus so that I can relive the spiritual and emotional process the Israelites experienced when they departed Egypt, moving from spiritual slavery to spiritual freedom, so too I am commanded with regard to Amalek. The memory must be active, concrete, and continually renewing itself. This is not historical memory, but rather a conscious memory that leads to action. I must take care lest I lose touch with the sources within my soul, particularly when I am "faint and weary," that is, when those sources are most vulnerable to an attack from without that would etch the fear in me for the rest of my life.

2

Good intentions are not enough. Indeed, the most difficult aspect of the *Sitra Ahra* is that we can never truly know where we stand. Varied and endlessly creative are the *Sitra Ahra*'s powers of camouflage. As Rabbi Nahman writes:

> Know that there are two kinds of palaces, and that they resemble each other. A king lives in one of them, while a slave lives in the second. In truth, there is certainly a great difference between the king's and the slave's chambers, but all the same, it is possible to confuse them.[15]

According to Rabbi Nahman, despite the profound difference in the essence of the two palaces, the palace of the king and the palace of the slave are nonetheless very similar. In the slave's palace too one finds many servants, and the cooperation among them gives the illusion that this is the king's palace:

> But know ... [that] there is a bond of the wicked inasmuch as many souls of wicked men join together out of which a house and home is formed for deceit.... Consider now that it is possible to confuse these two houses, that is, between truth and falsehood, for deceit makes itself resemble the truth. There, too, one finds a bond of many souls and a man could make a mistake and not know where the truth resides and how to approach it.[16]

What are we to do, dear Rabbi Nahman?

But Rabbi Nahman's writings are never that systematic. His teachings are scattered throughout various texts, often inaccessible, like the walls of Jericho that only fell to Joshua after he circled them seven times. Rabbi Nahman does not provide the reader with a clear methodology with which to distinguish between the palaces, only a cryptic remark:

> And know that there are two intelligences which are the aspect of behind and before.[17] That is, there is an intelligence which comes to a man in the course of time and as he ages and gets along in years, he knows more under the aspect of time will tell [in other words, patience]. This intelligence is the aspect of behind, because it comes delayed, since it requires time.[18]

The ruses of the *Sitra Ahra* are nothing more than our own self-delusions.

Man has two types of intelligence, two faculties of insight. A person who lives in a palace of falsehood and slavery will only gradually and after much time come to recognize his error. This man gains insight when he sees the fruit of his earlier decisions as they are reflected back to him in his children or the people around him. Only too late does he understand the castration and impotence of the social and emotional network on behalf of which he labored for so many years. But who wants to waste so many years of his life only to find out that he has been living a mistake? This is why Rabbi Nahman suggests that there is another type of insight, rooted in a person's ability to be attentive to even the slightest rustle of his heart: "But there is an intelligence which comes to a man in great abundance and quickness that lasts less than a minute because it is beyond time and doesn't need time."[19]

According to Rabbi Nahman, there can be flashes of intense intuition that are able to break through the psychic structures that we have built up over the years. They come from a place that is beyond time, a pure place, unsullied by circumstantial considerations, a place only of causes and effects. Rabbi Nahman calls such a flash "examination of the face" (*behinat panim*), an instantaneous and exhaustive reflection of the face of a person who is willing to look at them. For an instant, a person can see clearly the entire spectrum of his life through the prism of the complex he inhabits, even though he is still in the middle of the journey.

But the options Rabbi Nahman offers us are inherently passive, while I am searching for a deep insight that comes about as the result of my conscious initiative. I do not want to wait until the end of my days, but neither can I call forth flashes of profound intuition.

3

The moon that marks the beginning of Adar smiles down at me from on high. My daughter has given me an assignment, and so I am on a search for a Mulan costume. Mulan is a character in a Chinese folktale, a young woman who disguises herself as a warrior in order to keep her sick father from being drafted. She ends up saving the empire and falling in love with her dashing commander. Her disguise may have saved her sick father, but the price she must pay is her love. If she reveals her true identity to her commander, she will be severely punished.

My daughter's request sets me on a hunt for searching eyes and deceptive disguises in the classical Jewish sources, leading me to a figure whose very essence is the disguise. Like Queen Esther, Mulan's life and fate are intertwined in an identity that she has borrowed for herself. As I stand in line at the toy superstore, I realize that my daughter has sent me to purchase a costume of a girl who sets out on a journey in a costume. She is going to dress up as a character that is dressed up.

Once I have gotten past the requisite (and altogether superfluous) "educational" questions (Is this the kind of character I want to influence my daughter? Do I want her to think the only way to protect herself and her loved ones is by hiding her true identity?), I recall a similar event that occurred during Purim of 1977, when I was a still a child who never imagined he would be buying a Mulan costume for his daughter.

Already at the end of Tu Bishevat, the Jewish arbor day and a full month before Purim, my mother and brothers began to argue about whether it was appropriate for a child to dress up as a Hasidic master. My brothers, who were very strict about such matters, insisted that even though we were a Hasidic family of some repute, such a disguise would be tantamount to making fun of the institution of Hasidic leadership and of the particular Torah scholar selected. My mother sided with me, of course, and adopted my argument that many Jewish boys dress up as Mordechai, who was undoubtedly a great Torah scholar and an important Jewish leader. My brothers responded that the two cases are not analogous, since the standing of the present-day Hasidic leaders is not as firmly established as Mordechai's. Ultimately we reached a compromise: my brothers agreed to let me dress up as a Hasidic master, but not as any particular individual, lest it appear I was disparaging him.

Though still a child, I had the body of a young man and was fitted for the costume without difficulty. I borrowed an old Hasidic fur hat and a faded frock coat from my grandfather, and my mother decorated its collar with black fur. I wore my father's black slacks and a white shirt padded with a small pillow, giving me a respectable paunch. All that was needed was a fake gray beard, a walking stick with a metal ball handle, and of course the typical walk of Hasidic masters: a light patter on the tip of the toes that gives one the air of a spiritual angel who has happened into our world of lies.

Purim arrived. After hearing the Scroll of Esther recited in the synagogue, my friends and I set out on our exciting journey between the houses of Me'ah She'arim and the Hungarian quarter. There, as we well knew, they still practiced the Rabbinic ruling that on Purim, "give to whoever reaches out his hand." As in every year, we took advantage of this legal license to "mooch" and squirrel away pocket money to last the entire year. Already at the first house I knew something was wrong. My friends received a few coins and candies and were already hurrying off to knock on the next door and graciously provide the next family with an opportunity to fulfill the commandment of Purim charity, but I received very different treatment. Each of the families invited me in, seated me at their table, poured me a glass of wine, and somberly invited me to discuss matters of Torah. Purim money was clearly out of the question.

After this scenario repeated itself several times, my friends decided to abandon me rather than waste their precious time waiting for me to emerge from the house. Lonely, disgruntled, and more than a little tipsy, I made my way to my grandfather's house, which was in the same neighborhood. After patiently sitting through my complaints about the residents of his neighborhood, he sighed and said, "A person can get dressed up as anything he wants, except for a Hasidic master." "But why?" I asked, and I began to recite the halakhic approval I had received from an important Torah scholar, but he answered impatiently, "No, no. You cannot dress up as a Hasidic master. As soon as you wear a Hasidic master's clothes, you become a Hasidic master."

—

I have not dressed up since. Since that day, I have been yearning for the moment when I will be able to remove my various masks, to stop assuming postures to gain approval and success in a society that penalizes those who transgress its rules.

Evil is the eternal donner of disguises, and the most skilled. Unlike conceptions that represent evil as a diabolical or demonic force that does battle against God's eternal beneficence, much of the Jewish tradition locates the roots of evil within God and to a great extent within man. We are not dealing with a demon that approaches from without and tempts us into sin. Evil is manmade and inevitably personal. This evil is very difficult to detect, since it can present itself as a force of good. I am not referring to the most pronounced manifestations of evil, be it in murder or in corrupt and corrupting behavior, but rather the banal, everyday evil that chains man deep within his soul, turning the free man into a slave: a slave to the system into which he was born and in which he has lived all his life, and a slave to his own life circumstances. It is an evil found in the conceptual and emotional complex to which people bind themselves over the course of their lives, an evil born of a certain type of habituation, of a particular prism through which we see the world and ourselves. This prism blocks us from listening to our fellow man just as much as it blocks us from effecting change within ourselves, and this remains true even after we realize that the system we have constructed has become a mask that hides us from ourselves, a sterile disguise that provides neither joy nor vitality.

Rabbi Joshua Heschel of Apta teaches that to dress up at Purim is to reside in the gap between our daily disguises and the exaggerated, explicit disguise of the holiday.

> On account of this, we too must move beyond the bounds of reason, so we can annul evil completely. Indeed, the Talmudic sages alluded to this when they said, "It is incumbent on us to drink on Purim to the point of not knowing," that is to say, that we move beyond the bounds of reason and examine the world in its raw state, unable to distinguish between accursed Haman and blessed Mordechai. For in this space there exists the coincidence of opposites, which allows us to annul the evil within us. With good reason did the Jewish sages repeat throughout the ages that Purim is akin to *Yom Kippurim*, that is, Yom Kippur.[20]

The Rabbi of Apta is playing on the phonetic similarity between the two holidays to suggest that *Yom Kippurim*, the Jewish Day of Atonement, is merely a day *ki-Purim*, "like Purim," less sacred and less special than Purim itself. While Yom Kippur is a time to break with the behavioral patterns of our external existence—eating, drinking, sex, and more—Purim marks a more fundamental, internal break that manifests itself, paradoxically, in the holiday's emphasis on external identity and physical needs such as eating and drinking. Between these two masks, there exists, according to the Rabbi of Apta, a state of consciousness in which opposites coincide, an inchoate state of authentic change and transformation. This is a purely medial state, in which we are not bound by the external needs that force us to into disguises, nor by the borrowed identities we have taught ourselves to don.

The curious equation of Purim and Yom Kippur is more than a pun.[21] Both holidays focus on the theater of divine reversal, on the arena of good versus evil, where a swift, well-placed kick can transform good into evil or evil into good. The kick in question must be powered by the encounter with the supernal *sefirot*, first and foremost with *Binah*, the *sefirah* of repentance and reversal. Yom Kippur places the emphasis on reversing the *Sitra Ahra* that we have built up and fortified within our souls. On this day, we are called upon to purify ourselves under ideal conditions, as part of a spiritual retreat, and to renew contact with the *Binah* that resides within each of us. Purim, in contrast, is concerned with the need to reach the reversal point within *Malkhut*, the lived, social world. Haman after all (whom the Scroll of Esther symbolically identifies as an offspring of Agag, king of the Amalekites and the representative of the *Sitra Ahra*) permeates the space of the various social and public spheres, as political power becomes, over time, an instrument of violence, racism, and deprivation.

Purim offers a path to self-transformation within the hustle and bustle of daily life, far different from the optimal conditions of Yom Kippur. Here is Rabbi Yehudah Leib of Gur's commentary on the events described in the Scroll of Esther. The Hebrew phrase *amod al nafsham*, which describes the Jews' response to Haman's decrees, is an idiom that means "defended themselves." But the Rabbi of Gur interprets the phrase literally, "to stand on their souls":

> *Amod al nafsham* ... for the blotting out of Amalek involves self-sacrifice, a willingness to annul one's self to a particular point, namely, *hayyut*, vitality ... for it is doubtless impossible to blot out the name Amalek if one does not cleave to the point *hayyut*, which is located above the aspect of *nefesh*, soul, a place where the memory of Amalek does not exist and where no foreign power holds dominion. This is also the meaning of remembrance that occurs in the biblical pericope *Zakhor*, "remember," and refers to recollection in the depths of the heart, a recollection that is the proximate cause of action.[22]

The Jews, then, ascend, as it were, beyond their regular soul, beyond the place where they store up all the fears and desires that have been extinguished due to their constant, intractable defensiveness. Recollection, says Rabbi Yehudah Leib of Gur, does not refer to mere information, fragments of data floating through our brains, but rather to a deep knowledge that contains a push to action, like the memory of something that endangers our lives. Memory is at once internal and external, and its meaning manifests itself in the practical world of our daily lives. The Bible does not command us to hold a grudge against someone who has wronged us, but rather instructs us to adopt a life guided by memory. It is the internal memory of Amalek that produces the ability to defend against the evil of the *Sitra Ahra*'s complexes in the external world. Revisiting the original sources of our souls does not mean returning to a passive, naive state, but rather moves us to action in lived reality. Fear of this "Amalek" is not tantamount to stunned inaction in the face of the blows the world showers upon us; it is rather a catalyst, spurring us to harness the abilities we have acquired through difficult struggle against the *Sitra Ahra*. We must learn fear if we are to defeat it on its home turf.

Whenever anyone looks for Amalek, Amalek will be there. The notion that contingent reality governs me is the Amalek hidden within my fears and anxieties. We are commanded to remember the blotting out of Amalek through internal work—blotting out the Amalek within us, first and foremost in our hearts, and then through our actions. The memory that manifests itself in the blotting out of Amalek is not, then, a one-time mission, but rather a process that continues "for all generations."

This call to soar beyond my own time and space, to momentarily view reality in its totality, to recognize the myriad possibilities inherent in every situation, and how the change I make in myself can effect change in my surroundings, issues from the depths of the most secular holiday in the Jewish calendar. For Purim, despite the reading of the Scroll of Esther, is understood as a singularly secular celebration. God is never mentioned in the Scroll of Esther. Israel's redemption from the hand of Haman does not come about as the result of divine intervention or some glorious miracle, but as the result of Mordechai and Esther's political manipulations, and strategic realism. Both employ double agents within the court of Ahasuerus and exploit Esther's physical beauty and sexuality in order to undermine Haman's political standing and destroy him.

It is precisely the secular nature of Purim's carnivalesque reversal of values that traditional Jewish interpreters have identified as the *tikkun* for the golden calf episode. When the Israelites demanded a golden calf, they were denying the possibility of transcending their circumstances and the complex of forces that govern our daily lives. They refused to embrace the stunning power of the fiery epiphany on the mountain, an epiphany that tends to recede from our minds as soon as daily existence begins to weigh us down. The Talmud suggests that during the days of Mordechai and Esther, Israel accepted anew the original Sinaitic demand to live in freedom. Only now they did so willingly, and not because God "hung the mountain over them like a barrel."[23]

The plot of the Scroll of Esther makes no mention of divine intervention or miraculous occurrences. The events are all a result of human agency. The Scroll of Esther and the holiday of Purim remind us that people can change reality and transcend its limitations through their actions. The true, hidden root, dependent upon neither fate nor happenstance, is the root of all, and as such the source from which flow all contingent circumstances. As soon as we alter something at the root of all reality, in the supernal worlds, our reality will necessarily change. That is, sometimes visible reality is nothing more than the mimetic action of the *Sitra Ahra*. This is not to suggest that visible reality is necessarily negative, only that if one grasps our world for what it is, a derivative of the supernal worlds, it is possible to steer our reality and to comport ourselves properly within it, at which point it ceases to be the *Sitra Ahra*.

Returning to the biblical injunction to remember the forgetting of Amalek, it now appears to be predicated on a change in perspective. The commandment does not require ignoring life here on earth or relegating reality to the status of illusion. The material world deserves recognition as part of a broader system. It is *Malkhut*, an element of the ten *sefirot*. Kabbalistic texts generally recognize the world, in all its materiality, though they emphasize the importance of not surrendering to it. If you do so, you find yourself worshipping a reality that is nothing more than the distorted reflection of its supernal source. The question of perspective is critical: Do I take this cruel, hurtful reality to be the ultimate truth, thereby relegating all otherworldly forces to the status of empty fantasies, illusions? Or do I understand the existence of evil as a misapplication of other forces, positive but hidden, buried beneath the visible husk?

I do not believe that positive thinking alone can alter reality, so I turn to the Scroll of Esther for its powers of overturning, for its ability to reverse reality like the sleeve of a jacket. Then I will finally discover what my garment is made of, see its layers, its stitches, and its patches; then the true will be known as true and the seemingly true revealed as a mere counterfeit.

Rabbi Zadok Hakohen of Lublin, a nineteenth-century sage who started out as one of the greatest opponents of Hasidism and became one of the greatest Hasidic figures, underwent a radical transformation midway through his life.

> The sanctity of Purim lies in the following: to examine the invisible truth that is hidden within the imagination, until the imagination is once again a vessel for the truth within it, and so becomes secondary to the truth.... This is the reason one is obligated to become inebriated, for the drunk is full of imagination and is utterly without truthful thought, but for Jews imagination too is truth.[24]

According to Rabbi Zadok, Purim teaches us a great lesson about the workings of the imagination. We tend to see our fears and anxieties as an accurate reflection of external reality, while our abilities, ambitions, hope for change—these we relegate to the category of illusion. But in fact, the opposite is the case. Most of our fears are groundless, while our deepest hopes and most hidden dreams represent our most important

inner truth, which we need to nurture most and set free into the surrounding world. This is how Rabbi Zadok explains the commandment
to drink to the point of inebriation on Purim. Being drunk makes us
susceptible to illusions; it allows us to temporarily inhabit the gap that
opens up between our various identity costumes. Inebriation allows
for a new state of consciousness that blurs the difference between truth
and imagination. It unsettles what we know to be true and can open us
to the possibility that what we see when sober may not be true. In other
words, it provides a lesson in the relativism of truth. On Purim we are
commanded to drink until we can no longer differentiate between
Haman and Mordechai, that is, until we undermine our fixed notions
of truth and reality, a temporary suspension of sobriety that allows us
to distinguish between the merely visible and the truly real.

4

Like a new memory permeating the body, forgetting an incorporated
memory does not happen quickly or easily. This is why the kabbalists developed the *golem* method. This method—which has nothing
to do with the legendary Golem of Prague—draws its authority
from a statement in the Mishnah tractate *Avot* ("The Sayings of the
Fathers"):

> There are seven marks of the *golem* ["the clod"] and seven of
> the wise man. The wise man does not speak before one that is
> greater than he in wisdom; and he does not break into the words
> of his fellow; and he is not hasty in making an answer; he asks
> what is relevant and makes answer according to *halakhah*; and
> he speaks on the first point first and on the last point last; and
> of what he has heard no tradition, he says, "I have not heard";
> and he agrees to what is true. And the opposites of these are the
> marks of the *golem*.[25]

According to Rabbi Joshua Heschel of Apta, *golem* here is not a
disparaging term for a fool, but rather describes a primeval state that
allows for "conversion" from good to evil and, more importantly,
from evil to good:

There is a world known as *golem*, namely the world of *Hokhmah* that is the aspect of the letter *yod*, and this letter is the aspect of the *golem*, for *yod* appears as a small dot from which one can produce the form of any of the letters. And this is the meaning of "the opposites of these," namely, if you want to convert something to its opposite—this is achieved in *golem*. That is to say, you need to elevate it to the aspect of *golem*, and there you can convert it.[26]

The *golem*, says the Rabbi of Apta, is one of the highest levels of the divine *sefirot*, as well as a hidden essence within the human soul. It is the most elevated plane within *Hokhmah*, the *sefirah* represented by the letter *yod*, the first letter of the Tetragrammaton (YHWH), and the source of the entire sefirotic structure. The Hebrew word *golem* is a cognate of *gelem*, "raw material," something from which anything can be created. If we wish to convert evil into good, this can only be achieved in a state of *golem*, of raw material. To effect change in our world, which has already undergone the process of contraction and been given a particular form and image, it must first be returned to its primordial state, where it is still malleable:

> To better clarify this point, note that everything that has been formed into a particular form, can no longer receive another form, except if the first form has been corrupted and reverts to its *golem* state, without form or figure, and then the thing in question can be shaped according to our will. We know this from the testimony of the senses: if a person has a silver vessel and wants to make another vessel of it, it must first be smelted. The same is true in the supernal worlds, where they elevate something to the world of *Hokhmah*, which is also called *golem*, and only then can a new thing emerge.[27]

The conversions that take place in the space known as *golem* begin with a self-consciousness of change, pass through the raw mass of our emotions, and conclude by altering the internalization mechanisms of the soul. In traditional kabbalistic terms, the elements undergoing change are "letters" that have been ordered incorrectly, resulting in a series of missteps on the way to our inner truth:

This is also the esoteric teaching of confession. From the sin a person commits there emerges, through the arrangement of the letters, a prosecutor whose precise nature depends on the nature of the sin ... and when a person wants to undo that image or form, he must call up his memory and say, "I committed such-and-such sin." But this is only efficacious if he repents truly and completely in the depths of his heart—he cannot merely profess it. He elevates the image in question to the mind and thus *Hokhmah* is transformed into the aspect of *golem*, and the letters of the sin are inevitably sweetened.[28]

I now understand more fully the concept of repentance and the Talmudic claim that it can change the penitent's life narrative so that his "transgressions are accounted as merits." Every *sefirah* in the Tree of the *sefirot* allows me to understand and interpret my life from a new angle. Every act of repentance, every return to the source, every retelling and reinterpretation, leads to new forgiveness. By creating a new narrative in my soul, I can alter the course of my life as I had previously experienced it within me. Suddenly, the letters that had been misaligned when telling me my life story are reordered. I really am becoming a different person.

⌐

According to a number of great Hasidic masters, among them Rabbi Nahman of Breslov, the way to become a *golem* is to submit to the point of self-negation before a *tzaddik*—to find a truly great man and give him absolute control over my life. I must annul my own consciousness and become a reflection of his deeds and beliefs, doing whatever he tells me, without question and without reserve. This course of action is supposed to help me negate my ego, thereby clearing the way for me to build up, over time, a new emotional and intellectual complex that is not rooted in my personal limitations. According to this approach, the initial goal of my journey is not to discover the sefirotic system within me, but rather to adopt the sefirotic system of another, a reliable individual who can be counted on not to have erred in the maze of the ever-camouflaged *Sitra Ahra*.

Rabbi Nahman does not advocate this as a way for lost souls to latch onto an authoritative figure and thus avoid existential decisions. On the contrary, this self-negation allows us to shatter our false life-masks and grow our authentic faces. It is impossible to aim an arrow into fog, he says; we must have a clear target for the arrow of self-negation to strike. In order to renew our face, we must have a face:

> Regarding the matter of the *kabbalat panim* ["reception," but literally "receiving the face"] of a sage—the moon has no inherent illumination, rather receives all its light from the sun. In other words, because the moon is like a polished mirror it can receive light from the sun to shine onto the earth. But if its physical nature were coarse and dark, unpolished, it could not receive light from the sun at all.[29]

In order for the disciple to receive something from his master, he must make himself polished like the moon:

> The same is true of the master and his disciple, for they are like the sun and the moon. This is particularly the case if the disciple possesses a face, that is, if his face is radiant like a polished mirror. But if he has no face, that is, if his face is darkened, he cannot *lekabel panim* ["receive the face"], and the face of his master cannot be seen within him, for he is like one who faces a coarse and dark thing.[30]

But I have not found a person so great that he would be above suspicion of having erred in the maze of the *Sitra Ahra*. Indeed, even if I had met Rabbi Nahman himself—and I can certainly imagine myself becoming a fervent disciple of his—he would probably have told me, with his great integrity, that I cannot rely on him either. Error and confusion are a constant risk for even the greatest *tzaddik*, and no man knows his true place. Says Rabbi Nahman, "There are those who think they have made their way into the Holy of Holies, but in fact they remain utterly outside, for they have not even begun to grasp the truth."[31]

The Baal Shem Tov's student, the Maggid Dov Ber of Mezritch, developed a different approach that involves cleaving to God through prayer. Essentially, the Maggid proposes a form of meditation that requires one to focus on the letters and sounds of the prayer, while tuning out all thoughts extraneous to the prayer, ultimately reaching a state of self-oblivion. Indeed, the Maggid says, it is only when one forgets the words of a prayer that he truly begins to pray.[32] This is the state the Maggid characterizes as "nothingness," the state where we begin the liberation from the fetters of the *Sitra Ahra* and begin altering the very roots of our reality.

Even though most Jewish mystics and kabbalists employed meditation techniques of some sort, I have never come across a fully fleshed-out Jewish doctrine of meditation. As a result, I decide to try my luck with the techniques forged by the great masters of meditation—the mystics of the Far East. But after a few weeks of this sort of meditation, I realize that the ability to empty my consciousness is acquired over years, and no practitioner knows at the outset if he will ever attain this lofty goal. I am unable to distance myself from the daily troubles that bubble up through my consciousness one by one (though admittedly their pace has slowed). The mind is a wily trickster. Even when I try to combine meditation with yoga exercises, thoughts burst onto the scene, trying to control my movements, calculating my achievements and progress. And there are still many *Sitra Ahra* fears that well up within me.

Here is a test to gauge the fear within me: I will try to experience and document the fears I feel as soon as I set aside my daily concerns, my competitive urges, and my aggression: I fear death, diseases, car accidents, loneliness, being trapped in systems that close in on me from every direction. I am afraid of my daughters being harmed—God forbid—through pain or illness or some undiagnosed defect, or from a sick man assaulting them sexually; I fear they will be untalented or failures, or penniless as adults, or that I will not have enough money to support them while they are still under my care; I fear they will not have freedom, that they will marry men who will keep them in chains, like slaves; I fear they will be wicked or dishonest, that they will not know God, that they will never experience true prayer, that no one will recognize their worth, or worse—that they be worthless. Still more fears for myself: I fear that everyone will realize that I am a phony, a sham; that no one will want to listen to me; that they will speak of me behind my back. I fear that the State of Israel, my home, will not survive the waves of hostility battering it from without, or perhaps the sloth and corruption eating away at it from within. I fear that it will become a place that no longer has room for the Jewish tradition; that the ultra-Orthodox will be the only heirs to Judaism. I fear the Messiah will never come, and I fear the Messiah will come and I will have to confront the fact that I have lived my life in error—that the truth lies with my childhood tradition and that I broke with it for naught. I fear growing old, going completely bald, gaining weight, getting ugly; I fear my wife and my daughters and everyone around me rejecting me. I fear lest I become a millstone around my wife and daughters' neck; and I fear that when the time comes and they need to care for me, they will choose not to or will do so grudgingly, resenting and hating me and even hoping for my death. I fear my financial limitations will keep me from living comfortably; that I will not have enough money for proper care in my old age, that I will have to beg and plead for handouts or borrow money from friends and family. I fear my friends will betray me—that they will tell every Tom, Dick, and Harry what I have shared with them about myself. I fear my study of Kabbalah will lead me to terrible sins, that I am guilty of idolatry; that I am leading others into sin by introducing abominations and falsehoods into their mind—and for this I will have no place in the world to come. I am anxious that my parents, my brothers, my entire family is ashamed of me; that my parents will no longer appreciate me and will deny that we are related, that my brothers and sisters will stop inviting me to family events, denying my daughters contact with their family and closing a vista into other facets of the Jewish world. I am afraid of the forces of evil, if they exist, and of unfamiliar and unknown forces; I fear exposure to nature—insects and reptiles. I fear speaking the truth, and I fear writing about my fears. And I am startled by having exposed this list of my fears.

The Hasidic masters call such meditations "foreign thoughts," not because they are foreign to the human mind, but rather because they originate in the *Sitra Ahra*, the eternally foreign. To deal with these foreign thoughts they prescribe a process known as "ransoming of captives." One of the most impressive homilies about the "ransoming of captives" technique is in the writings of Rabbi Tzvi Elimelech of Dinov (1785–1841), a man of great courage. He left a steady job as a pulpit rabbi because he refused to sanction the practice of force-feeding geese. The halakhic prohibition against injuring animals was no empty slogan for him; it was a way of life. He believed every thought, every intuition that surfaces in our consciousness requires the "ransoming of captives"—even the pain of geese force-fed before slaughter.

Rabbi Tzvi Elimelech of Dinov considered every event that enters a person's consciousness a fragment of his soul that requires *tikkun*. Every thought is a beggar knocking on our door, pleading for a piece of bread or a coin:

> Thus they wrote that one should not reject the [foreign] thought outright, rather elevate it, and here lies the analogy with the ransoming [of] captives—a major commandment. For those letters are imprisoned by the *Sitra Ahra*, and they come to us seeking redemption from the hand of their enemy and safe passage back to their father's house. These letters are sparks that descended following the breaking of the vessels that occurred during the act of creation, along with those that have descended as a result of our many transgressions—the result of human actions throughout time, from generation to generation.[33]

Rabbi Tzvi Elimelech of Dinov warns us lest we reject these thoughts, urging us to accept them and make whole their deficiencies: "If the thought is lacking the light that illuminates the world of love, one should raise it up to that place."

But what am I to do with these captives? How can I feed them when my cupboard is bare? I myself have a surplus of deficits; I lack sufficient reserves of joy and love and grace to support all the captives that crowd onto my portals, now that I have freed them from the oblivion of their captivity.

5

As happens every year, the conclusion of Purim and imminent arrival of Passover send a shiver of unease down my spine. I do not know if this unease is part of my early childhood conditioning or perhaps has its roots in some adolescent conflict, but it is what drives me to promise my family, once again, a different Passover Seder. No more family dinners, with guests crammed around cramped tables; no more rushed, uninspired readings of the Haggadah. No. This year, Passover will be a holiday of liberty and choice. We will convene our close friends, read the ancient texts according to a new tradition we establish for ourselves, breaking with the uncompromising patterns of our forefathers; we will hold deep and meaningful conversations about freedom, about the enslaving frameworks that exist within us, as we celebrate the springtime of physical and spiritual rebirth.

Some of my friends would like to spend the Seder with me in the desert. I am assigned the textual component of the evening and set off on a rigorous study of the Passover Haggadah. I am quickly transported back to the days of my childhood preceding the holiday, the pre-Passover customs, the preparations that occupied my mother from the moment Purim ended, right up to Passover. Perhaps this is due to the two operations I underwent as a child, but the days leading up to Passover remind me of a series of preparations for a complex and risky medical procedure: the sterilization, the compulsive cleaning of every part of the house. If I entered a room or opened a closet that my mother and sisters had already cleaned, my punishment was to change my clothes, lest a leaven crumb sneak from the folds of my shirt into the cracks of the floorboards or the wood paneling. Scrubbed places were sealed off—no entry or exit was granted without thorough inspection. There were constant skirmishes and debates that accompanied the entire process, very much like the anxiety preceding the complicated "operation" that awaited us a few days hence, on the night of the Seder. The Jewish calendar terrorized my mother. She was forever convinced she would not have time to properly clean the house, sanitize the leavened dishes, and prepare the holiday dinner, even if she were given an additional week of preparation.

The atmosphere grew more tense as the night of Passover approached, what with the hunting for leaven, collecting the bread crumbs in a sealed wrapper in a corner, and the ceremonial burning of the leaven on the following morning. As the Passover Seder approached, my father and older brothers would don their *kittel*, a white robe that is also worn during the High Holy Days, Rosh Hashanah and Yom Kippur. And then came the operation itself: reading the Haggadah.

The anxiety these memories evoke in me only grows stronger today. The Haggadah is one of the most difficult and problematic public texts in the Jewish tradition. An evening that supposedly celebrates freedom has been set against the backdrop of a puerile and vindictive text, crammed with tales of persecution and hardship. The ungenerous spirit of the Haggadah is particularly evident in the baseless homilies about Laban the Aramean, who is said to have tried to kill Jacob and his entire family, and in the later series of homilies about Pharaoh's cruelty, culminating in the phrase "in every generation they arise to destroy us." These infantile revenge fantasies are exemplified in the Talmudic calculations of the precise number of plagues God visited upon Egypt: 10, 50, 200, 250, and so on. And I haven't even mentioned the harsh invocation "Pour out your wrath upon the nations that do not recognize you and upon the kingdoms that do not invoke your name." The core of the Haggadah (excluding the *Hallel*, the praise liturgy, which was not composed especially for Passover) is grating and hateful, infused with vengeance and evil. Even the traditional *piyyutim*, religious poems, composed after the Haggadah and then appended to it, are ghastly, bloodthirsty compositions. I had innumerable nightmares because of *Had Gadya*, a poem describing the successive killing of a baby goat, the cat that kills it, the dog that bites it, and so on. The images of the *shochet* (the ritual slaughterer) and of the angel of death hovered over my bed, and even God, who "slaughters the angel of death," did not comfort me.

Even granting that the sages of the Talmud composed the Haggadah to shock the children of future generations so that they never forget the Exodus, why choose texts of such poor literary quality? With the rich treasures of the Bible at their disposal, along with its exquisite commentaries and homilies, why did they select this motley crew of curious texts? A reader otherwise unfamiliar with Rabbinic midrash, whose exposure to it comes once a year from the Haggadah reading, will come away unimpressed. Who, after reading the Haggadah, is filled with desire to seek out and study additional midrashim like the ones that describe the exaggerated number of plagues God visited upon Egypt?

⌒

I resolve to find alternative literary sources to the traditional Haggadah but am daunted by the enormity of the task, which touches the core of the most meaningful commemorative night in the Jewish world. It cannot be undertaken lightly; I must investigate the matter thoroughly, maintaining a healthy distance from the current fashion of dispensing with core Jewish texts and customs due to some vague sense that they have lost their relevance. Toward this end, I want to isolate one of the core texts of the Haggadah, a midrash that appears early in the recounting of the Exodus narrative, a declarative text, not particularly charged, in fact rather innocent, through which the Talmudic sages sought to provide a broader social-historical framework to the Haggadah itself.

The passage follows the various declarations enjoined by the Bible: the statement that the matzah is the bread of affliction eaten by the Israelites as they departed Egypt (*ha lahma anya*, "This is the bread of affliction"), and the four questions recited by the children as a pedagogic telling of the Exodus narrative. At this point there appears a debate regarding the recounting of the Exodus at night:

> It happened that Rabbi Eliezer and Rabbi Yehoshua and Rabbi
> Elazar ben Azariah and Rabbi Akiva and Rabbi Tarfon were
> seated in Bnei Berak, recounting the story of the Exodus all
> night long, until their disciples said to them: Our masters, it is
> time to recite the morning *Shema*.[34]

On the face of it, this is an unremarkable story about the sages of the
Mishnah recounting the Exodus all night, so engrossed that they did
not notice dawn had broken. But the continuation of the story indicates this is not a routine occurrence, since it engendered controversy
among the sages of the day:

> Rabbi Elazar ben Azariah said: Behold, I am like a man of sev-
> enty but I did not merit that the Exodus be recounted at night.
> Until Ben Zoma explicated as follows: It is written "So that
> you remember the day of your exodus from Egypt all the days
> of your life." "The days of your life"—this is the days; "All the
> days of your life"—these are the nights. But the sages say: "The
> days of your life"—refers to this world; "All the days of your
> life"—refers to the messianic era."[35]

This debate appears in the Mishnah tractate *Berakhot* (Benedictions).
The Mishnah sages are debating the inclusion of the Exodus narrative
in the recitation of the evening *Shema*, a dispute that was decided as
a matter of law in Ben Zoma's favor, against the view of the majority
of the sages. Subsequent Mishnah commentators are united in understanding this dispute as revolving around the question of whether one
is obligated to recite the final section of the *Shema* liturgy at night, a
section that deals with the commandment to wear *tzitzit*, fringes, in
remembrance of the Exodus out of Egypt. The rabbis ask whether
this is appropriate, since the biblical commandment states explicitly
regarding the four fringes, "And you shall see it" (Number 15:39), but
in the darkness of the night one cannot see the fringes.

But it is perplexing that this dispute is cited in the Passover Haggadah. How is it relevant to the Seder? Such a narrow halakhic matter dealing with the evening prayers has no connection to the Seder
and certainly shouldn't be part of the core statement of the Haggadah.

Why does Rabbi Elazar ben Azariah, who serves as patriarch, accept Ben Zoma's view despite the resistance of the other sages? Ben Zoma was a largely unknown figure, a man who constantly searched for God, even as the world was collapsing around him; a sage who never resorted to easy solutions for his existential anguish, and as a result he eventually "lost his mind."[36]

I begin to understand the symbolic meaning of "night" in the sages' dispute and the reason Rabbi Elazar ben Azariah was so impressed with Ben Zoma's position. For if Ben Zoma holds that it is incumbent upon us to recall the freedom of the Exodus even in times of black night, then surely his view may be accepted. After all, he was not privileged and pampered; he was one of the sages whose probings led him into the black holes of servitude and fear. But even after suffering much sorrow and pain, he tries to remain optimistic: it is necessary to recall the Exodus during "the nights." This reading exposes another dimension to the dispute between Ben Zoma and the other sages: Can the night be seen as a starting point for renewal and redemption? Is our world under the dominion of evil and is there nothing to do but wait for salvation, the time when the gap between God and God's creation will be effaced? Or is there some way to lessen the distance between God and our life here on earth, some way to begin anew, despite everything?

Most of the sages who lived after the destruction of the Second Temple believed that there is nothing to do but wait for God to step in and redeem us. Ben Zoma, however, believed that night is a component of the redemption process, and thus it is incumbent upon us to mention freedom and redemption from the very outset of the process through to its conclusion, that is, from night into day.

This theological debate was at the same time a dispute over man's control over his own fate, over an active versus passive engagement of external reality, and to some extent over the meaning of the physical world. Is it a dark place, a place we must pass through with the utmost care until the Kingdom of Heaven is revealed anew? Or is this world intended from the moment of creation to be good, and it is incumbent upon us to struggle against the evil in it? The latter approach, which refuses to resign itself to the presence of evil in the world, is attributed to Ben Zoma in other Rabbinic sources:

> Ben Zoma says: ... Who is rich? He that rejoices in his portion, as it is written, "You shall eat the fruit of the labor of your hands; you shall be happy, and it shall go well with you" (Psalm 128:2). "You shall be happy"—in this world; "and it shall go well with you"—in the world to come.[37]

Man must find the light even when the world is engulfed in nocturnal darkness.

Ben Zoma holds that the redemptive process begins deep within the heart of darkness. The austere atmosphere of the Seder is, perhaps, intended as a tangible example of how the process of growth and rebirth has its genesis in the darkest and most difficult moment. Sometimes we must first understand that we are in the darkest "night," so that we can proceed to elevate ourselves from it. Perhaps it is best to use the Passover Seder to recall all the forms of evil contained in our imagination, so that we can be free of it the rest of the year.

6

Every year the same promises and the same plans; every year the same disappointment. When all was said and done, I again found myself seated around the same table, with the same relatives, reading the same Passover Haggadah. The very same Seder that reminded me of my past, invoking the same operating room atmosphere of the Passovers of my childhood. At the last minute I pulled back from the plan to celebrate Passover with a close circle of friends in a tent in the desert. And perhaps that is as it should be. Perhaps this is the night that I must traverse within myself in order to arrive at the light of day.

But my time is running out. Passover has come and gone, and summer will soon be upon us. I'm angry at summer and fear the exposure it constantly forces on me, the sweaty humiliation. It is as though all of creation is pointing at me and saying, "A stranger is in our midst."

The counting of the Omer has begun, the forty-nine days between Passover and Shavuot, Pentecost, the holiday of the first harvest and the Sinai epiphany:

> And from the day after the Sabbath, from the day on which you bring the sheaf of the elevation-offering, you shall count off seven weeks; they shall be complete. You shall count until the day after the seventh Sabbath, fifty days; then you shall present an offering of new grain to the Lord." (Leviticus 23:15–16)

The kabbalists have a field day with the counting of the Omer. Seven times seven: what could this signify if not the seven lower *sefirot* that govern our existence here on earth? Accordingly, each of the days of the counting of the Omer is dedicated to the *tikkun* of a different aspect of our lives as it relates to a different *sefirah* within us. According to the kabbalists, this is the proper preparation for Shavuot, when every Jew receives the Torah anew and produces his own individual interpretation of God.

My heart tells me that the counting of the Omer, understood as a process that occurs within the soul, represents a gradual ascent, that is, aims to bring me from the *Malkhut* within me to the *Binah* within me, where I can receive my own Torah anew. Lurianic Kabbalah, however, understands the process as moving in the other direction, beginning with *Hesed* and proceeding down the Tree of the *sefirot* until it lights upon the lowest, *Malkhut*.

In essence, Lurianic Kabbalah asserts that the hidden truth of the ascent lies along the path that leads to the lowest and most terrestrial. On the first day of the counting of the Omer they speak of *"Hesed that is within Hesed,"* examining the radical unboundedness hidden within the power of grace and generosity. The second day—*"Gevurah that is within Hesed"*—establishes internal borders to withstand the urge to burst forth even without set limits and appropriate vessels. On the third day they turn to *"Tiferet that is within Hesed,"* and so on, until they reach Shavuot, *"Malkhut that is within Malkhut."* This is the apex, the day in which all my vessels, even the most humble and earthly, are primed for the reception of my own personal Torah, as though I were standing today at the foot of Mount Sinai, smoke billowing from the mountaintop.

My entire life I have tried to "ascend," to flee my everyday life by elevating myself into the realm of the abstract. In kabbalistic parlance, the counting of the Omer requires that I descend, plunging into the depths of the physical and the material within myself and within my life history; that I scrutinize that realm and there perform my *tikkun*.

What God will I finally encounter when I descend to the base of my own personal Mount Sinai? A king? A friend? A companion? A partner? A tyrant? A merciful father, or perhaps an abusive father? Can all these aspects truly belong to a single God?

The sages of the Talmud tried to inject some order into the various aspects of the biblical God:

> "I am the Lord your God" (Exodus 20:2): Rabbi Haninah bar Pappa said: The Holy One appeared to Israel with a stern face, with a neutral face, with a friendly face, with a joyous face. The stern face is appropriate for the teaching of Scripture—when a man teaches Torah to his son, he must impress upon him his own awe of Torah; with a neutral face appropriate for the teaching of Mishnah; with a friendly face appropriate for the teaching of Talmud; with a joyous face appropriate for the teaching of Aggadah, the homiletic narratives. Therefore the Holy One said to them: Though you see Me in all these guises—"I am the Lord your God."[38]

According to Haninah bar Pappa, God chooses to reveal Himself in different aspects for pedagogic reasons, that is, to demonstrate the importance of donning a different face, as it were, at different stages of the educational process. The more difficult the material being studied, the more pleasant and inviting the teacher should be. Another view in the same Talmud passage, however, is that it is not all a matter of pedagogy, but rather each one of these modes of revelation represents a different aspect of God. Every individual experiences, actually sees, a particular aspect of God:

> Rabbi Levi said: The Holy One appeared to them as though He were a statue with faces on every side, so that though a thousand men might be looking at the statue, they would be led to believe that it was looking at each one of them. So, too, when the Holy One spoke, each and every person in Israel could say, "The Divine Word is addressing me." "I am the Lord your God" is a second person *plural* address; Scripture does not say "I am the Lord your God" in the singular.[39]

Another Talmudic sage was startled to hear Rabbi Levi's argument, fearing it might lead to anthropomorphism, and offered the following corrective: "Rabbi Yose bar Hanina said: The Divine Word spoke to each and every person according to his particular capacity."[40] This variegated epiphany is not, then, an expression of the diversity within God's image and ultimately tells us nothing about God Himself; it is rather a response to the different levels of receptivity and consciousness of every individual.

Later generations have tended to adopt Rabbi Yose bar Hanina's view that divine revelation is filtered through the prism of the individual or the group that experienced it. God, in other words, is immutable. But what makes God God is precisely the exercise of God's will, the divine decision to remove Himself from the vast reaches of His infinity and contract into the world. In other words, the varied forms in which God appears to individuals ultimately reflect variation and change within God Himself. God has no way to be God except through human consciousness, and as the latter changes and evolves, God too changes and evolves, thus manifesting new aspects of His being. Man imagines God in terms of his own cultural and conceptual world, and this imagined God *is* the true, absolute God. It is as though God were created anew for every individual in the image and form of that person. Human subjectivity is the true creator of God.

I have found an ancient midrash about Rabbi Shimon bar Yohai, citing Isaiah 43:12: "'You are My witnesses, says the Lord; and I am God.' Rabbi Shimon bar Yohai teaches: If you are My witnesses, I am God. If you are not My witnesses, I am not God."[41]

Rabbi Shimon bar Yohai seems to assert that if I, and the Jewish people as a whole, do not testify to God's existence, God cannot exist. Moreover, I console myself, this does not mean I have to be more righteous than Rabbi Shimon bar Yohai. I revere God sufficiently to offer my own individual interpretation of God's revelation; no one else can provide God with my interpretation, my witnessing. Like any human being, my humble imagining of God represents a unique interpretation of God's image, an interpretation woven into the great tapestry of mankind's God—thoughts, into all the possible revelations, into all possible life. The endless interpretations we offer to the concept of God *are* the manifestation of the never-ending identity of the all-creating force. Our interpretations endow God with His ever-renewing identity and existence.

The great kabbalists boldly gave voice to similar ideas. Here, for example, is Meir ibn Gabbai, one of the leading kabbalists of the fourteenth century, and his penetrating analysis of Psalm 121:5, "The Lord is your keeper; the Lord is your shadow at your right hand":

> What does "the Lord is your shadow" mean? It means *like* your shadow. Just as with the shadow, if you laugh it laughs back, and if you cry it cries back, and if you look at it with an angry face or a pleasant face—it reciprocates. So too the Holy One Blessed be He, "the Lord is your shadow"—as you are toward Him, so too He is to you.[42]

God captures His reflection from within me and integrates it into His own selfhood. God's comportment depends on my vision of Him.

Conceiving of God in this way is a revolution for me. We, humanity, do not revolve around God's axis, but rather God revolves around ours. In another passage, Ibn Gabbai characterizes this relationship as two taut strings on a single instrument; the vibrations of either one elicits a corresponding resonance in the other. In other words,

God and man are mutually interactive, influencing and altering one another in an ongoing dynamic. Even as we change God, the new image God dons makes its way back to us and helps to change and renew us. Significantly, this is not the idiosyncratic view of a radical thinker. Ibn Gabbai's teachings on this topic are quoted by Rabbi Israel Baal Shem Tov, the founder of Hasidism, by his disciples and by theirs, in turn.[43]

Each person's beliefs may create God, but there is also no deed that does not leave its mark in the world—for better or for worse. The most minute aspect of my actions will remain in the world long after I—and everyone touched by them—have breathed our last. Our every action and inaction roll on and on, leaving their mark on God; as long as man exists, God too exists. Nothing is ever truly lost, nothing fully forgotten within the endless reservoir of God's incessant transformation from "being" to "nothingness" and from "nothingness" to "being."

According to Abraham Joshua Heschel, one of the great religious thinkers of twentieth-century Judaism, the theological cry of the Bible is nothing less than God's endless call, asking me to create Him anew.[44] The cry against idolatry is not reducible to the theological preference of the one against the many, or of the true one against the false many; it is first and foremost the cry of the eternally renewing against those who would try to render God a fixed, fossilized entity. In the words of Moshe Idel, one of the greatest Kabbalah scholars in the world, "Judaism's most important contribution is the imperfect God, God who needs man," to be renewed.[45] Or as the philosopher Eliezer Schweid states, "The image of God that is woven in the space between me and the Infinite—that is the secret of true communication between us."[46]

In this sense, man holds tremendous power. But the corollary is true too: he has a tremendous responsibility over each and every action, over his life and the way he fashions his religious faith. But here the question arises: does the fact that I create God not mean that I am fossilizing God? If so, I am turning God into an idol. Only as long as I continue renewing myself is there a chance that I will avoid turning my God into an idol. The constant renewal of the image of God is directly tied to my own ability to renew myself, to smoothly transition between the various identities I have adopted over the course of my life. If I do not renew myself, my God will not experience renewal, and my worship will become idolatry.

It is my duty to submit to constant change and in so doing transform the image of God within me. But how great is the pleasure and vitality of all this change and renewal! As Rabbi Nahman of Breslov declared, "If I knew I was now standing at the same level as I was last year, I would want nothing to do with myself."[47]

7

In every generation there appears an individual, or perhaps a group, on whom God hangs His hopes: they will lead the way in providing God with the dynamism of His being. In every generation, the Bible provides a figure that animates God, resuscitating Him lest he become a dead deity. When Adam was in the Garden of Eden, he erred in choosing to eat of the fruit of the tree of knowledge of good and evil, a choice that the kabbalists interpret as opting for a life lived solely within contracted reality, divorced from constant contact with *Binah*, the supernal source of effluence and transformation. Abraham apparently failed too when he sought out a clear and understandable God, a God of unfettered *Hesed*.

The next station in God's journey of renewal finds expression in the life of Moses, and now God decides to establish a nation through Moses, an entire civilization that will continually revive and renew His image. Rather than being bound to the life cycle of every individual, living and dying over and over with their lives, God is determined to forge a culture that will constantly transform Him, a culture whose foundation is endless renewal.

In preparation for Shavuot, the commemoration of the giving of the Torah at Sinai, I turn once again to God's first, private revelation to

Moses at the burning bush, where He identifies Moses as the leader destined to lead the Israelites out of Egypt.

Moses, who fled Egypt after slaying an Egyptian man, took refuge in the desert and married Zipporah, the daughter of Jethro, a Midianite priest. One day, while herding his father-in-law's flocks, he saw a burning bush that was not consumed.

> God called to him out of the bush, "Moses, Moses!" And he said,
> "Here I am." Then he said, "Come no closer! Remove the sandals
> from your feet, for the place on which you are standing is holy
> ground." He said further, "I am the God of your father, the God
> of Abraham, the God of Isaac, and the God of Jacob." And Moses
> hid his face, for he was afraid to look at God. (Exodus 3:4–6)

God informs Moses that he has decided to take the Israelites out of Egypt, their house of bondage, into freedom, and asks him to serve as His elect messenger. But Moses is skeptical and cautious and in no rush to accept such a daring mission from a God he does not know: "Moses said to God, 'If I come to the Israelites and say to them, "The God of your ancestors has sent me to you," and they ask me, "What is His name?" what shall I say to them?'" (Exodus 3:13).

Why does Moses ask God for his name? God has just identified himself as the God of Abraham, Isaac, and Jacob. Why doesn't "the God of your ancestors" suffice? What does it mean that Moses is inquiring as to God's name? And I cannot help noticing that Moses addresses his divine interlocutor as *Elohim*, "God," even though God, speaking from His own divine self-consciousness, refers to Himself as *Adonai*, "Lord." Moses is clearly not satisfied with the name *Elohim* (even while using it to address God) and demands that God reveal His essence more fully. In the Bible, names are definitions, demarcating the essence of a man or of God. Viewed in this light, God's response is enigmatic: "God said to Moses, 'I will be what I will be.' He said further, 'Thus you shall say to the Israelites, "I will be has sent me to you"'" (Exodus 3:14).

God initially identifies Himself to Moses in a simple, straightforward way: "I am the God of your ancestors." But when Moses insists on hearing God's name, he receives a curious answer: "I will be what I will be." But God is not satisfied with this ambiguous response and amends His answer by omitting an important part of it: 'Thus you shall say to the Israelites, "I will be has sent me to you." But even this will not do, and God continues to redefine Himself: "God also said to Moses, 'Thus you shall say to the Israelites, "The Lord, the God of your ancestors, the God of Abraham, the God of Isaac, and the God of Jacob, has sent me to you": This is my name forever, and this my title for all generations'" (Exodus 3:15). Only now, on the third iteration, does God formulate a name that is accessible to the Israelites. He is "the Lord, the God of your ancestors."

These verses provide the reader with a brief glimpse into God's own deliberations as He tries to choose His name and define Himself. This revelation, the first in the book of Exodus, is really a renewal of the revelation process after many years with no contact between the God of Abraham, Isaac, and Jacob, and the patriarchs' descendants. It is portrayed as a very complex and tentative process. Preceding the rebirth of the nation, it marks a type of divine rebirth. It is as though the reader is allowed to watch, in real time, as God gazes at His new identity. God emerges, like a butterfly from its chrysalis, awakening from a long slumber and trying to define anew His essence and function, to become reacquainted with Himself.

What takes place in this process of divine reacquaintance? God answers this question quite literally: I will be what I will be, that is, I am whoever I am. Could the plain meaning of this answer be simply: "I do not know"? Could it be that Moses asks God, What is your name? and God essentially answers, I can don so many different aspects that I cannot commit to any one fixed identity. One of the authors of the Zohar, Rabbi Moshe de Leon, interprets the phrase "I will be what I will be" as "I currently am and will in the future construct my being; I will emanate all being into actuality," for "His being, may He be blessed, did not come into existence previously."[48] God's ambiguous answer does not mean He is too abstract for human understanding, but rather that He is not sure what He will be, since ultimately His being is contingent upon the development of human consciousness from one generation to the next and from one individual to the next.

As happens so often when we speak too honestly, God's strikingly frank revelation to Moses leads to serious trust issues. The biblical chapters recounting the Israelite Exodus out of Egypt concern questions of trust. Moses speaks to God of his concern that the Israelites will not believe him, so God provides him with signs and miracles, and the Israelites initially believe him but then lose faith. Later, during the desert wanderings, we see constant fluctuations in the Israelites' trust in God and in God's trust in the Israelites. Trust and mistrust are the key motifs in the national birth and maturation of Israel.

To my mind, the burning bush narrative, more than any other biblical text, holds the key to understanding God and trusting in Him. Moses does not ask whether what he observes is a divine revelation or perhaps some apparition, like the magic tricks practiced by Pharaoh's sorcerers. The question of trust is both much broader and much deeper than that. God reveals Himself in order to send Moses on a long and arduous mission to found a nation. This is a tremendously ambitious project that covers the transition from enslavement to freedom, the trek to the national homeland, and establishing new guidelines by which to live.

That is why, when Moses asks God's name, God does not provide a clear answer. Moses wants to know what type of divinity God will be two centuries hence, but God cannot even tell Moses who He will be in two days: "I will be what I will be." Moses does not ask, Are You or are You not God? but rather, Can I count on You when You are sending me off on this mission? But God cannot make any commitments regarding the future. Essentially, He responds: I know I will be something, but I do not know what. I can be God in countless ways, but I do not know what kind of God I will be in the future. Moses is struggling to decide whether he can begin a long-term relationship with such a God, to establish a covenant with the God of such a nebulous plan. After all, who is to say that after Moses leads Israel to Canaan, God will not demand something else or *be* someone else? God Himself does not know what the future will bring. He simply allows this new relationship to develop between Himself and His people, as it will shape Him anew generation after generation.

God's response "I will be what I will be" is one of the most tender and honest moments in the Bible. God knows He stands on the threshold of a new, dynamic relationship and is committed to staying open and flexible. But right after this honest moment of self-revelation, God comes to His senses and understands that this complex truth will not do—it is not the least bit reassuring and will not win much trust. After all, God is sending Moses to the Israelites, a people in a state of terrible distress, physically and psychologically enslaved. God understands this even as He is speaking and offers Moses a corrective: spare them the whole "I will be what I will be" story; offer them instead the abbreviated form, "I will be." But no sooner has he spoken than God understands that even this response is too vague, too nebulous, and He offers a further compromise. Moses is to introduce God to the Israelites as "the Lord, God of your ancestors," a phrase that encompasses all the attributes that surfaced from between the lines of God's dialogue with Moses.

But the tribulations of this ever-changing God do not end here. Though God has furnished Moses with signs and miracles to help him overcome the Israelites' lack of faith, Moses comes up with a new excuse: he is not suited to be God's messenger because he stutters. Moses carefully chooses the words by which to communicate to God that his speech is impeded: "O my Lord, I have never been eloquent, neither in the past nor even now that You have spoken to Your servant; but I am slow of speech and slow of tongue" (Exodus 4:10). In Hebrew, this verse has an unusually high number of words that begin or end with "m," probably the most difficult sound for stutterers. In other words, Moses puts on the full stutterer-show for God, and we have to assume it took him a good few minutes to finish the sentence. But, as we know, God is not impressed and duly instructs Moses to conscript his brother, Aaron, as his spokesman.

The narrative then turns to one of the oddest episodes in the Bible:

> Moses went back to his father-in-law Jethro and said to him, "Please let me go back to my kindred in Egypt and see whether they are still living." And Jethro said to Moses, "Go in peace." The Lord said to Moses in Midian, "Go back to Egypt; for all those who were seeking your life are dead." So Moses took his wife and his sons, put them on a donkey, and went back to the land of Egypt; and Moses carried the staff of God in his hand.... On the way, at a place where they spent the night, the Lord met him and tried to kill him. But Zipporah took a flint and cut off her son's foreskin, and touched his feet with it, and said, "Truly you are a bridegroom of blood to me!" So he let him alone. It was then she said, "A bridegroom of blood by circumcision." (Exodus 4:18–20, 4:24–26)

One day God speaks to Moses as a true friend, with astounding openness, discussing matters of identity alongside historic missions and grand promises. Now suddenly He wants to kill him? One thing this passage makes clear: Moses had not circumcised his son. Circumcision, then, is likely the key to the entire obscure episode, since it concludes the story and immediately causes God to let Moses be.

The Talmudic sages tried to unravel this mysterious tale:

> "On the way, at a place where they spent the night"—circumcision is dear to God since He did not allow Moses to tarry in its completion even an hour. Therefore, when Moses was journeying and stopped at the inn and lazily put off circumcising his son, Eliezer, immediately ... "the Lord met him and tried to kill him"—even though He was a messenger of mercy, all the same "he tried to kill him"; "But Zipporah took a flint"—and how did Zipporah know that Moses's life was in danger on account of circumcision? An angel came and swallowed Moses from his head down to his circumcised member. When Zipporah saw that he swallowed him up to that point, she realized that Moses's injury had to do with circumcision, for she recognized the great power of circumcision was preventing the angel from

swallowing Moses any further. Immediately, she "cut off her son's foreskin and touched his feet with it, and said, 'Truly you are a bridegroom of blood to me!'" She said: You will be my bridegroom, you are given to me by the power of this circumcision blood since I fulfilled the commandment without delay. "A bridegroom of blood by circumcision," announcing the power of circumcision by asserting, My bridegroom was condemned to death for his lazy tarrying in fulfilling this commandment. Were it not for her, he would not have survived.[49]

In other words, God cannot wait even a moment for Moses to circumcise his son, but Moses tarries. God appears to Moses in the form of an angel and wants to kill him. How does Zipporah know that she must circumcise her son in order to save her husband's life? The biblical account of this eerie encounter provides few details, so the Talmudic exegetes complete the picture: Zipporah saw an angel (or a serpent) swallowing Moses from his head to the site of circumcision. In other words, Moses's uncircumcised son is the root of the matter.

I have never taken the Rabbis' Bible exegesis at face value. Repeated readings have taught me that they were genuinely wise readers, who concealed their thoughts between the lines, sometimes under the guise of curious legends and dicta. At first blush, this story appears rather ridiculous. But maybe Moses's "laziness" regarding his son's circumcision should be interpreted as his ambivalence or even resistance to accepting God's covenant, a covenant that will endure over the course of his son's life. I see here a clear echo to Abraham's resistance to establishing the "Covenant Between the Pieces" with God, a fixed covenant with a God that is endlessly changing. When Abraham flees from the Void Space within the Divine, he is instructed to circumcise himself and his son. Moses is perhaps a more responsible figure than Abraham, for he does not rush to maintain even this already established covenant.

That Moses avoids circumcising his son is undoubtedly a mark of his ambivalence. He is not sure if he should include his children in the relationship he maintains with God. God has revealed to Moses the true nature of things, that God's paths are unknown and forever changing, and Moses, in response, fails to circumcise his son. God is so angered by Moses's refusal to enter into a relationship with Him, especially when this refusal was preceded by God's honest self-revelation, that in His rage He wishes to kill Moses. Zipporah quickly grasps what is occurring and circumcises her son. This is a terrible theological and ideological battle between God and Moses, which is resolved by a third, unanticipated player. Thus, Zipporah becomes the first to establish the covenant between Israel and the new God who is revealed in Egypt.

The speed with which God sets the Israelites at the foot of Mount Sinai, so soon after the Exodus, is undoubtedly a reflection of His own urgent need to be renewed and revived. The Bible describes a rushed God, determined to accomplish His goal and place an entire nation at Sinai, so He can then declare His identity: "I am the Lord your God, who brought you out of the land of Egypt, out of the house of slavery; you shall have no other gods before me" (Exodus 20:2–3). Traditional interpreters and Bible scholars alike have noted that the Decalogue is not phrased as a legal document; it is not, in other words, another collection of laws like those found in the Bible and the surrounding ancient cultures. No, the Sinai epiphany has, it seems, one purpose and one purpose only: to lay out the ground rules of the unique God of Israel.

This is a God who addresses the individual ("your God" is second person singular in the Hebrew) as a free man or woman ("who brought you out of the land of Egypt, out of the house of slavery"); a God whose most sublime form of revelation comes in a "face-to-face" encounter. Since the encounter is with the "face," with the ultimate mark of the personal, it is not surprising that Israel is prohibited from worshipping graven images, frozen depictions of the Divine, with no possibility of renewal and rebirth; a God who commands that we not take in vain our language and our speech, the tools with which we create our world and our thoughts ("You shall not take the name of the Lord your God in vain"); a God who worries lest we forget that creation is an ongoing process in which we are partners, so He asks us to sanctify one day of the week to remember and remind others that it is possible to change pace, that we can all take a break from the ongoing race ("Remember the Sabbath day and keep it holy"); a God who forbids us to forget our past ("Honor your father and your mother, so that your days may be long in the land the Lord God has given you"), since the sustained presence of our specific cultural heritage is the only guarantor of a long life "in the land" God has given us; a God who forbids us to take another person's life, since all men are created in God's image, and all men guarantee God's perpetual change ("You shall not murder"); a God who forbids us to steal from ourselves and from others, who obligates us to create our lives for ourselves; a God who instructs us not to steal, not to covet, not to commit adultery, not to adopt false identities that are not the product of our own self-renewal, since only self-renewal allows God His true liberty, and us ours.

The Decalogue is not a set of laws. The Ten Commandments lay the groundwork for any future revelation, any future renewal. The Ten Commandments are the periodic table for any person who hopes to receive divine revelation within himself and to continue evolving, lest he turn into a graven human who worships a frozen god.

8

What would my good friend say about this discourse on faith, when he is doing all he can to restore basic sensory perception to his paralyzed daughter? She is breathing on her own, but the left side of her body does not respond to her brain's commands, and she still cannot talk. Is it even possible for me to speak with him of my very flexible notion of faith when he so desperately needs every possible shred of clear, solid faith?

Apparently not. I do not know any of us who could retain our sanity in such difficult times without a very solid foundation of faith. He would probably repeat the same thing he said to me a few years back: that he feels sorry for people like me, forever trying to navigate between the religious and the secular, who cannot fully enjoy either world without being haunted by a sense of guilt.

Suddenly, I understand the Israelites who received the Ten Commandments at Sinai and immediately turned to worship the golden calf. I would have joined them, too, were I compelled to live in constant fear of an inscrutable future. When God announced Himself as a personal deity, one whose image and future are contingent on the future consciousness of human beings, the Israelites mistakenly thought they could shape God in the form that best suited them at the moment, one familiar to them from the time as slaves in Egypt. There are scholars who identify the golden calf with the sacred Egyptian bull, chosen on the basis of miraculous signs, whose gait and direction were used for divination by its priests. Perhaps, then, Israel cannot bear this ever-changing God whose own fate is unknown, and turn instead to an unambiguous god who knows their fate. They beseech Aaron, the priest, saying, "Come, make gods for us, who shall go before us" (Exodus 32:1).

If mine is a personal God, a God I can shape as I see fit, why not shape Him with the same ease, the same comfort that I enjoy right now? Given my fears and anxieties about the future, why must I set out on a journey through the Void, why shape myself anew, suffering the excruciating pain of shedding my old skin, and only then dare to shape the image of my God? Why not shorten the process and shape Him right now, skipping the process of renewal and regrowth?

Worshipping the golden calf means living according to a clear plan, working toward a set, determined future. This is the constant temptation for any free person who has received the great gift of a free God: the temptation to remain as I am, to shape the image of God within me and the image of God within God based on the mask I have on right now.

For the kabbalists, the Israelites worship the golden calf not because they immediately forget the Sinai epiphany or because they suddenly experience a terrible spiritual descent. Nor are they grasping after a tangible object, a statue, to hold onto. It is rather God's awesome epiphany that reveals to them the gap between the heavenly worlds and our earthly reality, and the ensuing realization that they will have to inhabit this gap from that point on. The Israelites are privy to a revelation and spiritual ascent like no other, but they also come to see reality differently. There can no longer be a clear, unambiguous God in their daily lives. Indeed the world of revelation and the experience of the quotidian world are sundered: there exists a sublime God who may occasionally break into our reality to cause miracles, but our world is fundamentally divorced from God and is governed by its own rules. Moreover, physical reality requires a dividing screen, a visible, tangible mask, something we can point to and lean on and depend on over time.

The Israelites divide existence into two realms: God, who is in a perpetual state of self-renewal, on one side, and God's frozen manifestation within our lived reality, on the other. They believe not that there are two gods (though many people interpret the golden calf episode in this manner), but rather that humanity is trapped in the physical world, with no channels of communication to what lies beyond our world. In this sense, the golden calf is not the result of their having forgotten the Sinai epiphany, but on the contrary, of their having experienced it.

After the Sinai epiphany, the Israelites grasp for the first time what they are up against, what is being asked of them. They understand that they are dealing with a God they must shape over and over again from within themselves, a dynamic and self-renewing God that becomes a graven image when we try to define or fossilize Him. The golden calf episode is, as it were, their protest: we inhabit the physical world and cannot maintain open lines of communication with such a God. God has no permanent place in our world because He lacks a clear definition. But reality demands of us clearly demarcated vessels, unambiguous formulas and definitions. The human mind cannot maintain itself in a state of constant chaos. We may be able to grasp the sublime from time to time, granted occasional flashes, special moments of revelation. But the giving of the Ten Commandments on Sinai made a very different set of demands: to live our daily lives while maintaining a constant dialogue with this unknowable God.

It is not for naught that Zachariah describes the end-time as follows: "On that day, the Lord will be one and His name one" (Zachariah 14:9). The prophet is suggesting not that there will be no idols or competing deities, but rather that God's name, which is now bifurcated, will be made whole and united. But the fracture the golden calf caused in God's name will not heal easily; its rehabilitation requires the efforts of many generations.

Following the Israelites' decision to worship the golden calf, God asks Moses to carve a new set of tablets, completely different from the first. These tablets are not God's handiwork. God remains hidden, no longer willing to reveal Himself "face-to-face." They are the product of Moses's human labor. This is why the second set of tablets communicates not universal instructions amenable to various personal interpretations, but rather clear directives: to conquer, to expel, to divide, to avoid the idolatry of the Canaanites.[50] Directives suited for a clear-cut reality, with an ominous promise of pain and danger at every step. The realms are clearly demarcated.

The divine project known as "the Sinai epiphany" is based on a divine call to Israel to accept the mission of becoming a nation that lives outside of reality or, more precisely, on the threshold of reality. Only this type of dynamic existence can serve as a relay station of sorts between God and the world, since the abstract infinite cannot manifest itself in our material existence; it cannot penetrate into created reality. God leads Israel out of Egypt as part of a plan to separate one group from among the nations and have it plant one foot in terrestrial life, the other beyond quotidian reality. Only a group such as this could heal, could effect a *tikkun*, in God's bifurcated name.

The Israelites, however, reject this role; they refuse to serve as the bridge between chaotic infinity and the finitude of material reality. There would be a price to pay: a life without clear and certain knowledge, without clearly demarcated vessels, a life situated within the material though an existential abyss yawned at their feet. A life of eternal twilight, a nether reality in a no-man's-land neither here nor there; in short, life in the Void. Such a life is terribly difficult and complex, but it is the only life in which I can take root and bloom.

The golden calf episode and the breaking of the first set of tablets mark a turning point in the history of the biblical God and a profound rupture in the history of Israel, a radical shift from one form of revelation to another. The generation of the Exodus was sentenced to death in the desert, but not as some pedagogic punishment for the golden calf. There *is* no punishment for such an act. The golden calf episode transforms the state of the God-man relationship from one that does not require clear rules and regulations ("face-to-face") to one in which man, awash in the quotidian, cannot survive without them. And so Israel received laws and continues receiving laws. Many laws.

Even if the second set of tablets contains the same familiar text of the Decalogue, its meaning is now radically different. No longer an infinite interpretive freedom ("freedom [*herut*] on the tablets" in the Rabbinic phrase, punning on "engraved [*harut*] on the tablets")[51], these are clear, unequivocal laws, delivered in a voice that bespeaks violence, separation, and intimidation.

From this point on, the work of effecting *tikkun* in God becomes much more complicated. As soon as one begins to work within a model of laws and definitions, it grows increasingly difficult to break out of it. The only way to do so is by carving out of our imprisoning concrete reality some point of contact with the Void of infinite possibilities. Mired as we are in laws and regulations, we can hardly ignore them, but we can stretch their boundaries and so renew ourselves, a little each day.

There is a wonderful reading of the golden calf episode in the teachings of Rabbi Moshe Hayyim Efraim of Sadilkov, one of the founders of Hasidism. He links God's instruction that Moses make a second set of tablets, *pesol lekha* ("fashion for yourself"; Exodus 34:1), with *lekh lekha* ("Go forth!"; Genesis 12:1), with which God sent Abraham on his journey to the Void Space. The key word is the emphatic *lekha*:

> For this word is recognized as alluding to the idea that every Jew
> has a root and a letter in the Torah, as per the saying "The Torah,

the Holy One blessed be He, and Israel—are all one,"[52] and when a Jew sins, God forbid, he blemishes the letter of the Torah to which he is bound, casting a pall upon its light, but when he repents it returns to its original state and illuminates the light of Torah anew. And this is alluded to in the Torah's account following the sin of the golden calf ... as it is written, "Cut two tablets of stone like the former ones, and I will write on the tablets the words that were on the former tablets, which you broke" (Exodus 34:1), that is, letters and words that existed previously but that you broke.[53]

Rabbi Efraim of Sadilkov reads "fashion for yourself" as an active command that spans all generations and marks the beginning of the hard labor required to retrieve the original source of the letters. It is incumbent upon us to search the harsh laws of the second tablets and recover from them the now lost sense they possessed, prior to the golden calf episode. The process of repentance is understood here as a return to the original state of things, an individual process, which is why God says "fashion *for yourself*." Each of us has our own process of *tikkun*. Each of us must extract our own face from the laws. For what is a law? A generally applicable, public instruction. Repentance is the process by which we extract from these general rules our own private meaning.

The shift from the first set of tablets to the second is simultaneously a shift from personal interpretive freedom to public law enforcement. The *tikkun*, however, moves in the opposite direction, from the social to the individual, from the fixed and fossilized to the dynamic and changing.

We create God anew in every generation, every day, and every hour, and thus God and man find themselves in a state of interdependence and reciprocal reflection. Every era and every aspect of Jewish culture create a new God. We experience a new aspect of God every time, and this is perhaps the secret vitality of Judaism. The God of Israel can don a new face through the mind and heart of every believer, young and old alike.

We each carry within us, from early childhood, a different image of God. The question is whether the portrait of God we carry in our hearts changes over time or, like an undeveloped fetus preserved in formaldehyde, remains unchanged over time even as we grow and mature. Now, if the unchanged and unevolved portrait of God is best suited for me, it is no wonder I cannot use it over the course of the new trials, difficulties, and joys that are part of my life. No, I cannot live my life fully with fossilized images of some god who has not matured since my childhood. These images of the Divine will forever condemn me to life with the god of the golden calf.

What God will I choose for myself on the eve of Shavuot, the holiday of the first fruit of the harvest, the holiday of the new offering I must bring from the fresh harvest of my land?

9

It is the eve of the new month of Elul. Twenty years exactly since the Elul when I left the yeshiva, never to return. I am on my way back from the modest celebration my friend hosted, giving thanks for his daughter's recovery from her accident nearly a year ago. Eleven long months of unremitting agony, daily fluctuations between life and death, between guarded optimism and total despair. His close family, a few friends, and the doctors who cared for his daughter, both in the hospital and in the rehabilitation clinic—all have been invited to celebrate the miracle, before our hearts grow accustomed to the girl's astounding transformation.

Magnanimity and humility permeate the modest banquet hall in the ultra-Orthodox Jerusalem neighborhood of Me'ah She'arim, generally the site of bar mitzvah and bris celebrations for low-income families. A leading expert on neurosurgery speaks plainly in the presence of his junior colleagues of how my friend's faith-based decision not to allow his daughter's head to be operated on was apparently the best possible choice. My friend's daughter then recites, her voice cracking, the *Hagomel*, the traditional blessing for those who have survived danger. Her vocal chords have not fully healed from the pulmonary fluids that entered her throat, and her left limbs have not regained full movement. But my friend whispers in her ear, promising her he will always care for her more than for any of her seven siblings.

Suddenly I see a man, roughly my age, his black hair beginning to gray and his beard whitening. I recognize him instantly, a friend from my lost world, my best friend and roommate throughout my yeshiva years. For years we slept with our beds facing each other, on either side of the window. He was my partner in late-morning study, and we often wandered together through the hills surrounding the yeshiva. He even came from Bnei Berak once to sleep over at my parents' house, while the yeshiva was on break.

I call out to him. He takes hesitant steps in my direction. I do not understand his hesitation. "It's me, Dov"—I get up and stretch my hand out to him. He stops in his tracks, observes me silently, and finally admits, "I did not recognize you." "How could you not recognize me?" I press him. "I haven't changed that much." He quickly explains that he had imagined me quite differently.

We stop speaking and step out of the hall. I offer to drive him to Bnei Berak; we could use the ride as an opportunity to renew our acquaintance. I apologize and make a call on my cell phone, canceling an appointment scheduled for later in the day. He is struck by my manners. "You're too courteous," he says. "But I was always like that," I respond, perplexed. He does not agree: "You were never so restrained, so withdrawn." "How was I?" I ask; I really do not remember. "You were always like the sun, shining, bursting forth, open and burning and bright," he says. Then he pauses before continuing: "Until you extinguished yourself."

"What do you mean? Why do you say that?" I protest, remembering his old betrayal, forging my signature twenty years ago, though I immediately decide to hold my tongue. I discreetly take out a small tape recorder that I carry with me to my lectures, and I press "record." This time, I decide, I'll be silent, I will only listen. I won't argue, won't flaunt my erudition and abilities. I will be attentive to my very core.

I listen silently. He speaks of how, with my help, he was able to transform himself from a taciturn, brooding teenager to an open and confident young man. He reminds me how I convinced him to come jogging with me every night, a couple of miles around the yeshiva town; how I collected statements by halakhic authorities supporting the position that it is a religious obligation to strengthen the body in order to better serve God and study Torah. He also reminds me of our long nature walks, and my old hobby—scaling steep rocks and high walls. "And then you changed," he suddenly thunders at me. "You began to fast, you stopped speaking for months. You became a *tzaddik*," he says, emphasizing the last word. "You became someone you weren't."

The space between us grows more transparent, more diaphanous. I open the car window a bit, but the wind's howl is deafening. I close the window and cannot restrain myself. "It's precisely the opposite. It was during my time as a '*tzaddik*' that I felt closest to my true essence, closest to God. Nothing was fake." My voice grows hoarse; I am almost shouting. "Are you suggesting—are you suggesting that all this happened when I was alienated from myself, when I was not being who I truly am?" He corrects himself immediately. "Perhaps I misspoke. I never thought you lied or faked anything. I think you neglected or suppressed an important and authentic aspect of yourself. It was clear to me that you would pay a high price."

10

We are in the midst of Elul, but I do not feel the old shudders that reverberated in me during all the Eluls of my youth: the Elul when I arrived at the yeshiva, twelve and a half years old and alone, with only an old suitcase; the Elul when I changed course and began my fasts and ascetic exercises; the Elul when I hurried out of the yeshiva, never to return.

This Elul, my heart has grown dull. Every day, I sink deeper into the facial nerve pains that have grown increasingly severe of late. I have no faith in the path I have traveled over the past year, in the journey into my Voids. I go to yet another doctor in the hope that he will diagnose me and relieve these pains. He recommends that I have all my old fillings and root canals reopened. But my pains only grow worse. I spend my days taking double doses of painkillers. Every night I collapse into my bed early, falling asleep only to wake up after midnight, restless. My heart has grown callous and uncaring, my decisions are not decisions, my thoughts are not thoughts, and already Rosh Hashanah leaps toward me like the grasshoppers in my backyard. I have not been able to prepare my heart for the upcoming Jewish New Year or give myself a full account of the one that passed.

On the last evening of the passing year, I drive to Jerusalem to visit my parents and wish them *shanah tovah*, a good new year. I arrive a little early and go to a Sephardic synagogue by their house to hear the *Selihot* service—the penitential liturgy recited on the days leading up to the High Holy Days. "Master of forgiveness, who examines our inner thoughts, revealer of deep secrets," I permit myself to hum along with the congregation. When we come to the verses that conclude the *Selihot* service—"The Lord reigns, the Lord did reign, the Lord will reign forever and ever" recited aloud several times—my mouth suddenly rebels. How can I lie, pretending to accept God's kingship, when I reject the king-slave relationship altogether? I have traveled too far to define my relationship with God in these terms.

How, then, should it be defined? Here again is the question I have been struggling with all year. What am I to Him? What is He to me? What narrative will I tell myself in the coming year? Who will be my God, even if only for the immediate future? I do not have a faith "narrative" like my good friend, whose daughter's life is no longer in danger.

The consoling autumn of this hilltop city cannot becalm my restless state. I conclude the *Selihot* and, as is customary, walk with one part of the congregation and stand before another group that is now seated on the synagogue benches. For the purpose of this service, the sitting group serves as a makeshift Jewish court, whose function is to annul the oaths of those standing before them.

"Hearken, expert judges," I call out with the rest of the standing group, accepting the authority of regular congregants who happened to pass by the synagogue and joined the service: "All personal oaths and pledges, obligations, or swears, that I have vowed, whether in a dream or awake ... I request that they be annulled and regret all the matters, whether pertaining to monies, or to the body, or to the soul—I regret them all.... And though by law the one who regrets his oaths and wishes them annulled must enumerate them, know this, sirs, they cannot be enumerated for they are many, nor do I ask you to annul oaths that cannot be annulled—so please consider them as though I had enumerated them."

After briefly adjourning, and without pretrial deliberations or expert testimonies, the sitting judges declare the annulment, repeating the formula three times, as if to force it into the depths of our consciousness: "Let them all be annulled for you, all forgiven, all permitted. There exists no oath or pledge or obligation or vow or prohibition or curse. There is only forgiveness and absolution and reprieve. As they are annulled by this earthly court, so let them be annulled in the heavenly court."

During Rosh Hashanah I spend many hours meditating on the holiday liturgy. This is the first time in twenty years that I really try to understand the idea of God's kingship, a motif that recurs in many Rosh Hashanah prayers and liturgical poems. In my prayers back then, God was still a high and mighty king, the sovereign of the universe. All things were God's and anything I took from the world I took from Him, with no hope of ever repaying Him. What have I to do with this king? I ask myself, and refuse to recite the words that may have been appropriate two millennia ago but mean little to anyone who did not grow up in a monarchy. My meditation on kingship is followed by a meditation on memory, another important component of the traditional Rosh Hashanah service, the memory of the binding of Isaac, the memory of the merits of the patriarchs, of Abraham, Isaac, and Jacob, of Joseph and David, recalled throughout the synagogue service.

But I am not in synagogue. This Rosh Hashanah I am praying at home, sitting in the garden and reading the High Holy Day prayer book, waiting until I feel ready to blow the shofar for my wife and daughters. The hoarse voice rising from the depths of my being, channeled through the depths of the ram's horn, bursting from the shofar's mouth like a wordless lament, awakens in me the memory of my conversation of a month earlier with my old friend.

Only now can I reflect on how strongly I resisted his perspective, resisted listening openly to the view of a person who was so very present in my life back then, that when I thought I was getting in touch with my most authentic inner self I was actually turning my back on a no less important and no less authentic part of myself. I spent most of the past year becoming conscious of my body, yet I remain too stiff-necked to admit it to myself: he is right and I am wrong. I remain steadfast, refusing to let him rob me of the pure, virginal tears, pouring forth from me in the prayers of my youth. My body cries out, my pains grow stronger, but still I continue to quarrel with his claims, a supplicant grasping the horns of the memory altar, doing anything to avoid having to confess to him, in my heart: you are right.

The voice of another's blood cries out to me from my childhood, another that I have suppressed and covered over.

Twenty years after that formative year, I find myself willing to accept God as king as well. It is not that I have condemned myself to slavery or declared myself the king's son or close friend. I see God now as a king in exile, my partner in the need to annul childhood oaths, a fellow traveler in the exilic journey through the world of *Malkhut*: the world of deeds, of contractions, of ends, of suffering and of limitations.

Our bloody wounds bandaged, God and I wander hither and yon, sometimes drawing near, other times marching side by side, searching for healing, for redemption, for a new name. Thus, we grope along in the moonlight, turning to an ancient sun whose light has dimmed, both praying that it shine again. Like two sojourners, we hope to meet up from time to time and mutter to each other the words that absolve one of transgressions committed against his fellow man: "You are forgiven, you are forgiven, you are forgiven."

The Ten Sefirot

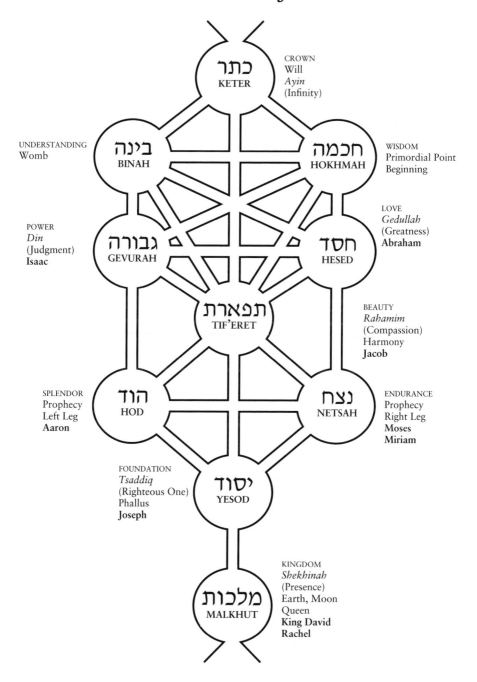

כתר
KETER

CROWN
Will
Ayin
(Infinity)

בינה
BINAH

UNDERSTANDING
Womb

חכמה
HOKHMAH

WISDOM
Primordial Point
Beginning

LOVE
Gedullah
(Greatness)
Abraham

POWER
Din
(Judgment)
Isaac

גבורה
GEVURAH

חסד
HESED

תפארת
TIF'ERET

BEAUTY
Rahamim
(Compassion)
Harmony
Jacob

SPLENDOR
Prophecy
Left Leg
Aaron

הוד
HOD

נצח
NETSAH

ENDURANCE
Prophecy
Right Leg
Moses
Miriam

FOUNDATION
Tsaddiq
(Righteous One)
Phallus
Joseph

יסוד
YESOD

KINGDOM
Shekhinah
(Presence)
Earth, Moon
Queen
King David
Rachel

מלכות
MALKHUT

Acknowledgments

Some journeys never end, and that appears to be the fate of the one I sought to recount in this book. I do not have more answers today than when I set off, but I have gained some insight into the narrations and the emanations that make up my life. I hope and pray that this journey will help other travelers, and will allow me to set off on future journeys more easily, unencumbered by the heavy cargo I shouldered this time around.

Many have accompanied me on this journey, and I offer them my heartfelt thanks. First and foremost, I thank the many Jewish sages over the centuries, whose teachings I hungrily consume and whose influence on my life and my Jewish identity I feel each and every day. I am referring particularly to the great masters of Kabbalah and of Hasidic thought, in all their manifold systems and doctrines, without whom I cannot conceive of my own Jewishness. Of these, allow me to note a small number, a tiny fraction, really, whose influence on my life is particularly marked: Rabbi Azriel of Gerona, the authors of the Zohar, Rabbi Moshe Cordovero, Rabbi Isaac Luria and his disciples, and Rabbi Moshe Hayyim Luzzatto. And from among the great Hasidic masters: the Maggid Dov Baer of Mezritch, Rabbi Moshe Hayyim Efraim of Sadilkov, Rabbi Joshua Heschel of Apta, Rabbi Yehudah Leib of Gur, Rabbi Pinchas of Koretz, and Rabbi Menachem Mendel of Kotzk. And, of course, Rabbi Nahman of Breslov, whose writings have held me in their grip for many years now. I must not omit from this list some of the great Jewish thinkers of recent generations: Rabbi Abraham Joshua Heschel, Martin Buber, Rabbi Abraham Isaac Kook, and Arthur Green. Many scholars of Kabbalah and Hasidism have illuminated my path with their studies: Gershom Scholem, Joseph Weiss, Isaiah Tishby, Yehuda Liebes,

Moshe Idel, Haviva Pedaya, and many others, more than can be listed here. Needless to say, responsibility for errors and misunderstandings lies with me alone.

Boundless thanks to my friend and editor, Avraham Shapira, a unique midwife of Jewish culture and Jewish literature. His encouragement and the breadth of his erudition were a constant support throughout this journey. Countless thanks also to George S. Eltman, Deborah Harris, and Stuart Matlins for editing this English edition. My heartfelt thanks to my students and colleagues at BINA's Beit Midrash (Tel-Aviv). Through shared study we arrived at important insights into Kabbalah and Hasidism. The administrators and faculty of this center welcomed me with an open heart, and it was under its auspices that much of this book was composed.

To my wife, Carmit, and our daughters—eternal love.

Notes

Chapter One
Keter—Invisible Beginnings

1. See M. Halamish, Hannah Kasher, and Yohanan Silman, eds., *The Faith of Abraham* (Ramat Gan: Bar-Ilan University Press, 2002).

2. Maimonides, *Code of Jewish Law* (*Mishneh Torah*), Laws of Idolatry 1:3.

3. Dov Elbaum, *Zman Elul* (Tel Aviv: Am Oved, 1997).

4. Some scholars argue that the term derives from *mispar* ("number"), others connect it with "sphere," and still others with "sapphire."

5. According to Nahmanides's commentary on *Sefer Yetzirah*. See Gershom Scholem, *Origins of the Kabbalah*, trans. Allan Arkush (Princeton, NJ: Princeton University Press, 1987), 365–475; on the concept of "contraction" (*tzimtzum*), see Moshe Idel, "On the History of the Term *Tzimtzum* in Kabbalistic and Scholarly Literature" (Hebrew), *Jerusalem Studies in Jewish Thought* 10 (1992): 59–72.

6. *Sefer Yetzirah*, 2.6, from Aryeh Kaplan, *Sefer Yetzirah: The Book of Creation* (York Beach, ME: Samuel Weiser, 1997), 131.

7. See the discussion in Gershom Scholem, *Major Trends in Jewish Mysticism* (New York: Schocken Books, 1954), 325–350.

8. This concept is first advanced in *Midrash Tanhuma*, pericope *Pikude*, 3. Later kabbalistic thinkers transform the equation such that one can gain insights into the nature and character of God by observing human beings. See, e.g., Zohar III, 33b.

9. *Genesis Rabbah* 9:2.

10. The traditional interpretation of this verse is found in the Babylonian Talmud, *Pesahim* 50a.

11. Zohar III, 103a.

12. Isaiah Tishby, *The Doctrine of Evil and the Husks* (Kelippot) *in Lurianic Kabbalah* (Hebrew) (Jerusalem: Schocken Books, 1942).

13. "*Derush Heftzi Bah*," 1c, discussed in Tishby, *Doctrine of Evil*, 56–61.

Chapter Two
Hokhmah—The Abyss from Which None Ever Returns

1. Joseph ibn Tabul, Luria's student, wrote a commentary on the same verse in his essay "*Sod ha-Tanin*"; see also Gershom Scholem, *Sabbatai Sevi*, trans. R. J. Zwi Werblowsky (Princeton, NJ: Princeton University Press, 1976), 298–300.

2. *Likkute Moharan* 64, trans. Moshe Mykoff (Jerusalem and New York: Breslov Research Institute, 2003), with minor modifications. The passage in question is found in vol. 7, p. 384.

3. In other words, the two opposites that encompass the entire creation. According to Rabbi Hayyim Vital, there is an equal distance from *Ein Sof* to all the points of the circles that God vacated and each element of created reality. See *Etz ha-Hayyim*, the Teaching of the Circles and the Straight Line, first Sanctuary, Adam Kadmon, Branch 2.

4. The term "measures" refers to time and space, or perhaps to time and the divine *sefirot* that express this new space.

5. *Likkute Moharan* B, 84.

6. Ibid.

7. "Intellect and letters" refers to the letters of Hebrew and the discursive, rational thought that is based on language and finds expression in letters.

8. *Likkute Moharan* 64 (Mykoff, 7:392–394).

9. "Cross" in the sense of "pass over," that is, to go past the problem without ignoring it. There may also be an allusion to "Across the River," a kabbalistic term for *Binah*. See, e.g., the river imagery associated with *Binah* in Isaiah Tishby, *The Wisdom of the Zohar*, trans. David Goldstein (Portland, OR: Littman Library, 1989), 1:350–351.

10. *Likkute Moharan* 64 (Mykoff, 7:396–398).

11. See in particular the studies of Joseph Weiss, *Studies in Breslav Hasidism* (Hebrew) (Jerusalem: Mosad Bialik, 1975); Arthur Green, *Tormented Master: A Life of Rabbi Nahman of Bratslav* (New York: Schocken Books, 1981); Tzvi Mark, *Mysticism and Madness in the Writings of Rabbi Nahman of Breslav* (Hebrew) (Tel Aviv: Alma and Am Oved, 2003).

12. The terminology follows the *"Ra'ayah Mehemana"* passage in Zohar III, 225a, and *Tikkunei ha-Zohar*, 5a.

13. *Likkute Moharan* 64 (Mykoff, 7:398–399).

14. Rabbi Nahman does not employ the Lurianic terminology of the "straight line" penetrating the "circle," but there is no reason to think that he denied its validity. To my mind, Rabbi Nahman avoids these terms because he considers them too rudimentary, since the question does not deal with the process of creation but rather with what lies beyond it.

15. "Intellect" here refers to human thought, which is also derived from letters, that is, from a discursive contraction. In this Rabbi Nahman follows the famous passage from Zohar II, 23a–b: "'The Enlightened will shine' (Daniel 12:3)—Who are the Enlightened? It is the wise man who, of himself, looks upon things that cannot be expressed orally" (see Tishby, *Wisdom of the Zohar*, 1:322–324). In this sense, the Void Space does not even contain that symbolic conceptualization of reality.

16. According to Rabbi Nahman's interpretation, this Talmudic phrase means "thus it emanated, thus it was revealed, in Thought."

17. *Likkute Moharan* B, 84.

18. According to the Aharon Applefeld, *Sippur Hayyim* (Tel Aviv: Keter, 1999), 150.

19. From the writings of his disciples it is clear that Rabbi Nahman held Cordovero's teachings in the highest regard.

20. Following the Zohar interpretation that associates the Hebrew name of God, *Elohim*, with the words *mi eleh* ("who are these"), which are made up of the same letters. According to the Zohar, the *sefirot* can be divided into two groups: those that can be referred to ("these") and those about whom one can only ask ("who"). See Tishby, *Wisdom of the Zohar*, 1:331.

21. See Moshe Cordovero's commentary to *Sefer Yetzirah* ("The Book of Creation"), chap. 1, sec. 7.

22. The higher aspect of *Hokhmah*, which is tied to *Keter*.

23. Joseph Gikatilla, *Gates of Light*, Gate Nine. An English translation exists (Joseph Gikatilla, *Gates of Light*, trans. Avi Weinstein [Lanham, MD: AltaMira, 1994], 337–338) but the translation here is by Azzan Yadin.

24. *Likkute Moharan* (Mykoff, 11:172).

25. See *Sichot ha-Ran* 77.

26. *Likkute Moharan* 64 (Mykoff, 7:411–413).

27. Ibid. (7:413).

28. Rabbi Nahman here alters the traditional sense of "actions." Though it generally refers to the practical commandments, Rabbi Nahman uses it to refer to the creation of the world and perhaps to the tales of actions, *ma'asiyot*, that he told toward the end of his life.

29. *Likkute Moharan* 64 (Mykoff, 7:419).

30. For additional discussion of this silence, see Melilah Hellner-Eshed on the Zohar's vocabulary of the mystical experience, *A River Issues from Eden: On the Language of Mystical Experience in the Zohar* (Tel Aviv: Alma and Am Oved, 2005), 412–414.

31. *Likkute Moharan*, 64, 5 (Mykoff, 7:425).

32. Ibid. (7:423).

Chapter Three
Binah—The Sound of a Serpent Shedding Its Skin

1. Rabbi Nahmnan made this statement to his disciples prior to deciding to have one of his manuscripts burned.

2. Palestinian Talmud, *Pe'ah* 3a.

3. Zohar I, 38a. And see Yoni Garb, "The Mystery of Faith in the Zohar," in *On Faith*, eds. Moshe Halbertal, David Kurzweil and Avi Sagi (Jerusalem: Keter, 2005 [Hebrew]), 297.

4. See Gershom Scholem, "New Fragments from the Writings of Rabbi Azriel of Gerona," in *Studies in Memory of A. Gulak and S. Klein* (Jerusalem: Hebrew University, 1942), 207. Elsewhere, Scholem notes the similarity between Rabbi Azriel's position and that of Scotus Erigena in *De divisione naturae* 1:72. See Scholem, *Origins of the Kabbalah*, 440–442.

5. There were kabbalists who understood the Hebrew word for "faith," *emunah*, as tied to *omenet*, a midwife, the body from which all reality nurses its sustenance. See Gershom Scholem, *Be-ikvot Mashiach* (Jerusalem: Tarshish, 1944), 39.

6. Rabbi Hayyim Vital, *Sha'ar Hakavanot*, "Nocturnal Meditations," Homily 3.

7. For Luria, faith is also found in *Malkhut*, since in his system each *sefirah* divides into ten internal *sefirot*. Thus, *Binah* or *Hokhmah* within *Malkhut* represents the location of faith.

8. Zohar I, 122b; 76b; 79b; *Zohar Hadash*, pericope *Lekh Lekha*, 30b, and Ruth 82a.

9. See *Likkute Moharan*, 275 (Mykoff, 11:346–348). Needless to say, the Hebrew word for "free," *hofshi*, did not then carry the sense of "secular," as it does in certain circles today.

10. Natan of Nemirov, *The Praise of Rabbi Nachman* (Lembers, 1876), paragraph 34.

11. *Genesis Rabbah* 68:9: "The Holy One blessed be He is the place of the world, but the world is not His place."

12. Zohar III, 168a.

13. Babylonian Talmud, *Yoma* 20b.

14. See Yehudah Liebes's fascinating article, "'Two Young Roes of a Doe': The Secret Sermon of Isaac Luria before His Death," *Jerusalem Studies in Jewish Thought* 10 (1992): 113–169.

15. Rabbi Meir Nahum of Chernobyl, *Maor va-Shemesh*, pericope *Aharei Mot*, s.v. "*ve-nire'h.*"

16. Rabbi Hayyim Vital, *Sha'ar Hagilgulim*, introduction 17.

17. Rabbi Moshe Hayyim Luzzatto's commentary to Leviticus, pericope *Behar*, s.v. "*ve-kidashtem.*"

Chapter Four
Hesed—The Fiery Sword of Abraham

1. Moses Maimondes, *Mishneh Torah, The Laws of Idolatry*, trans. Eliyahu Touger (New York and Jerusalem: Maznaim, 1990), 22–23.

2. Zohar I, 78a, trans. Harry Sperling and Maurice Simon, *The Zohar* (London: Soncino, 1932), 1:264.

3. In kabbalistic symbolism, the name *Elohim* also refers to *Binah*, the *sefirah* that borders on the Void Space.

4. *Sefer ha-Bahir* §190 (Kaplan, 75).

5. *Tikkunei ha-Zohar* 90a. This book was composed by an anonymous mystic who apparently lived about a hundred years after the composition of the Zohar. It is characterized by uncompromisingly mystical interpretations of the Bible and greatly influenced later kabbalists and Hasidic thinkers.

6. See Nahmanides's sharp rebuke in his commentary to Genesis 19:8: "This is nothing more than wickedness."

7. See Martin Buber, *Tales of the Hasidim: The Early Masters*, trans. O. Marx (New York: Schocken Books, 1957), 65.

Chapter Five
Gevurah—Isaac's Ashes Lie Heaped upon the Altar

1. For an earlier, less comprehensive discussion of Isaac's life, see my book *My Life with the Forefathers* (Tel Aviv: Am Oved, 2000).

2. The phrase "fear of Isaac" originates in Genesis 31:53, where "Jacob swore by the fear of his father Isaac." Abraham ibn Ezra interprets this as an allusion to the binding, and I find this reading compelling. But it is only in an early liturgical poem (traditionally attributed to Rav Amram Gaon, but apparently of earlier provenance) that "fear of Isaac" comes to refer to Isaac, just as the other phrases in the *piyyut* refer to the other patriarchs.

3. *Genesis Rabbah* 65.

4. The kabbalistic transformation of *Gevurah* into a force of evil and impurity is a complex issue unto itself, which I discuss in greater detail in chapter 10. Here I am focusing only on the basic identification between Isaac and this *sefirah*.

5. This identification occurs throughout the Zohar but is particularly common in the pericopes *Vayehi* and *Pinhas*. As a rule, I am not concerned with the structures the kabbalists "impose" on the patriarchs as much as the interpretive associations that might result from these identifications. Still, it should be noted that these kabbalistic structures, and *Sefer ha-Bahir* in particular, which identify Abraham, Isaac, and Jacob with *Hesed*, *Gevurah*, and *Tiferet*, respectively, understand Isaac as having had this *sefirah* imposed upon him. Abraham, by contrast, is said to have taken *Hesed* for himself. This, in any case, is the reading in Rabbi Joseph Gikatilla, *Gates of Light*, chap. 5.

6. I am well aware of the harmonistic explanations put forth by traditional commentators as to the location of Abraham, Sarah, and Isaac. To my mind, the plain sense of the biblical narrative makes these interpretations improbable.

7. As many commentators have noted, this is the site where Hagar, Ishmael's mother, encounters the angel after she was driven out by Abraham and Sarah.

8. The dictum of the sages, originally made in a different context, is apt: "The chatter of the fathers' servants is better than the children's learning" (*Genesis Rabbah* 60:11). See also Nehama Leibowitz, *New Studies in Bereshit* (Hebrew) (Jerusalem: Ha-Histadrut ha-Zionit, 1996), 162, who examines the discrepancies in the servant's account but explains them differently.

9. I find the traditional interpretation of Rebecca's response as an indication of "modesty" completely implausible.

10. I am following Nahmanides, who, in his commentary to the Torah, notes the depletion of Abraham's inheritance. He does not allude to Isaac's "character" as a contributing factor.

11. This is the prevalent opinion among most source critical scholars.

12. Note the language of Genesis 26:1: "There was a famine in the land—aside from the previous famine that had occurred in the days of Abraham—and Isaac went to Abimelech the king of the Philistines, in Gerar."

13. This reading of Isaac's sojourn among the Philistines may shed light on God's commandment at the beginning of the journey to Gerar: "Do not go down to Egypt; stay in the land that I point out to you" (Genesis 26:2). The psychological process of exposing scars must be undertaken with great care.

14. Rabbi Moshe Hayyim Luzzatto's commentary to Genesis, pericope *Toledot*.

15. Ibid.

16. *Likkute Moharan* 61 (Mykoff, 7:250–252).

17. "Isaac pleaded with the Lord on behalf of his wife, because she was barren; and the Lord responded to his plea and his wife, Rebecca, conceived" (Genesis 25:21). Unlike the prayers of Abraham and Jacob, the Bible does not quote the content of Isaac's plea, but only the circumstances surrounding it.

18. Babylonian Talmud, *Eruvin* 13a.

Chapter Six
Tiferet—Integrity beyond Truth

1. Joshua Heschel of Apta, *Ohev Israel*, New Selections to the Book of Genesis.

2. Moses Maimonides, *The Commentary to Mishnah Aboth*, Mishnah 2:5, trans. Arthur David (New York: Bloch, 1968), 33.

3. Rabbi Moshe Hayyim Efraim of Sadilkov, *Degel Mahane Efraim*, pericope *Vayishlah*, s.v. "*vaye'avek.*"

4. See Zohar I, 174a for a discussion of these shifts.

5. The Babylonian Talmud (*Berakhot* 13a–b) states explicitly that the shift from Jacob to Israel was not absolute: "Not that 'Jacob' was wholly uprooted, but that 'Israel' became the main name, and 'Jacob' relegated to secondary status." The Talmud goes on to say that after the night at the Yabbok ford, 'Israel' reverted to 'Jacob,' and so on.

6. See the impressive psychoanalytic discussion in Erich Neumann's article in *Keshet* 10 (1961).

Chapter Seven
Netzah—Miriam, Prophetess of Water

1. *Genesis Rabbah* 65:20.

2. Babylonian Talmud, *Hagigah* 14b.

3. Babylonian Talmud, *Berakhot* 61b. Translation based on H. N. Bialik and Y. H. Ravnitzky, *The Book of Legends*, trans. William G. Braude (New York: Schocken Books, 1992), 238.

4. Babylonian Talmud, *Eruvin* 21b, following Bialik and Ravnitzky, *Book of Legends*, 237.

5. Babylonian Talmud, *Menahot* 29b.

6. Babylonian Talmud, *Shabbat* 31a.

7. *Genesis Rabbah* 24:7.

8. Mishnah *Yadayim* 3:5.

9. Mishnah *Gittin* 9:10.

10. Moses Maimonides, *Mishneh Torah*, The Laws of Repentance, 10.3, trans. Eliyahu Touger (New York and Jerusalem: Maznaim, 1987), 222.

11. Moses Maimonides, *Mishneh Torah*, The Laws of Personality Developments, 4:19, trans. Eliyahu Touger and Ze'ev Abramson (New York and Jerusalem: Maznaim, 1989), 78.

12. Babylonian Talmud, *Nedarim* 9b.

13. *Sifre Zuta* 12, s.v. "*va-tedabber.*"

14. Tosefta *Sukkah* 3:11.

15. The original justification was Moses's striking the rock instead of speaking with it.

16. *Mekhilta of Rabbi Ishmael*, Shirata 3 (Lauterbach ed., 2:24).

Chapter Eight
Hod—Bar Yohai, the New Interpreter of the Body

1. This is, e.g., the interpretation of Rabbi Joseph Gikatilla in chap. 2 of *Gates of Light* (p. 62 in the English Weinstein ed.).

2. Zohar III, 127 (Tishby, *Wisdom of the Zohar*, 1:155–156).

3. See the Babylonian Talmud, *Eruvin* 21b: "Rabba expounded: What is the meaning of the verse 'Come, my beloved, let us go into the field; let us lodge among the towns. Let us go early to the vineyards; let us see if the vine has flowered, if its blossoms have opened, if the pomegranates are in bloom. There I will give my love to you' (Song of Songs 7:12-13)? 'Come, my beloved, let us go into the field'—the Congregation of Israel said to the Holy One blessed be He, 'Master of the World, do not judge me as You would the city dwellers, who are mired in thievery and sexual transgressions, and false vows and perjury'; 'let us go into the field'—'Come, I will show you Torah scholars who devoted themselves to their studies despite their poverty'; 'let us lodge among the towns'—do not read *kefarim* ("towns") but rather *koferim* ("heretics"), those to whom you have granted beneficence, but they have denied your existence; 'Let us go early to the vineyards'—this refers to the houses of prayer and the houses of study."

4. Zohar III, 127 (Tishby, *Wisdom of the Zohar*, 1:156).

5. This is why traditional translations of the Zohar from Aramaic to Hebrew omit the *Idra Rabba* altogether.

6. Zohar III, 127.

7. Babylonian Talmud, *Shabbat* 33b (Bialik and Ravnitzky, *Book of Legends*, 249).

8. Ibid.

9. Babylonian Talmud, *Shabbat* 33b (Bialik and Ravnitzky, *The Book of Legends*, 250).

10. Zohar I, 171a (Sperling and Simon trans., 2.153–154). Needless to say, the Zohar does not understand this as a sign of Moses's weakness, as per my interpretation in the previous chapter.

11. Zohar I, 171a (Sperling and Simon trans., 2.154).

12. See Zohar I, 171a and 203b.

13. Rabbi Yehudah Leib of Gur, *Sefat Emet*, to Genesis, pericope *Vayishlah*.

14. *Likkute Moharan*, 22 (Mykoff, 3:341).

15. Ibid. (3:341–343).

16. Ibid. (3:343).

17. Tishby, *Wisdom of the Zohar*, 1:364–365.

18. Ibid., 1:365.

19. Ibid.

Chapter Nine
Yesod—All the Dreams

1. Rashi's interpretation is alluded to in *Yalkut Shimoni* to Proverbs, 26, paragraph 561.

2. *Genesis Rabbah* 98:18.

3. This discussion is from the Babylonian Talmud, *Sotah* 36b.

4. The phrase "his bow remained taut" can be vocalized so as to read "his bow returned," which the Rabbis then interpret as an indication that Joseph's "bow," that is, his penis, returned to its previous state.

5. Babylonian Talmud, *Yoma* 86a.

6. Following Benno Jacob, the Bible scholar. See also Leibowitz, *New Studies in Bereshit*, 301, though she ultimately rejects this approach.

7. Zohar I, 191b (Pritzker Edition, trans. Daniel C. Matt, [Palo Alto, CA: Stanford University Press], 2004, 3.169–170).

8. *Genesis Rabbah* 89:6.

9. See, e.g., Hayyim Vital, *Sha'ar ha-Pesukim*, pericope *Vayeshev*, s.v. *"ve-zeh biu'ro."*

10. *Likkute Moharan Tanyana*, 67.

11. *Likkute Moharan* 19 (Mykoff, 3:120).

12. The Hebrew *lishbor shever* means "to purchase food," but *shever* also means "break, rupture," so the passage can be interpreted as the brothers coming to Egypt to break with the rupture that occurred in their life when they sold Joseph into slavery.

Chapter Ten
Malkhut—All the Fears

1. Babylonian Talmud, *Yoma* 86b.

2. In *Megid Mesharim*, Rabbi Joseph Karo holds conversations with the Mishnah, which reveals to him supernal secrets. See also Rabbi Joseph Gikatilla's *Sha'are Tzedek*, and the discussion in Moshe Idel, *Le Porte della Giustizia* (Milan: Adelphi, 2001).

3. One example is the Baal Shem Tov's "Epistle on the Ascent of the Soul," first published at the end of Rabbi Jacob Joseph of Polonnoye's *Ben Porat Yosef* (Korets, 1781). For a comprehensive discussion of this epistle, see Haviva Pedaya, "The Besht's Epistle on Holiness," *Zion* 70 (2005): 311–354.

4. "Essay on the Emanation of the Left Side by Rabbi Isaac ben Jacob Hakohen," published by Gershom Scholem in *Mada'ei ha-Yahadut* 2 (1927): 244–264.

5. See Tishby, *Wisdom of the Zohar*, 2:454 ("*Sitra ahra* is to the *sefirot* as the ape is to man").

6. The *Sitra Ahra*'s only authentic power is the particle of creativity it has as a result of its links with the positive aspects of *Gevurah*. As noted, God's contraction into an identifiable entity required the creation of a limiting and containing element that carries within it a kernel of finitude. The forces of the *Sitra Ahra* use this creative kernel, radicalize it, and enhance it, until it leaves the bounds of the divine system, becoming its own system, self-centered and egoistic, that follows its own rules.

7. Zohar II, 103a.

8. See *Peri Etz ha-Hayyim*, "*Sha'ar ha-Tefilin*" 12.

9. The account of the four who entered the *pardes* (orchard) is found in the Babylonian Talmud, *Hagigah* 14b–15a. A shorter and altogether different version is found in Tosefta *Hagigah* 2:2.

10. Zohar II, 242b–246b (Paul Levertoff trans. in Matt, *The Zohar*, 4.325; translation altered). In this sense, male and female symbolize the evil that bursts forth from man and the evil that man internalizes from other sources, respectively.

11. See Hizkuni's commentary to Genesis 45:24: "'Do not *rogez* on the way'—do not be fearful of anything." See also Rabbi David Kimchi's commentary to 1 Samuel 14:15, "the land was *rogez*," and M. Kedari, *Dictionary of Biblical Hebrew* (Ramat Gan: Bar Ilan University Press, 2006), 987.

12. See Zohar II, 87a.

13. Rashi to Deuteronomy 25:10: "This refers to a chance occurrence," and similarly Rabbenu Bahya and Rabbi Shemuel ben Meir in their commentaries. The kabbalists connect the root *k-r-h*, "occur," to *keri*, "nocturnal emission," interpreted as an encounter with the forces of evil and impurity. See, e.g., Zohar II, 195a.

14. *Pesikta of Rav Kahana* 3:16: "R. Berechiah said in the name of R. Abba bar Kahan: As long as Amalek's seed endures in the world, it is—if one dare speak thus—as though a pennant hid God's face. Once the seed of Amalek perish, 'your Teacher will not hide himself any more, but your eyes shall see your Teacher' (Isaiah 30:20)," in *Pesikta de-Rab Kahana*, trans. William G. Braude and Israel J. Kapstein (Philadelphia: Jewish Publication Society, 2002), 76.

15. Martin Irving Mantel, *Rabbi Nachman of Bratzlav's Tales: A Critical Translation from the Yiddish with Annotations and Commentary* (dissertation, Princeton University, 1977), 297; translation altered.

16. Ibid., 298.

17. Rabbi Nahman here alludes to the verse "You hem me in, behind and before, and lay your hand on me" (Psalm 139:5), which the Rabbis interpret as a reference to the two faces of the androgynous Adam, prior to the creation of Eve.

18. Mantel, *Rabbi Nachman's Tales*, 298.

19. Ibid., 298–299. Note further Rabbi Nahman's assertion that "through the commandment of ransoming captives one becomes worthy of distinguishing between those two houses mentioned above, between truth and deceit, between the king and the slave, the aspect of cursedness of 'Cursed be Canaan; lowest of slaves shall he be to his brothers' (Genesis 9:25)" (ibid., 298).

20. Rabbi Joshua Heschel of Apta, *Ohev Yisrael*, Zekhor and Purim, s.v. "*ve-al pi zeh neva'er ketzat inyanei purim.*"

21. Following *Tikkunei ha-Zohar*, *tikkun* 21, 57b. It is worth noting that this source too speaks of costumes, linking the special Yom Kippur garments of the high priest to Queen Esther's garments. This may be one of the earliest theological sources for the tradition of dressing up at Purim, a custom that spread throughout the Jewish world beginning in the Middle Ages.

22. Rabbi Yehudah Leib of Gur, *Sefat Emet* to Exodus, the Purim homily. I heard a different interpretation of this phrase in tragic circumstances, when the author David Grossman eulogized his son, Uri, of blessed memory, who was killed in battle in the summer of 2006. According to Grossman, *la'amod al nefesh* means to obstinately hold to the sensitivity and compassion within us, and resist our own tendencies toward violence and aggression.

23. Babylonian Talmud, *Shabbat* 88a.

24. Rabbi Zadok Hakohen of Lublin, *Resisei Lailah*, 58.

25. Mishnah *Avot* 5:7 (Danby translation).

26. Joshua Heschel of Apta, *Ohev Yisrael*, Zekhor and Purim, s.v. "*Pirkei de-Rabbi Eliezer.*" He cites this interpretation in the name of the Maggid of Mezritch, the great disciple of the Baal Shem Tov, who turned Hasidism into a mass movement.

27. Ibid.

28. Ibid.

29. *Likkute Moharan*, 153 (Mykoff 10:234).

30. Ibid. (10:234–236).

31. *Likkute Moharan*, 245 (Mykoff 11:220).

32. Several passages attest to this view in the writings of the Maggid of Mezritch, i.e., *Magid Devarav le-Ya'akov* and *Likkute Amarim*. See the copious citations collected in Rivka Schatz-Uffenheimer, *Hasidism as Mysticism: Quietistic Elements in Eighteenth Century Hasidic Thought*, trans. Jonathan Chipman (Princeton, NJ: Princeton University Press, 1993), especially chaps. 2 and 7.

33. Rabbi Tzvi Elimelech of Dinov, *Igra de-Kallah*, 323a.

34. From the Passover Haggadah.

35. From the Passover Haggadah, following Mishnah *Berakhot* 1:5.

36. See the Babylonian Talmud, *Hagigah* 15a–b.

37. Mishnah *Avot* 4:1 (Danby trans.).

38. *Pesikta of Rav Kahana* 12:25 (Braude and Kapstein, 333).

39. Ibid.

40. Ibid.

41. *Sifre Deuteronomy* 346. The same midrash appears in *Pesikta of Rav Kahana* 12:6 and was discussed at length by the German Jewish philosopher Franz Rosenzweig, "Atheistic Theology," in *Franz Rosenzweig: Philosophical and Theological Writings*, ed. and trans. Paul Franks and Michael L. Morgan (Indianapolis: Hackett, 2000), 10–24.

42. Meir ibn Gabbai, *Tola'at Ya'akov*, 4a, and see Moshe Idel, *Kabbalah: New Perspectives* (New Haven: Yale University Press, 1988), 173–178.

43. See, e.g., Rabbi Levi Yitzhak of Berditchev, *Kedushat Levi*, 39c; and Idel, *Kabbalah: New Perspectives*, 178–179.

44. See Abraham Joshua Heschel, *God in Search of Man* (New York: Farrar Straus, 1955).

45. In *Questions Concerning God* (Hebrew), eds. Yizhar Hess and Elazar Sturm (Jerusalem: Shorashim, 1998), 133.

46. Ibid., 35–36.

47. *The Praise of Rabbi Nachman*, paragraph 34.

48. Moses de Leon, *Shekel ha-Kodesh*, ed. Charles Mopsik (Los Angeles: Cherub, 1995), 3.

49. *Exodus Rabbah* 5:8.

50. See Exodus 34:10–17.

51. See, e.g., *Exodus Rabbah* 32:1 and many parallels.

52. Zohar III, 273.

53. Moshe Hayyim Efraim of Sadilkov, *Degel Mahane Efraim*, pericope *Ki Tisa*.

AVAILABLE FROM BETTER BOOKSTORES.
TRY YOUR BOOKSTORE FIRST.

Bible Study / Midrash

Passing Life's Tests: Spiritual Reflections on the Trial of Abraham, the Binding of Isaac *By Rabbi Bradley Shavit Artson, DHL*
Invites us to use this powerful tale as a tool for our own soul wrestling, to confront our existential sacrifices and enable us to face—and surmount—life's tests.
6 x 9, 176 pp, Quality PB, 978-1-58023-631-7 **$18.99**

The Messiah and the Jews: Three Thousand Years of Tradition, Belief and Hope *By Rabbi Elaine Rose Glickman; Foreword by Rabbi Neil Gillman, PhD; Preface by Rabbi Judith Z. Abrams, PhD*
Explores and explains an astonishing range of primary and secondary sources, infusing them with new meaning for the modern reader.
6 x 9, 192 pp, Quality PB, 978-1-58023-690-4 **$16.99**

Speaking Torah: Spiritual Teachings from around the Maggid's Table—in Two Volumes *By Arthur Green, with Ebn Leader, Ariel Evan Mayse and Or N. Rose*
The most powerful Hasidic teachings made accessible—from some of the world's preeminent authorities on Jewish thought and spirituality.
Volume 1—6 x 9, 512 pp, Hardcover, 978-1-58023-668-3 **$34.99**
Volume 2—6 x 9, 448 pp, Hardcover, 978-1-58023-694-2 **$34.99**

Masking and Unmasking Ourselves: Interpreting Biblical Texts on Clothing & Identity *By Dr. Norman J. Cohen*
Presents ten Bible stories that involve clothing in an essential way, as a means of learning about the text, its characters and their interactions.
6 x 9, 240 pp, HC, 978-1-58023-461-0 **$24.99**

The Genesis of Leadership: What the Bible Teaches Us about Vision, Values and Leading Change *By Rabbi Nathan Laufer; Foreword by Senator Joseph I. Lieberman*
6 x 9, 288 pp, Quality PB, 978-1-58023-352-1 **$18.99**

Hineini in Our Lives: Learning How to Respond to Others through 14 Biblical Texts and Personal Stories *By Rabbi Norman J. Cohen, PhD* 6 x 9, 240 pp, Quality PB, 978-1-58023-274-6 **$16.99**

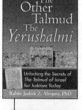

The Modern Men's Torah Commentary: New Insights from Jewish Men on the 54 Weekly Torah Portions *Edited by Rabbi Jeffrey K. Salkin*
6 x 9, 368 pp, HC, 978-1-58023-395-8 **$24.99**

Moses and the Journey to Leadership: Timeless Lessons of Effective Management from the Bible and Today's Leaders *By Rabbi Norman J. Cohen, PhD*
6 x 9, 240 pp, Quality PB, 978-1-58023-351-4 **$18.99**; HC, 978-1-58023-227-2 **$21.99**

The Other Talmud—The Yerushalmi: Unlocking the Secrets of The Talmud of Israel for Judaism Today *By Rabbi Judith Z. Abrams, PhD*
6 x 9, 256 pp, HC, 978-1-58023-463-4 **$24.99**

Sage Tales: Wisdom and Wonder from the Rabbis of the Talmud
By Rabbi Burton L. Visotzky 6 x 9, 256 pp, HC, 978-1-58023-456-6 **$24.99**

The Torah Revolution: Fourteen Truths That Changed the World
By Rabbi Reuven Hammer, PhD 6 x 9, 240 pp, HC, 978-1-58023-457-3 **$24.99**

The Wisdom of Judaism: An Introduction to the Values of the Talmud
By Rabbi Dov Peretz Elkins 6 x 9, 192 pp, Quality PB, 978-1-58023-327-9 **$16.99**

Or phone, fax, mail or e-mail to: **JEWISH LIGHTS Publishing**
Sunset Farm Offices, Route 4 • P.O. Box 237 • Woodstock, Vermont 05091
Tel: (802) 457-4000 • Fax: (802) 457-4004 • www.jewishlights.com
Credit card orders: (800) 962-4544 (8:30AM–5:30PM EST Monday–Friday)
Generous discounts on quantity orders. SATISFACTION GUARANTEED. Prices subject to change.

Congregation Resources

Jewish Megatrends: Charting the Course of the American Jewish Future
By Rabbi Sidney Schwarz; Foreword by Ambassador Stuart E. Eizenstat
Visionary solutions for a community ripe for transformational change—from fourteen leading innovators of Jewish life.
6 x 9, 288 pp, HC, 978-1-58023-667-6 **$24.99**

Relational Judaism: Using the Power of Relationships to Transform the Jewish Community *By Dr. Ron Wolfson*
How to transform the model of twentieth-century Jewish institutions into twenty-first-century relational communities offering meaning and purpose, belonging and blessing.
6 x 9, 288 pp, HC, 978-1-58023-666-9 **$24.99**

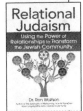

Revolution of Jewish Spirit: How to Revive *Ruakh* in Your Spiritual Life, Transform Your Synagogue & Inspire Your Jewish Community
By Rabbi Baruch HaLevi, DMin, and Ellen Frankel, LCSW; Foreword by Dr. Ron Wolfson
A practical and engaging guide to reinvigorating Jewish life. Offers strategies for sustaining and expanding transformation, impassioned leadership, inspired programming and inviting sacred spaces.
6 x 9, 224 pp, Quality PB Original, 978-1-58023-625-6 **$19.99**

Building a Successful Volunteer Culture: Finding Meaning in Service in the Jewish Community *By Rabbi Charles Simon; Foreword by Shelley Lindauer; Preface by Dr. Ron Wolfson*
6 x 9, 192 pp, Quality PB, 978-1-58023-408-5 **$16.99**

The Case for Jewish Peoplehood: Can We Be One?
By Dr. Erica Brown and Dr. Misha Galperin; Foreword by Rabbi Joseph Telushkin
6 x 9, 224 pp, HC, 978-1-58023-401-6 **$21.99**

Empowered Judaism: What Independent Minyanim Can Teach Us about Building Vibrant Jewish Communities *By Rabbi Elie Kaunfer; Foreword by Prof. Jonathan D. Sarna*
6 x 9, 224 pp, Quality PB, 978-1-58023-412-2 **$18.99**

Finding a Spiritual Home: How a New Generation of Jews Can Transform the American Synagogue *By Rabbi Sidney Schwarz*
6 x 9, 352 pp, Quality PB, 978-1-58023-185-5 **$19.95**

Inspired Jewish Leadership: Practical Approaches to Building Strong Communities
By Dr. Erica Brown 6 x 9, 256 pp, HC, 978-1-58023-361-3 **$27.99**

Jewish Pastoral Care, 2nd Edition: A Practical Handbook from Traditional & Contemporary Sources *Edited by Rabbi Dayle A. Friedman, MSW, MAJCS, BCC*
6 x 9, 528 pp, Quality PB, 978-1-58023-427-6 **$35.00**

Jewish Spiritual Direction: An Innovative Guide from Traditional and Contemporary Sources
Edited by Rabbi Howard A. Addison, PhD, and Barbara Eve Breitman, MSW
6 x 9, 368 pp, HC, 978-1-58023-230-2 **$30.00**

A Practical Guide to Rabbinic Counseling
Edited by Rabbi Yisrael N. Levitz, PhD, and Rabbi Abraham J. Twerski, MD
6 x 9, 432 pp, HC, 978-1-58023-562-4 **$40.00**

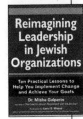

Professional Spiritual & Pastoral Care: A Practical Clergy and Chaplain's Handbook
Edited by Rabbi Stephen B. Roberts, MBA, MHL, BCJC
6 x 9, 480 pp, HC, 978-1-59473-312-3 **$50.00**

Reimagining Leadership in Jewish Organizations: Ten Practical Lessons to Help You Implement Change and Achieve Your Goals *By Dr. Misha Galperin*
6 x 9, 192 pp, Quality PB, 978-1-58023-492-4 **$16.99**

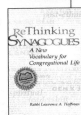

Rethinking Synagogues: A New Vocabulary for Congregational Life
By Rabbi Lawrence A. Hoffman, PhD 6 x 9, 240 pp, Quality PB, 978-1-58023-248-7 **$19.99**

Spiritual Community: The Power to Restore Hope, Commitment and Joy
By Rabbi David A. Teutsch, PhD
5½ x 8½, 144 pp, HC, 978-1-58023-270-8 **$19.99**

Spiritual Boredom: Rediscovering the Wonder of Judaism *By Dr. Erica Brown*
6 x 9, 208 pp, HC, 978-1-58023-405-4 **$21.99**

The Spirituality of Welcoming: How to Transform Your Congregation into a Sacred Community *By Dr. Ron Wolfson* 6 x 9, 224 pp, Quality PB, 978-1-58023-244-9 **$19.99**

Bar / Bat Mitzvah

The Mitzvah Project Book
Making Mitzvah Part of Your Bar/Bat Mitzvah ... and Your Life
By Liz Suneby and Diane Heiman; Foreword by Rabbi Jeffrey K. Salkin; Preface by Rabbi Sharon Brous
The go-to source for Jewish young adults and their families looking to make the world a better place through good deeds—big or small.
6 x 9, 224 pp, Quality PB Original, 978-1-58023-458-0 **$16.99** *For ages 11–13*

The Bar/Bat Mitzvah Memory Book, 2nd Edition: An Album for Treasuring the Spiritual Celebration
By Rabbi Jeffrey K. Salkin and Nina Salkin
8 x 10, 48 pp, 2-color text, Deluxe HC, ribbon marker, 978-1-58023-263-0 **$19.99**

For Kids—Putting God on Your Guest List, 2nd Edition: How to Claim the Spiritual Meaning of Your Bar or Bat Mitzvah *By Rabbi Jeffrey K. Salkin*
6 x 9, 144 pp, Quality PB, 978-1-58023-308-8 **$15.99** *For ages 11–13*

The Jewish Prophet: Visionary Words from Moses and Miriam to Henrietta Szold and A. J. Heschel *By Rabbi Dr. Michael J. Shire*
6½ x 8½, 128 pp, 123 full-color illus., HC, 978-1-58023-168-8 **$14.95**

Putting God on the Guest List, 3rd Edition: How to Reclaim the Spiritual Meaning of Your Child's Bar or Bat Mitzvah *By Rabbi Jeffrey K. Salkin*
6 x 9, 224 pp, Quality PB, 978-1-58023-222-7 **$16.99**
       Teacher's Guide: 8½ x 11, 48 pp, PB, 978-1-58023-226-5 **$8.99**

Teens / Young Adults

Text Messages: A Torah Commentary for Teens
Edited by Rabbi Jeffrey K. Salkin
Shows today's teens how each Torah portion contains worlds of meaning for them, for what they are going through in their lives, and how they can shape their Jewish identity as they enter adulthood.
6 x 9, 304 pp (est), HC, 978-1-58023-507-5 **$24.99**

Hannah Senesh: Her Life and Diary, the First Complete Edition
By Hannah Senesh; Foreword by Marge Piercy; Preface by Eitan Senesh; Afterword by Roberta Grossman
6 x 9, 368 pp, b/w photos, Quality PB, 978-1-58023-342-2 **$19.99**

I Am Jewish: Personal Reflections Inspired by the Last Words of Daniel Pearl
Edited by Judea and Ruth Pearl 6 x 9, 304 pp, Deluxe PB w/ flaps, 978-1-58023-259-3 **$19.99**
Download a free copy of the *I Am Jewish Teacher's Guide* at www.jewishlights.com.

The JGirl's Guide: The Young Jewish Woman's Handbook for Coming of Age
By Penina Adelman, Ali Feldman and Shulamit Reinharz
6 x 9, 240 pp, Quality PB, 978-1-58023-215-9 **$14.99** *For ages 11 & up*
       Teacher's & Parent's Guide: 8½ x 11, 56 pp, PB, 978-1-58023-225-8 **$8.99**

The JGuy's Guide: The GPS for Jewish Teen Guys
By Rabbi Joseph B. Meszler, Dr. Shulamit Reinharz, Liz Suneby and Diane Heiman
6 x 9, 208 pp, Quality PB Original, 978-1-58023-721-5 **$16.99**
       Teacher's Guide: 8½ x 11, 30pp, PB, 978-1-58023-773-4 **$8.99**

Tough Questions Jews Ask, 2nd Edition: A Young Adult's Guide to Building a Jewish Life *By Rabbi Edward Feinstein*
6 x 9, 160 pp, Quality PB, 978-1-58023-454-2 **$16.99** *For ages 11 & up*
       Teacher's Guide: 8½ x 11, 72 pp, PB, 978-1-58023-187-9 **$8.95**

Pre-Teens

Be Like God: God's To-Do List for Kids
By Dr. Ron Wolfson
Encourages kids ages eight through twelve to use their God-given superpowers to find the many ways they can make a difference in the lives of others and find meaning and purpose for their own.
7 x 9, 144 pp, Quality PB, 978-1-58023-510-5 **$15.99** *For ages 8–12*

The Book of Miracles: A Young Person's Guide to Jewish Spiritual Awareness
By Lawrence Kushner, with all-new illustrations by the author.
6 x 9, 96 pp, 2-color illus., HC, 978-1-879045-78-1 **$16.95** *For ages 9–13*

Spirituality / Crafts

Jewish Threads: A Hands-On Guide to Stitching Spiritual Intention into Jewish Fabric Crafts *By Diana Drew with Robert Grayson*
Learn how to make your own Jewish fabric crafts with spiritual intention—a journey of creativity, imagination and inspiration. Thirty projects.
7 x 9, 288 pp, 8-page color insert, b/w illus., Quality PB Original, 978-1-58023-442-9 **$19.99**

Beading—The Creative Spirit: Finding Your Sacred Center through the Art of Beadwork *By Wendy Ellsworth*
Invites you on a spiritual pilgrimage into the kaleidoscope world of glass and color.
7 x 9, 240 pp, 8-page full-color insert, b/w photos and diagrams, Quality PB, 978-1-59473-267-6 **$18.99***

Contemplative Crochet: A Hands-On Guide for Interlocking Faith and Craft *By Cindy Crandall-Frazier; Foreword by Linda Skolnik*
Will take you on a path deeper into your crocheting and your spiritual awareness.
7 x 9, 208 pp, b/w photos, Quality PB, 978-1-59473-238-6 **$16.99***

The Knitting Way: A Guide to Spiritual Self-Discovery
By Linda Skolnik and Janice MacDaniels
Shows how to use knitting to strengthen your spiritual self.
7 x 9, 240 pp, b/w photos, Quality PB, 978-1-59473-079-5 **$16.99***

The Painting Path: Embodying Spiritual Discovery through Yoga, Brush and Color *By Linda Novick; Foreword by Richard Segalman*
Explores the divine connection you can experience through art.
7 x 9, 208 pp, 8-page full-color insert, b/w photos, Quality PB, 978-1-59473-226-3 **$18.99***

The Quilting Path: A Guide to Spiritual Self-Discovery through Fabric, Thread and Kabbalah *By Louise Silk* Explores how to cultivate personal growth through quilt making. 7 x 9, 192 pp, b/w photos, Quality PB, 978-1-59473-206-5 **$16.99***

Travel / History

Israel—A Spiritual Travel Guide, 2nd Edition: A Companion for the Modern Jewish Pilgrim *By Rabbi Lawrence A. Hoffman, PhD*
Helps today's pilgrim tap into the deep spiritual meaning of the ancient—and modern—sites of the Holy Land.
4¾ x 10, 256 pp, Illus., Quality PB, 978-1-58023-261-6 **$18.99**
Also Available: **The Israel Mission Leader's Guide** 5½ x 8½, 16 pp, PB, 978-1-58023-085-8 **$4.95**

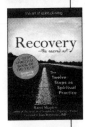

On the Chocolate Trail: A Delicious Adventure Connecting Jews, Religions, History, Travel, Rituals and Recipes to the Magic of Cacao
By Rabbi Deborah R. Prinz
Take a delectable journey through the religious history of chocolate—a real treat!
6 x 9, 272 pp w/ 20+ b/w photographs, Quality PB, 978-1-58023-487-0 **$18.99**

Twelve Steps

Recovery—The Sacred Art: The Twelve Steps as Spiritual Practice
By Rami Shapiro; Foreword by Joan Borysenko, PhD
Draws on insights and practices of different religious traditions to help you move more deeply into the universal spirituality of the Twelve Step system.
5½ x 8½, 240 pp, Quality PB Original, 978-1-59473-259-1 **$16.99***

100 Blessings Every Day: Daily Twelve Step Recovery Affirmations, Exercises for Personal Growth & Renewal Reflecting Seasons of the Jewish Year *By Rabbi Kerry M. Olitzky; Foreword by Rabbi Neil Gillman, PhD* 4½ x 6½, 432 pp, Quality PB, 978-1-879045-30-9 **$16.99**

Recovery from Codependence: A Jewish Twelve Steps Guide to Healing Your Soul
By Rabbi Kerry M. Olitzky 6 x 9, 160 pp, Quality PB, 978-1-879045-32-3 **$13.95**

Twelve Jewish Steps to Recovery, 2nd Edition: A Personal Guide to Turning from Alcoholism & Other Addictions—Drugs, Food, Gambling, Sex...
By Rabbi Kerry M. Olitzky and Stuart A. Copans, MD; Preface by Abraham J. Twerski, MD
6 x 9, 160 pp, Quality PB, 978-1-58023-409-2 **$16.99**

*A book from SkyLight Paths, Jewish Lights' sister imprint

Life Cycle
Marriage / Parenting / Family / Aging

The New Jewish Baby Album: Creating and Celebrating the Beginning of a Spiritual Life—A Jewish Lights Companion
By the Editors at Jewish Lights; Foreword by Anita Diamant; Preface by Rabbi Sandy Eisenberg Sasso
A spiritual keepsake that will be treasured for generations. More than just a memory book, *shows you how—and why it's important*—to create a Jewish home and a Jewish life. 8 x 10, 64 pp, Deluxe Padded HC, Full-color illus., 978-1-58023-138-1 **$19.95**

The Jewish Pregnancy Book: A Resource for the Soul, Body & Mind during Pregnancy, Birth & the First Three Months *By Sandy Falk, MD, and Rabbi Daniel Judson, with Steven A. Rapp* Medical information, prayers and rituals for each stage of pregnancy. 7 x 10, 208 pp, b/w photos, Quality PB, 978-1-58023-178-7 **$16.95**

Celebrating Your New Jewish Daughter: Creating Jewish Ways to Welcome Baby Girls into the Covenant—New and Traditional Ceremonies *By Debra Nussbaum Cohen; Foreword by Rabbi Sandy Eisenberg Sasso* 6 x 9, 272 pp, Quality PB, 978-1-58023-090-2 **$18.95**

The New Jewish Baby Book, 2nd Edition: Names, Ceremonies & Customs—A Guide for Today's Families *By Anita Diamant* 6 x 9, 320 pp, Quality PB, 978-1-58023-251-7 **$19.99**

Parenting as a Spiritual Journey: Deepening Ordinary and Extraordinary Events into Sacred Occasions *By Rabbi Nancy Fuchs-Kreimer, PhD* 6 x 9, 224 pp, Quality PB, 978-1-58023-016-2 **$17.99**

Parenting Jewish Teens: A Guide for the Perplexed
By Joanne Doades Explores the questions and issues that shape the world in which today's Jewish teenagers live and offers constructive advice to parents. 6 x 9, 176 pp, Quality PB, 978-1-58023-305-7 **$16.99**

Judaism for Two: A Spiritual Guide for Strengthening and Celebrating Your Loving Relationship *By Rabbi Nancy Fuchs-Kreimer, PhD, and Rabbi Nancy H. Wiener, DMin; Foreword by Rabbi Elliot N. Dorff, PhD*
Addresses the ways Jewish teachings can enhance and strengthen committed relationships. 6 x 9, 224 pp, Quality PB, 978-1-58023-254-8 **$16.99**

The Creative Jewish Wedding Book, 2nd Edition: A Hands-On Guide to New & Old Traditions, Ceremonies & Celebrations *By Gabrielle Kaplan-Mayer* 9 x 9, 288 pp, b/w photos, Quality PB, 978-1-58023-398-9 **$19.99**

Divorce Is a Mitzvah: A Practical Guide to Finding Wholeness and Holiness When Your Marriage Dies *By Rabbi Perry Netter; Afterword by Rabbi Laura Geller* 6 x 9, 224 pp, Quality PB, 978-1-58023-172-5 **$16.95**

Embracing the Covenant: Converts to Judaism Talk About Why & How
By Rabbi Allan Berkowitz and Patti Moskovitz 6 x 9, 192 pp, Quality PB, 978-1-879045-50-7 **$16.95**

The Guide to Jewish Interfaith Family Life: An InterfaithFamily.com Handbook
Edited by Ronnie Friedland and Edmund Case
6 x 9, 384 pp, Quality PB, 978-1-58023-153-4 **$18.95**

A Heart of Wisdom: Making the Jewish Journey from Midlife through the Elder Years
Edited by Susan Berrin; Foreword by Rabbi Harold Kushner
6 x 9, 384 pp, Quality PB, 978-1-58023-051-3 **$18.95**

Introducing My Faith and My Community: The Jewish Outreach Institute Guide for the Christian in a Jewish Interfaith Relationship
By Rabbi Kerry M. Olitzky 6 x 9, 176 pp, Quality PB, 978-1-58023-192-3 **$16.99**

Making a Successful Jewish Interfaith Marriage: The Jewish Outreach Institute Guide to Opportunities, Challenges and Resources *By Rabbi Kerry M. Olitzky with Joan Peterson Littman* 6 x 9, 176 pp, Quality PB, 978-1-58023-170-1 **$16.95**

A Man's Responsibility: A Jewish Guide to Being a Son, a Partner in Marriage, a Father and a Community Leader *By Rabbi Joseph B. Meszler* 6 x 9, 192 pp, Quality PB, 978-1-58023-435-1 **$16.99**

So That Your Values Live On: Ethical Wills and How to Prepare Them
Edited by Rabbi Jack Riemer and Rabbi Nathaniel Stampfer
6 x 9, 272 pp, Quality PB, 978-1-879045-34-7 **$18.99**

Holidays / Holy Days

Prayers of Awe Series

An exciting new series that examines the High Holy Day liturgy to enrich the praying experience of everyone—whether experienced worshipers or guests who encounter Jewish prayer for the very first time.

May God Remember: Memory and Memorializing in Judaism—*Yizkor*
Edited by Rabbi Lawrence A. Hoffman, PhD
Examines the history and ideas behind *Yizkor*, the Jewish memorial service, and this fascinating chapter in Jewish piety.
6 x 9, 304 pp, HC, 978-1-58023-689-8 **$24.99**

We Have Sinned—Sin and Confession in Judaism: *Ashamnu* and *Al Chet*
Edited by Rabbi Lawrence A. Hoffman, PhD 6 x 9, 304 pp, HC, 978-1-58023-612-6 **$24.99**

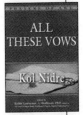

Who by Fire, Who by Water—*Un'taneh Tokef*
Edited by Rabbi Lawrence A. Hoffman, PhD
6 x 9, 272 pp, Quality PB, 978-1-58023-672-0 **$19.99**; HC, 978-1-58023-424-5 **$24.99**

All These Vows—*Kol Nidre*
Edited by Rabbi Lawrence A. Hoffman, PhD 6 x 9, 288 pp, HC, 978-1-58023-430-6 **$24.99**

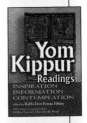

Rosh Hashanah Readings: Inspiration, Information and Contemplation
Yom Kippur Readings: Inspiration, Information and Contemplation
Edited by Rabbi Dov Peretz Elkins; Section Introductions from Arthur Green's These Are the Words
Rosh Hashanah: 6 x 9, 400 pp, Quality PB, 978-1-58023-437-5 **$19.99**
Yom Kippur: 6 x 9, 368 pp, Quality PB, 978-1-58023-438-2 **$19.99**; HC, 978-1-58023-271-5 **$24.99**

Reclaiming Judaism as a Spiritual Practice: Holy Days and Shabbat
By Rabbi Goldie Milgram 7 x 9, 272 pp, Quality PB, 978-1-58023-205-0 **$19.99**

The Sabbath Soul: Mystical Reflections on the Transformative Power of Holy Time
Selection, Translation and Commentary by Eitan Fishbane, PhD
6 x 9, 208 pp, Quality PB, 978-1-58023-459-7 **$18.99**

Shabbat, 2nd Edition: The Family Guide to Preparing for and Celebrating the Sabbath
By Dr. Ron Wolfson 7 x 9, 320 pp, Illus., Quality PB, 978-1-58023-164-0 **$21.99**

Hanukkah, 2nd Edition: The Family Guide to Spiritual Celebration
By Dr. Ron Wolfson 7 x 9, 240 pp, Illus., Quality PB, 978-1-58023-122-0 **$18.95**

Passover

My People's Passover Haggadah
Traditional Texts, Modern Commentaries
Edited by Rabbi Lawrence A. Hoffman, PhD, and David Arnow, PhD
A diverse and exciting collection of commentaries on the traditional Passover Haggadah—in two volumes!
Vol. 1: 7 x 10, 304 pp, HC, 978-1-58023-354-5 **$24.99**
Vol. 2: 7 x 10, 320 pp, HC, 978-1-58023-346-0 **$24.99**

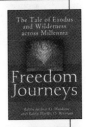

Creating Lively Passover Seders, 2nd Edition: A Sourcebook of Engaging Tales, Texts & Activities *By David Arnow, PhD* 7 x 9, 464 pp, Quality PB, 978-1-58023-444-3 **$24.99**

Freedom Journeys: The Tale of Exodus and Wilderness across Millennia
By Rabbi Arthur O. Waskow and Rabbi Phyllis O. Berman
6 x 9, 288 pp, HC, 978-1-58023-445-0 **$24.99**

Leading the Passover Journey: The Seder's Meaning Revealed, the Haggadah's Story Retold *By Rabbi Nathan Laufer*
6 x 9, 224 pp, Quality PB, 978-1-58023-399-6 **$18.99**

Passover, 2nd Edition: The Family Guide to Spiritual Celebration
By Dr. Ron Wolfson with Joel Lurie Grishaver 7 x 9, 416 pp, Quality PB, 978-1-58023-174-9 **$19.95**

The Women's Passover Companion: Women's Reflections on the Festival of Freedom
Edited by Rabbi Sharon Cohen Anisfeld, Tara Mohr and Catherine Spector; Foreword by Paula E. Hyman
6 x 9, 352 pp, Quality PB, 978-1-58023-231-9 **$19.99**; HC, 978-1-58023-128-2 **$24.95**

The Women's Seder Sourcebook: Rituals & Readings for Use at the Passover Seder
Edited by Rabbi Sharon Cohen Anisfeld, Tara Mohr and Catherine Spector
6 x 9, 384 pp, Quality PB, 978-1-58023-232-6 **$19.99**

Ecology / Environment

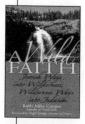

A Wild Faith: Jewish Ways into Wilderness, Wilderness Ways into Judaism
By Rabbi Mike Comins; Foreword by Nigel Savage 6 x 9, 240 pp, Quality PB, 978-1-58023-316-3 **$16.99**

Ecology & the Jewish Spirit: Where Nature & the Sacred Meet
Edited by Ellen Bernstein 6 x 9, 288 pp, Quality PB, 978-1-58023-082-7 **$18.99**

Torah of the Earth: Exploring 4,000 Years of Ecology in Jewish Thought
Vol. 1: Biblical Israel & Rabbinic Judaism; Vol. 2: Zionism & Eco-Judaism
Edited by Rabbi Arthur Waskow Vol. 1: 6 x 9, 272 pp, Quality PB, 978-1-58023-086-5 **$19.95**
Vol. 2: 6 x 9, 336 pp, Quality PB, 978-1-58023-087-2 **$19.95**

The Way Into Judaism and the Environment *By Jeremy Benstein, PhD*
6 x 9, 288 pp, Quality PB, 978-1-58023-368-2 **$18.99**; HC, 978-1-58023-268-5 **$24.99**

Graphic Novels / Graphic History

The Adventures of Rabbi Harvey: A Graphic Novel of Jewish Wisdom and Wit in the
Wild West *By Steve Sheinkin* 6 x 9, 144 pp, Full-color illus., Quality PB, 978-1-58023-310-1 **$16.99**

Rabbi Harvey Rides Again: A Graphic Novel of Jewish Folktales Let Loose in the
Wild West *By Steve Sheinkin* 6 x 9, 144 pp, Full-color illus., Quality PB, 978-1-58023-347-7 **$16.99**

Rabbi Harvey vs. the Wisdom Kid: A Graphic Novel of Dueling Jewish Folktales in
the Wild West *By Steve Sheinkin*
6 x 9, 144 pp, Full-color illus., Quality PB, 978-1-58023-422-1 **$16.99**

The Story of the Jews: A 4,000-Year Adventure—A Graphic History Book
By Stan Mack 6 x 9, 288 pp, Illus., Quality PB, 978-1-58023-155-8 **$16.99**

Grief / Healing

Judaism and Health: A Handbook of Practical, Professional and Scholarly
Resources *Edited by Jeff Levin, PhD, MPH, and Michele F. Prince, LCSW, MAJCS*
Foreword by Rabbi Elliot N. Dorff, PhD
Explores the expressions of health in the form of overviews of research studies,
first-person narratives and advice. 6 x 9, 448 pp, HC, 978-1-58023-714-7 **$50.00**

Facing Illness, Finding God: How Judaism Can Help You and Caregivers Cope
When Body or Spirit Fails *By Rabbi Joseph B. Meszler*
6 x 9, 208 pp, Quality PB, 978-1-58023-423-8 **$16.99**

Grief in Our Seasons: A Mourner's Kaddish Companion *By Rabbi Kerry M. Olitzky*
4½ x 6½, 448 pp, Quality PB, 978-1-879045-55-2 **$15.95**

Healing and the Jewish Imagination: Spiritual and Practical Perspectives on
Judaism and Health *Edited by Rabbi William Cutter, PhD*
6 x 9, 240 pp, Quality PB, 978-1-58023-373-6 **$19.99**

Healing from Despair: Choosing Wholeness in a Broken World
By Rabbi Elie Kaplan Spitz with Erica Shapiro Taylor; Foreword by Abraham J. Twerski, MD
5½ x 8½, 208 pp, Quality PB, 978-1-58023-436-8 **$16.99**

Healing of Soul, Healing of Body: Spiritual Leaders Unfold the Strength & Solace
in Psalms *Edited by Rabbi Simkha Y. Weintraub, LCSW*
6 x 9, 128 pp, 2-color illus. text, Quality PB, 978-1-879045-31-6 **$16.99**

Midrash & Medicine: Healing Body and Soul in the Jewish Interpretive Tradition
Edited by Rabbi William Cutter, PhD; Foreword by Michele F. Prince, LCSW, MAJCS
6 x 9, 352 pp, Quality PB, 978-1-58023-484-9 **$21.99**

Mourning & Mitzvah, 2nd Edition: A Guided Journal for Walking the Mourner's
Path through Grief to Healing *By Rabbi Anne Brener, LCSW*
7½ x 9, 304 pp, Quality PB, 978-1-58023-113-8 **$19.99**

Tears of Sorrow, Seeds of Hope, 2nd Edition: A Jewish Spiritual Companion
for Infertility and Pregnancy Loss *By Rabbi Nina Beth Cardin*
6 x 9, 208 pp, Quality PB, 978-1-58023-233-3 **$18.99**

A Time to Mourn, a Time to Comfort, 2nd Edition: A Guide to Jewish
Bereavement *By Dr. Ron Wolfson; Foreword by Rabbi David J. Wolpe*
7 x 9, 384 pp, Quality PB, 978-1-58023-253-1 **$21.99**

When a Grandparent Dies: A Kid's Own Remembering Workbook for Dealing
with Shiva and the Year Beyond *By Nechama Liss-Levinson, PhD*
8 x 10, 48 pp, 2-color text, HC, 978-1-879045-44-6 **$15.95** *For ages 7–13*

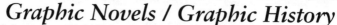

Social Justice

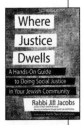

Where Justice Dwells
A Hands-On Guide to Doing Social Justice in Your Jewish Community
By Rabbi Jill Jacobs; Foreword by Rabbi David Saperstein
Provides ways to envision and act on your own ideals of social justice.
7 x 9, 288 pp, Quality PB Original, 978-1-58023-453-5 **$24.99**

There Shall Be No Needy
Pursuing Social Justice through Jewish Law and Tradition
By Rabbi Jill Jacobs; Foreword by Rabbi Elliot N. Dorff, PhD; Preface by Simon Greer
Confronts the most pressing issues of twenty-first-century America from a deeply Jewish perspective. 6 x 9, 288 pp, Quality PB, 978-1-58023-425-2 **$16.99**

There Shall Be No Needy Teacher's Guide 8½ x 11, 56 pp, PB, 978-1-58023-429-0 **$8.99**

Conscience
The Duty to Obey and the Duty to Disobey
By Rabbi Harold M. Schulweis
Examines the idea of conscience and the role conscience plays in our relationships to government, law, ethics, religion, human nature, God—and to each other.
6 x 9, 160 pp, Quality PB, 978-1-58023-419-1 **$16.99**; HC, 978-1-58023-375-0 **$19.99**

Judaism and Justice
The Jewish Passion to Repair the World
By Rabbi Sidney Schwarz; Foreword by Ruth Messinger
Explores the relationship between Judaism, social justice and the Jewish identity of American Jews. 6 x 9, 352 pp, Quality PB, 978-1-58023-353-8 **$19.99**

Spirituality / Women's Interest

New Jewish Feminism
Probing the Past, Forging the Future
Edited by Rabbi Elyse Goldstein; Foreword by Anita Diamant
Looks at the growth and accomplishments of Jewish feminism and what they mean for Jewish women today and tomorrow.
6 x 9, 480 pp, HC, 978-1-58023-359-0 **$24.99**

The Divine Feminine in Biblical Wisdom Literature
Selections Annotated & Explained
Translation & Annotation by Rabbi Rami Shapiro
5½ x 8½, 240 pp, Quality PB, 978-1-59473-109-9 **$16.99**
(A book from SkyLight Paths, Jewish Lights' sister imprint)

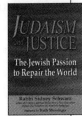

The Quotable Jewish Woman
Wisdom, Inspiration & Humor from the Mind & Heart
Edited by Elaine Bernstein Partnow
6 x 9, 496 pp, Quality PB, 978-1-58023-236-4 **$19.99**

The Women's Haftarah Commentary
New Insights from Women Rabbis on the 54 Weekly Haftarah Portions, the 5 Megillot & Special Shabbatot
Edited by Rabbi Elyse Goldstein
Illuminates the historical significance of female portrayals in the Haftarah and the Five Megillot. 6 x 9, 560 pp, Quality PB, 978-1-58023-371-2 **$19.99**

The Women's Torah Commentary
New Insights from Women Rabbis on the 54 Weekly Torah Portions
Edited by Rabbi Elyse Goldstein
Over fifty women rabbis offer inspiring insights on the Torah, in a week-by-week format.
6 x 9, 496 pp, Quality PB, 978-1-58023-370-5 **$19.99**; HC, 978-1-58023-076-6 **$34.95**

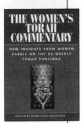

See Passover for *The Women's Passover Companion: Women's Reflections on the Festival of Freedom* and *The Women's Seder Sourcebook: Rituals & Readings for Use at the Passover Seder.*

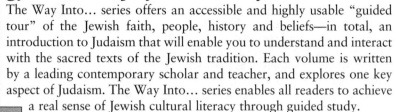

Theology / Philosophy / The Way Into... Series

The Way Into... series offers an accessible and highly usable "guided tour" of the Jewish faith, people, history and beliefs—in total, an introduction to Judaism that will enable you to understand and interact with the sacred texts of the Jewish tradition. Each volume is written by a leading contemporary scholar and teacher, and explores one key aspect of Judaism. The Way Into... series enables all readers to achieve a real sense of Jewish cultural literacy through guided study.

The Way Into Encountering God in Judaism
By Rabbi Neil Gillman, PhD
For everyone who wants to understand how Jews have encountered God throughout history and today.
6 x 9, 240 pp, Quality PB, 978-1-58023-199-2 **$18.99**; HC, 978-1-58023-025-4 **$21.95**
Also Available: **The Jewish Approach to God:** A Brief Introduction for Christians
By Rabbi Neil Gillman, PhD
5½ x 8½, 192 pp, Quality PB, 978-1-58023-190-9 **$16.95**

The Way Into Jewish Mystical Tradition
By Rabbi Lawrence Kushner
Allows readers to interact directly with the sacred mystical texts of the Jewish tradition. An accessible introduction to the concepts of Jewish mysticism, their religious and spiritual significance, and how they relate to life today.
6 x 9, 224 pp, Quality PB, 978-1-58023-200-5 **$18.99**

The Way Into Jewish Prayer
By Rabbi Lawrence A. Hoffman, PhD
Opens the door to 3,000 years of Jewish prayer, making anyone feel at home in the Jewish way of communicating with God.
6 x 9, 208 pp, Quality PB, 978-1-58023-201-2 **$18.99**

The Way Into Jewish Prayer Teacher's Guide
By Rabbi Jennifer Ossakow Goldsmith
8½ x 11, 42 pp, PB, 978-1-58023-345-3 **$8.99**
Download a free copy at www.jewishlights.com.

The Way Into Judaism and the Environment
By Jeremy Benstein, PhD
Explores the ways in which Judaism contributes to contemporary social-environmental issues, the extent to which Judaism is part of the problem and how it can be part of the solution.
6 x 9, 288 pp, Quality PB, 978-1-58023-368-2 **$18.99**; HC, 978-1-58023-268-5 **$24.99**

The Way Into *Tikkun Olam* (Repairing the World)
By Rabbi Elliot N. Dorff, PhD
An accessible introduction to the Jewish concept of the individual's responsibility to care for others and repair the world.
6 x 9, 304 pp, Quality PB, 978-1-58023-328-6 **$18.99**

The Way Into Torah
By Rabbi Norman J. Cohen, PhD
Helps guide you in the exploration of the origins and development of Torah, explains why it should be studied and how to do it.
6 x 9, 176 pp, Quality PB, 978-1-58023-198-5 **$16.99**

The Way Into the Varieties of Jewishness
By Sylvia Barack Fishman, PhD
Explores the religious and historical understanding of what it has meant to be Jewish from ancient times to the present controversy over "Who is a Jew?"
6 x 9, 288 pp, Quality PB, 978-1-58023-367-5 **$18.99**; HC, 978-1-58023-030-8 **$24.99**

Theology / Philosophy

Believing and Its Tensions: A Personal Conversation about God, Torah, Suffering and Death in Jewish Thought
By Rabbi Neil Gillman, PhD
Explores the changing nature of belief and the complexities of reconciling the intellectual, emotional and moral questions of Gillman's own searching mind and soul.
5½ x 8½, 144 pp, HC, 978-1-58023-669-0 **$19.99**

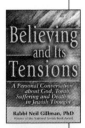

God of Becoming and Relationship: The Dynamic Nature of Process Theology   *By Rabbi Bradley Shavit Artson, DHL*
Explains how Process Theology breaks us free from the strictures of ancient Greek and medieval European philosophy, allowing us to see all creation as related patterns of energy through which we connect to everything.
6 x 9, 208 pp, HC, 978-1-58023-713-0 **$24.99**

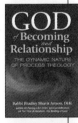

The Other Talmud—*The Yerushalmi*: Unlocking the Secrets of The Talmud of Israel for Judaism Today   *By Rabbi Judith Z. Abrams, PhD*
A fascinating—and stimulating—look at "the other Talmud" and the possibilities for Jewish life reflected there.   6 x 9, 256 pp, HC, 978-1-58023-463-4 **$24.99**

The Way of Man: According to Hasidic Teaching
By Martin Buber; New Translation and Introduction by Rabbi Bernard H. Mehlman and Dr. Gabriel E. Padawer; Foreword by Paul Mendes-Flohr
An accessible and engaging new translation of Buber's classic work—*available as an e-book only*.   E-book, 978-1-58023-601-0 Digital List Price **$14.99**

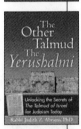

The Death of Death: Resurrection and Immortality in Jewish Thought
By Rabbi Neil Gillman, PhD   6 x 9, 336 pp, Quality PB, 978-1-58023-081-0 **$18.95**

Doing Jewish Theology: God, Torah & Israel in Modern Judaism *By Rabbi Neil Gillman, PhD*
6 x 9, 304 pp, Quality PB, 978-1-58023-439-9 **$18.99**; HC, 978-1-58023-322-4 **$24.99**

From Defender to Critic: The Search for a New Jewish Self
By Dr. David Hartman   6 x 9, 336 pp, HC, 978-1-58023-515-0 **$35.00**

The God Who Hates Lies: Confronting & Rethinking Jewish Tradition
By Dr. David Hartman with Charlie Buckholtz   6 x 9, 208 pp, HC, 978-1-58023-455-9 **$24.99**

A Heart of Many Rooms: Celebrating the Many Voices within Judaism
By Dr. David Hartman   6 x 9, 352 pp, Quality PB, 978-1-58023-156-5 **$19.95**

Jewish Theology in Our Time: A New Generation Explores the Foundations and Future of Jewish Belief   *Edited by Rabbi Elliot J. Cosgrove, PhD; Foreword by Rabbi David J. Wolpe; Preface by Rabbi Carole B. Balin, PhD*   6 x 9, 240 pp, Quality PB, 978-1-58023-630-1, **$19.99**; HC, 978-1-58023-413-9 **$24.99**

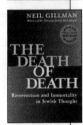

Maimonides—Essential Teachings on Jewish Faith & Ethics: The Book of Knowledge & the Thirteen Principles of Faith—Annotated & Explained
Translation and Annotation by Rabbi Marc D. Angel, PhD
5½ x 8½, 224 pp, Quality PB Original, 978-1-59473-311-6 **$18.99***

Maimonides, Spinoza and Us: Toward an Intellectually Vibrant Judaism
By Rabbi Marc D. Angel, PhD 6 x 9, 224 pp, HC, 978-1-58023-411-5 **$24.99**

Our Religious Brains: What Cognitive Science Reveals about Belief, Morality, Community and Our Relationship with God
By Rabbi Ralph D. Mecklenburger; Foreword by Dr. Howard Kelfer; Preface by Dr. Neil Gillman
6 x 9, 224 pp, HC, 978-1-58023-508-2 **$24.99**

Your Word Is Fire: The Hasidic Masters on Contemplative Prayer
Edited and translated by Rabbi Arthur Green, PhD, and Barry W. Holtz
6 x 9, 160 pp, Quality PB, 978-1-879045-25-5 **$16.99**

I Am Jewish
Personal Reflections Inspired by the Last Words of Daniel Pearl
Almost 150 Jews—both famous and not—from all walks of life, from all around the world, write about many aspects of their Judaism.
Edited by Judea and Ruth Pearl   6 x 9, 304 pp, Deluxe PB w/ flaps, 978-1-58023-259-3 **$19.99**
Download a free copy of the *I Am Jewish Teacher's Guide* at www.jewishlights.com.

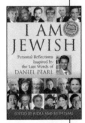

*A book from SkyLight Paths, Jewish Lights' sister imprint

Spirituality / Prayer

Davening: A Guide to Meaningful Jewish Prayer
By Rabbi Zalman Schachter-Shalomi with Joel Segel; Foreword by Rabbi Lawrence Kushner
A fresh approach to prayer for all who wish to appreciate the power of prayer's poetry, song and ritual, and to join the age-old conversation that Jews have had with God. 6 x 9, 240 pp, Quality PB, 978-1-58023-627-0 **$18.99**

Jewish Men Pray: Words of Yearning, Praise, Petition, Gratitude and Wonder from Traditional and Contemporary Sources
Edited by Rabbi Kerry M. Olitzky and Stuart M. Matlins; Foreword by Rabbi Bradley Shavit Artson, DHL
A celebration of Jewish men's voices in prayer—to strengthen, heal, comfort, and inspire—from the ancient world up to our own day.
5 x 7¼, 400 pp, HC, 978-1-58023-628-7 **$19.99**

Making Prayer Real: Leading Jewish Spiritual Voices on Why Prayer Is Difficult and What to Do about It *By Rabbi Mike Comins* 6 x 9, 320 pp, Quality PB, 978-1-58023-417-7 **$18.99**

Witnesses to the One: The Spiritual History of the *Sh'ma*
By Rabbi Joseph B. Meszler; Foreword by Rabbi Elyse Goldstein
6 x 9, 176 pp, Quality PB, 978-1-58023-400-9 **$16.99**; HC, 978-1-58023-309-5 **$19.99**

My People's Prayer Book Series: Traditional Prayers, Modern Commentaries *Edited by Rabbi Lawrence A. Hoffman, PhD*
Provides diverse and exciting commentary to the traditional liturgy. Will help you find new wisdom in Jewish prayer, and bring liturgy into your life. Each book includes Hebrew text, modern translations and commentaries from all perspectives of the Jewish world.

Vol. 1—The *Sh'ma* and Its Blessings
  7 x 10, 168 pp, HC, 978-1-879045-79-8 **$29.99**
Vol. 2—The *Amidah* 7 x 10, 240 pp, HC, 978-1-879045-80-4 **$24.95**
Vol. 3—*P'sukei D'zimrah* (Morning Psalms)
  7 x 10, 240 pp, HC, 978-1-879045-81-1 **$29.99**
Vol. 4—*Seder K'riat Hatorah* (The Torah Service)
  7 x 10, 264 pp, HC, 978-1-879045-82-8 **$29.99**
Vol. 5—*Birkhot Hashachar* (Morning Blessings)
  7 x 10, 240 pp, HC, 978-1-879045-83-5 **$24.95**
Vol. 6—*Tachanun* and Concluding Prayers
  7 x 10, 240 pp, HC, 978-1-879045-84-2 **$24.95**
Vol. 7—Shabbat at Home 7 x 10, 240 pp, HC, 978-1-879045-85-9 **$24.95**
Vol. 8—*Kabbalat Shabbat* (Welcoming Shabbat in the Synagogue)
  7 x 10, 240 pp, HC, 978-1-58023-121-3 **$24.95**
Vol. 9—Welcoming the Night: *Minchah* and *Ma'ariv* (Afternoon and Evening Prayer) 7 x 10, 272 pp, HC, 978-1-58023-262-3 **$24.99**
Vol. 10—Shabbat Morning: *Shacharit* and *Musaf* (Morning and Additional Services) 7 x 10, 240 pp, HC, 978-1-58023-240-1 **$29.99**

Spirituality / Lawrence Kushner

I'm God; You're Not: Observations on Organized Religion & Other Disguises of the Ego
6 x 9, 256 pp, Quality PB, 978-1-58023-513-6 **$18.99**; HC, 978-1-58023-441-2 **$21.99**

The Book of Letters: A Mystical Hebrew Alphabet
Popular HC Edition, 6 x 9, 80 pp, 2-color text, 978-1-879045-00-2 **$24.95**
Collector's Limited Edition, 9 x 12, 80 pp, gold-foil-embossed pages, w/ limited-edition silkscreened print, 978-1-879045-04-0 **$349.00**

The Book of Miracles: A Young Person's Guide to Jewish Spiritual Awareness
6 x 9, 96 pp, 2-color illus., HC, 978-1-879045-78-1 **$16.95** *For ages 9–13*

God Was in This Place & I, i Did Not Know: Finding Self, Spirituality and Ultimate Meaning 6 x 9, 192 pp, Quality PB, 978-1-879045-33-0 **$16.95**

Honey from the Rock: An Introduction to Jewish Mysticism
6 x 9, 176 pp, Quality PB, 978-1-58023-073-5 **$16.95**

Invisible Lines of Connection: Sacred Stories of the Ordinary
5½ x 8½, 160 pp, Quality PB, 978-1-879045-98-9 **$16.99**

The Way Into Jewish Mystical Tradition
6 x 9, 224 pp, Quality PB, 978-1-58023-200-5 **$18.99**; HC, 978-1-58023-029-2 **$21.95**

Meditation

The Magic of Hebrew Chant: Healing the Spirit, Transforming the Mind, Deepening Love
By Rabbi Shefa Gold; Foreword by Sylvia Boorstein
Introduces this transformative spiritual practice as a way to unlock the power of sacred texts and make prayer and meditation the delight of your life. Includes musical notations. 6 x 9, 352 pp, Quality PB, 978-1-58023-671-3 **$24.99**

The Magic of Hebrew Chant Companion—The Big Book of Musical Notations and Incantations
8½ x 11, 154 pp, PB, 978-1-58023-722-2 **$19.99**

Jewish Meditation Practices for Everyday Life
Awakening Your Heart, Connecting with God
By Rabbi Jeff Roth
Offers a fresh take on meditation that draws on life experience and living life with greater clarity as opposed to the traditional method of rigorous study.
6 x 9, 224 pp, Quality PB, 978-1-58023-397-2 **$18.99**

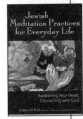

Discovering Jewish Meditation, 2nd Edition
Instruction & Guidance for Learning an Ancient Spiritual Practice
By Nan Fink Gefen, PhD 6 x 9, 208 pp, Quality PB, 978-1-58023-462-7 **$16.99**

The Handbook of Jewish Meditation Practices
A Guide for Enriching the Sabbath and Other Days of Your Life
By Rabbi David A. Cooper 6 x 9, 208 pp, Quality PB, 978-1-58023-102-2 **$16.95**

Meditation from the Heart of Judaism
Today's Teachers Share Their Practices, Techniques, and Faith
Edited by Avram Davis 6 x 9, 256 pp, Quality PB, 978-1-58023-049-0 **$16.95**

Ritual / Sacred Practices

God in Your Body: Kabbalah, Mindfulness and Embodied Spiritual Practice
By Jay Michaelson
The first comprehensive treatment of the body in Jewish spiritual practice and an essential guide to the sacred. 6 x 9, 272 pp, Quality PB, 978-1-58023-304-0 **$18.99**

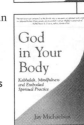

The Book of Jewish Sacred Practices: CLAL's Guide to Everyday & Holiday Rituals & Blessings *Edited by Rabbi Irwin Kula and Vanessa L. Ochs, PhD*
6 x 9, 368 pp, Quality PB, 978-1-58023-152-7 **$18.95**

The Jewish Dream Book: The Key to Opening the Inner Meaning of Your Dreams
By Vanessa L. Ochs, PhD, with Elizabeth Ochs; Illus. by Kristina Swarner
8 x 8, 128 pp, Full-color illus., Deluxe PB w/ flaps, 978-1-58023-132-9 $16.95

Jewish Ritual: A Brief Introduction for Christians
By Rabbi Kerry M. Olitzky and Rabbi Daniel Judson
5½ x 8½, 144 pp, Quality PB, 978-1-58023-210-4 **$14.99**

The Rituals & Practices of a Jewish Life: A Handbook for Personal Spiritual Renewal *Edited by Rabbi Kerry M. Olitzky and Rabbi Daniel Judson*
6 x 9, 272 pp, Illus., Quality PB, 978-1-58023-169-5 **$18.95**

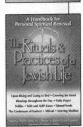

The Sacred Art of Lovingkindness: Preparing to Practice
By Rabbi Rami Shapiro 5½ x 8½, 176 pp, Quality PB, 978-1-59473-151-8 **$16.99**
(A book from SkyLight Paths, Jewish Lights' sister imprint)

Mystery & Detective Fiction

Criminal Kabbalah: An Intriguing Anthology of Jewish Mystery & Detective Fiction *Edited by Lawrence W. Raphael; Foreword by Laurie R. King*
All-new stories from twelve of today's masters of mystery and detective fiction— sure to delight mystery buffs of all faith traditions.
6 x 9, 256 pp, Quality PB, 978-1-58023-109-1 **$16.95**

Mystery Midrash: An Anthology of Jewish Mystery & Detective Fiction
Edited by Lawrence W. Raphael; Preface by Joel Siegel
6 x 9, 304 pp, Quality PB, 978-1-58023-055-1 **$16.95**

Spirituality

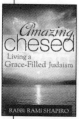

Amazing Chesed: Living a Grace-Filled Judaism
By Rabbi Rami Shapiro Drawing from ancient and contemporary, traditional and non-traditional Jewish wisdom, reclaims the idea of grace in Judaism.
6 x 9, 176 pp, Quality PB, 978-1-58023-624-9 **$16.99**

Jewish with Feeling: A Guide to Meaningful Jewish Practice
By Rabbi Zalman Schachter-Shalomi with Joel Segel
Takes off from basic questions like "Why be Jewish?" and whether the word God still speaks to us today and lays out a vision for a whole-person Judaism.
5½ x 8½, 288 pp, Quality PB, 978-1-58023-691-1 **$19.99**

Perennial Wisdom for the Spiritually Independent: Sacred Teachings— Annotated & Explained *Annotation by Rami Shapiro; Foreword by Richard Rohr*
Weaves sacred texts and teachings from the world's major religions into a coherent exploration of the five core questions at the heart of every religion's search.
5½ x 8½, 336 pp, Quality PB Original, 978-1-59473-515-8 **$16.99**

Aleph-Bet Yoga: Embodying the Hebrew Letters for Physical and Spiritual Well-Being
By Steven A. Rapp; Foreword by Tamar Frankiel, PhD, and Judy Greenfeld; Preface by Hart Lazer
7 x 10, 128 pp, b/w photos, Quality PB, Lay-flat binding, 978-1-58023-162-6 **$16.95**

A Book of Life: Embracing Judaism as a Spiritual Practice
By Rabbi Michael Strassfeld 6 x 9, 544 pp, Quality PB, 978-1-58023-247-0 **$19.99**

Bringing the Psalms to Life: How to Understand and Use the Book of Psalms
By Rabbi Daniel F. Polish, PhD 6 x 9, 208 pp, Quality PB, 978-1-58023-157-2 **$16.95**

Does the Soul Survive? A Jewish Journey to Belief in Afterlife, Past Lives & Living with Purpose *By Rabbi Elie Kaplan Spitz; Foreword by Brian L. Weiss, MD*
6 x 9, 288 pp, Quality PB, 978-1-58023-165-7 **$18.99**

Entering the Temple of Dreams: Jewish Prayers, Movements and Meditations for the End of the Day *By Tamar Frankiel, PhD, and Judy Greenfeld*
7 x 10, 192 pp, illus., Quality PB, 978-1-58023-079-7 **$16.95**

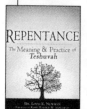

First Steps to a New Jewish Spirit: Reb Zalman's Guide to Recapturing the Intimacy & Ecstasy in Your Relationship with God *By Rabbi Zalman M. Schachter-Shalomi with Donald Gropman* 6 x 9, 144 pp, Quality PB, 978-1-58023-182-4 **$16.95**

Foundations of Sephardic Spirituality: The Inner Life of Jews of the Ottoman Empire
By Rabbi Marc D. Angel, PhD 6 x 9, 224 pp, Quality PB, 978-1-58023-341-5 **$18.99**

God & the Big Bang: Discovering Harmony between Science & Spirituality
By Dr. Daniel C. Matt 6 x 9, 216 pp, Quality PB, 978-1-879045-89-7 **$18.99**

God in Our Relationships: Spirituality between People from the Teachings of Martin Buber *By Rabbi Dennis S. Ross* 5½ x 8½, 160 pp, Quality PB, 978-1-58023-147-3 **$16.95**

The Jewish Lights Spirituality Handbook: A Guide to Understanding, Exploring & Living a Spiritual Life *Edited by Stuart M. Matlins*
6 x 9, 456 pp, Quality PB, 978-1-58023-093-3 **$19.99**

Judaism, Physics and God: Searching for Sacred Metaphors in a Post-Einstein World
By Rabbi David W. Nelson 6 x 9, 352 pp, Quality PB, inc. reader's discussion guide,
978-1-58023-306-4 **$18.99**; HC, 352 pp, 978-1-58023-252-4 **$24.99**

Meaning & Mitzvah: Daily Practices for Reclaiming Judaism through Prayer, God, Torah, Hebrew, Mitzvot and Peoplehood *By Rabbi Goldie Milgram*
7 x 9, 336 pp, Quality PB, 978-1-58023-256-2 **$19.99**

Repentance: The Meaning and Practice of Teshuvah
By Dr. Louis E. Newman; Foreword by Rabbi Harold M. Schulweis; Preface by Rabbi Karyn D. Kedar
6 x 9, 256 pp, HC, 978-1-58023-426-9 **$24.99** Quality PB, 978-1-58023-718-5 **$18.99**

The Sabbath Soul: Mystical Reflections on the Transformative Power of Holy Time
Selection, Translation and Commentary by Eitan Fishbane, PhD
6 x 9, 208 pp, Quality PB, 978-1-58023-459-7 **$18.99**

Tanya, the Masterpiece of Hasidic Wisdom: Selections Annotated & Explained
Translation & Annotation by Rabbi Rami Shapiro; Foreword by Rabbi Zalman M. Schachter-Shalomi
5½ x 8½, 240 pp, Quality PB, 978-1-59473-275-1 **$16.99**

These Are the Words, 2nd Edition: A Vocabulary of Jewish Spiritual Life
By Rabbi Arthur Green, PhD 6 x 9, 320 pp, Quality PB, 978-1-58023-494-8 **$19.99**

Inspiration

Into the Fullness of the Void: A Spiritual Autobiography *By Dov Elbaum*
The spiritual autobiography of one of Israel's leading cultural figures that provides insights and guidance for all of us. 6 x 9, 304 pp, Quality PB Original, 978-1-58023-715-4 **$18.99**

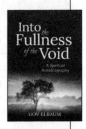

Saying No and Letting Go: Jewish Wisdom on Making Room for What Matters Most
By Rabbi Edwin Goldberg, DHL; Foreword by Rabbi Naomi Levy
Taps into timeless Jewish wisdom that teaches how to "hold on tightly" to the things that matter most while learning to "let go lightly" of the demands and worries that do not ultimately matter. 6 x 9, 192 pp, Quality PB, 978-1-58023-670-6 **$16.99**

The Bridge to Forgiveness: Stories and Prayers for Finding God and Restoring Wholeness *By Rabbi Karyn D. Kedar* 6 x 9, 176 pp, Quality PB, 978-1-58023-451-1 **$16.99**

The Empty Chair: Finding Hope and Joy—Timeless Wisdom from a Hasidic Master, Rebbe Nachman of Breslov *Adapted by Moshe Mykoff and the Breslov Research Institute*
4 x 6, 128 pp, Deluxe PB w/ flaps, 978-1-879045-67-5 **$9.99**

A Formula for Proper Living: Practical Lessons from Life and Torah
By Rabbi Abraham J. Twerski, MD 6 x 9, 144 pp, HC, 978-1-58023-402-3 **$19.99**

The Gentle Weapon: Prayers for Everyday and Not-So-Everyday Moments—
Timeless Wisdom from the Teachings of the Hasidic Master, Rebbe Nachman of Breslov
Adapted by Moshe Mykoff and S. C. Mizrahi, together with the Breslov Research Institute
4 x 6, 144 pp, Deluxe PB w/ flaps, 978-1-58023-022-3 **$9.99**

The God Upgrade: Finding Your 21st-Century Spirituality in Judaism's 5,000-Year-Old Tradition *By Rabbi Jamie Korngold; Foreword by Rabbi Harold M. Schulweis*
6 x 9, 176 pp, Quality PB, 978-1-58023-443-6 $15.99

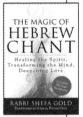

God Whispers: Stories of the Soul, Lessons of the Heart *By Rabbi Karyn D. Kedar*
6 x 9, 176 pp, Quality PB, 978-1-58023-088-9 **$15.95**

God's To-Do List: 103 Ways to Be an Angel and Do God's Work on Earth
By Dr. Ron Wolfson 6 x 9, 144 pp, Quality PB, 978-1-58023-301-9 **$16.99**

Happiness and the Human Spirit: The Spirituality of Becoming the Best You Can Be
By Rabbi Abraham J. Twerski, MD
6 x 9, 176 pp, Quality PB, 978-1-58023-404-7 **$16.99**; HC, 978-1-58023-343-9 **$19.99**

Life's Daily Blessings: Inspiring Reflections on Gratitude and Joy for Every Day, Based on Jewish Wisdom *By Rabbi Kerry M. Olitzky* 4½ x 6½, 368 pp, Quality PB, 978-1-58023-396-5 **$16.99**

The Magic of Hebrew Chant: Healing the Spirit, Transforming the Mind, Deepening Love *By Rabbi Shefa Gold; Foreword by Sylvia Boorstein*
6 x 9, 352 pp, Quality PB, 978-1-58023-671-3 **$24.99**

Restful Reflections: Nighttime Inspiration to Calm the Soul, Based on Jewish Wisdom
By Rabbi Kerry M. Olitzky and Rabbi Lori Forman-Jacobi 5 x 8, 352 pp, Quality PB, 978-1-58023-091-9 **$16.99**

Sacred Intentions: Morning Inspiration to Strengthen the Spirit, Based on Jewish Wisdom
By Rabbi Kerry M. Olitzky and Rabbi Lori Forman-Jacobi 4½ x 6½, 448 pp, Quality PB, 978-1-58023-061-2 **$16.99**

The Seven Questions You're Asked in Heaven: Reviewing and Renewing Your Life on Earth *By Dr. Ron Wolfson* 6 x 9, 176 pp, Quality PB, 978-1-58023-407-8 **$16.99**

Kabbalah / Mysticism

Ehyeh: A Kabbalah for Tomorrow
By Rabbi Arthur Green, PhD 6 x 9, 224 pp, Quality PB, 978-1-58023-213-5 **$18.99**

The Gift of Kabbalah: Discovering the Secrets of Heaven, Renewing Your Life on Earth
By Tamar Frankiel, PhD 6 x 9, 256 pp, Quality PB, 978-1-58023-141-1 **$16.95**

Jewish Mysticism and the Spiritual Life: Classical Texts, Contemporary Reflections *Edited by Dr. Lawrence Fine, Dr. Eitan Fishbane and Rabbi Or N. Rose*
6 x 9, 256 pp, HC, 978-1-58023-434-4 **$24.99**; Quality PB, 978-1-58023-719-2 **$18.99**

Seek My Face: A Jewish Mystical Theology *By Rabbi Arthur Green, PhD*
6 x 9, 304 pp, Quality PB, 978-1-58023-130-5 **$19.95**

Zohar: Annotated & Explained *Translation & Annotation by Dr. Daniel C. Matt; Foreword by Andrew Harvey* 5½ x 8½, 176 pp, Quality PB, 978-1-893361-51-5 **$16.99**
(A book from SkyLight Paths, Jewish Lights' sister imprint)

See also *The Way Into Jewish Mystical Tradition* in The Way Into... Series.

JEWISH LIGHTS BOOKS ARE AVAILABLE FROM BETTER BOOKSTORES. TRY YOUR BOOKSTORE FIRST.

About Jewish Lights

People of all faiths and backgrounds yearn for books that attract, engage, educate, and spiritually inspire.

Our principal goal is to stimulate thought and help all people learn about who the Jewish People are, where they come from, and what the future can be made to hold. While people of our diverse Jewish heritage are the primary audience, our books speak to people in the Christian world as well and will broaden their understanding of Judaism and the roots of their own faith.

We bring to you authors who are at the forefront of spiritual thought and experience. While each has something different to say, they all say it in a voice that you can hear.

Our books are designed to welcome you and then to engage, stimulate, and inspire. We judge our success not only by whether or not our books are beautiful and commercially successful, but by whether or not they make a difference in your life.

For your information and convenience, at the back of this book we have provided a list of other Jewish Lights books you might find interesting and useful. They cover all the categories of your life:

Bar/Bat Mitzvah	Life Cycle
Bible Study / Midrash	Meditation
Children's Books	Men's Interest
Congregation Resources	Parenting
Current Events / History	Prayer / Ritual / Sacred Practice
Ecology / Environment	Social Justice
Fiction: Mystery, Science Fiction	Spirituality
Grief / Healing	Theology / Philosophy
Holidays / Holy Days	Travel
Inspiration	Twelve Steps
Kabbalah / Mysticism / Enneagram	Women's Interest

Stuart M. Matlins, Publisher

Or phone, fax, mail or e-mail to: **JEWISH LIGHTS Publishing**
Sunset Farm Offices, Route 4 • P.O. Box 237 • Woodstock, Vermont 05091
Tel: (802) 457-4000 • Fax: (802) 457-4004 • www.jewishlights.com
Credit card orders: **(800) 962-4544** (8:30AM–5:30PM EST Monday–Friday)
Generous discounts on quantity orders. SATISFACTION GUARANTEED. Prices subject to change.

For more information about each book, visit our website at www.jewishlights.com